Race Car Aerodynamics

Designing for Speed

by Joseph Katz

www.
BentleyPublishers
.com

Selected Books and Repair Information From Bentley Publishers

Driving

The Unfair Advantage *Mark Donohue*
ISBN 0-8376-0073-1(hc); 0-8376-0069-3(pb)

Going Faster! Mastering the Art of Race Driving *The Skip Barber Racing School*
ISBN 0-8376-0227-0

A French Kiss With Death: Steve McQueen and the Making of *Le Mans*
Michael Keyser ISBN 0-8376-0234-3

The Technique of Motor Racing
Piero Taruffi ISBN 0-8376-0228-9

Sports Car and Competition Driving
Paul Frère with foreword *by Phil Hill*
ISBN 0-8376-0202-5

Engineering

Supercharged! Design, Testing, and Installation of Supercharger Systems
Corky Bell ISBN 0-8376-0168-1

Maximum Boost: Designing, Testing, and Installing Turbocharger Systems
Corky Bell ISBN 0-8376-0160-6

Bosch Fuel Injection and Engine Management *Charles O. Probst, SAE*
ISBN 0-8376-0300-5

Other Enthusiast Titles

Jeep CJ Rebuilder's Manual: 1946–1971
Moses Ludel ISBN 0-8376-1037-0

Jeep CJ Rebuilder's Manual: 1972–1986
Moses Ludel ISBN 0-8376-0151-70

Jeep Owner's Bible™ *Moses Ludel*
ISBN 0-8376-0154-1

Mercedes-Benz E-Class Owner's Bible™ 1986–1995 *Bentley Publishers*
ISBN 0-8376-0230-0

Road & Track Illustrated Automotive Dictionary *John Dinkel* ISBN 0-8376-0143-6

Audi

Audi A4 Repair Manual: 1996–2001, 1.8L turbo, 2.8L, including Avant and quattro
Bentley Publishers ISBN 0-8376-0371-4

Audi A4 1996–2001, S4 2000–2001 Official Factory Repair Manual on CD-ROM
Audi of America ISBN 0-8376-0833-3

Audi A6 Sedan 1998–2002, Avant 1999–2002, allroad quattro 2001–2002, S6 Avant 2002 Official Factory Repair Manual on CD-ROM *Audi of America*
ISBN 0-8376-0836-8

BMW

BMW 5 Series Service Manual: 1997–2002 525i, 528i, 530i, 540i, Sedan, Sport Wagon
Bentley Publishers ISBN 0-8376-0317-X

BMW 3 Series Enthusiast's Companion™
Jeremy Walton ISBN 0-8376-0220-3

BMW 6 Series Enthusiast's Companion™
Jeremy Walton ISBN 0-8376-0193-2

BMW 3 Series (E46) Service Manual: 1999–2001, 323i, 325i, 325xi, 328i, 330i, 330xi Sedan, Coupe, Convertible, Sport Wagon
Bentley Publishers ISBN 0-8376-0320-X

BMW 3 Series (E36) Service Manual: 1992–1998, 318i/is/iC, 323is/iC, 325i/is/iC, 328i/is/iC, M3 *Bentley Publishers*
ISBN 0-8376-0326-9

BMW 5 Series Service Manual: 1989–1995 525i, 530i, 535i, 540i, including Touring
Bentley Publishers ISBN 0-8376-0319-6

BMW 7 Series Service Manual: 1988–1994, 735i, 735iL, 740i, 740iL, 750iL
Bentley Publishers ISBN 0-8376-0328-5

Chevrolet

Zora Arkus-Duntov: The Legend Behind Corvette *Jerry Burton* ISBN 0-8376-0858-9

Corvette from the Inside: The 50-Year Development History *Dave McLellan*
ISBN 0-8376-0859-7

Corvette by the Numbers: The Essential Corvette Parts Reference 1955–1982:
Alan Colvin ISBN 0-8376-0288-2

Chevrolet by the Numbers 1965–1969: The Essential Chevrolet Parts Reference
Alan Colvin ISBN 0-8376-0956-9

Corvette Fuel Injection & Electronic Engine Management 1982–2001:
Charles O. Probst, SAE ISBN 0-8376-0861-9

Corvette 427: Practical Restoration of a '67 Roadster *Don Sherman*
ISBN 0-8376-0218-1

Ford

The Official Ford Mustang 5.0 Technical Reference & Performance Handbook: 1979–1993 *Al Kirschenbaum*
ISBN 0-8376-0210-6

Ford F-Series Pickup Owner's Bible™
Moses Ludel ISBN 0-8376-0152-5

Ford Fuel Injection and Electronic Engine Control: 1988–1993 *Charles O. Probst, SAE*
ISBN 0-8376-0301-3

Ford Fuel Injection and Electronic Engine Control: 1980–1987 *Charles O. Probst, SAE*
ISBN 0-8376-0302-1

Porsche

Porsche: Excellence Was Expected
Karl Ludvigsen ISBN 0-8376-0235-1

Porsche Carrera 964 and 965, 1989–1994 Technician's Handbook: Without Guesswork™ *Bentley Publishers*
ISBN 0-8376-0292-0

Porsche 911 Carrera Service Manual: 1984–1989 *Bentley Publishers*
ISBN 0-8376-0291-2

Porsche 911 SC Coupe, Targa, and Cabriolet Service Manual: 1978–1983
Bentley Publishers ISBN 0-8376-0290-4

Volkswagen

Volkswagen Sport Tuning for Street and Competition *Per Schroeder*
ISBN 0-8376-0161-4

Battle for the Beetle
Karl Ludvigsen ISBN 08376-0071-5

Jetta, Golf, GTI Service Manual: 1999–2003 1.8L turbo, 1.9L TDI diesel, 2.0L gasoline, 2.8L VR6, *Bentley Publishers*
ISBN 0-8376-0323-4

New Beetle Service Manual: 1998–2002 1.8L turbo, 1.9L TDI diesel, 2.0L gasoline
Bentley Publishers ISBN 0-8376-0376-5

New Beetle 1998–2002 Official Factory Repair Manual on CD-ROM
Volkswagen of America ISBN 0-8376-0838-4

Passat Service Manual: 1998–2002, 1.8L turbo, 2.8L V6, 4.0L W8, including wagon and 4MOTION *Bentley Publishers*
ISBN 0-8376-0393-5

Passat 1998–2002 Official Factory Repair Manual on CD-ROM
Volkswagen of America ISBN 0-8376-0837-6

New Beetle Service Manual: 1998–1999, 2.0L Gasoline, 1.9L TDI Diesel, 1.8L Turbo *Bentley Publishers*
ISBN 0-8376-0385-4

Jetta, Golf, GTI, Cabrio Service Manual: 1993–1999, including Jetta*III* and Golf*III**
Bentley Publishers ISBN 0-8376-0366-8

Eurovan Official Factory Repair Manual: 1992–1999 *Volkswagen of America*
ISBN 0-8376-0335-8

Eurovan 1992–2002 Official Factory Repair Manual on CD-ROM
Volkswagen of America ISBN 0-8376-0835-X

Jetta, Golf, GTI 1993–1999, Cabrio 1995–2002 Official Factory Repair Manual on CD-ROM *Volkswagen of America*
ISBN 0-8376-0834-1

Jetta, Golf, GTI Service Manual: 1985–1992 Gasoline, Diesel, and Turbo Diesel, including 16V *Bentley Publishers*
ISBN 0-8376-0342-0

Super Beetle, Beetle and Karmann Ghia Official Service Manual: Type 1, 1970–1979 *Volkswagen of America*
ISBN 0-8376-0096-0

Race Car Aerodynamics

Designing for Speed

by Joseph Katz

B www.
BentleyPublishers
.com

B BENTLEY PUBLISHERS | Automotive Books & Manuals

Bentley Publishers, a division of Robert Bentley, Inc.
1734 Massachusetts Avenue
Cambridge, MA 02138 USA
800-423-4595 / 617-547-4170

Information that makes
the difference®

www.
BentleyPublishers
.com

Copies of this book may be purchased from selected booksellers, or directly from the publisher by mail. The publisher encourages comments from the reader of this book. These communications have been and will be considered in the preparation of this and other manuals. Please write to Bentley Publishers at the address listed on the top of this page or e-mail us through our website.

Since this page cannot legibly accommodate all the copyright notices, the caption credits listing the source of the photographs or illustrations used constitutes an extension of the copyright page.

Library of Congress Cataloging-in-Publication Data

Katz, Joseph, 1947–
    Race car aerodynamics : designing for speed / by Joseph Katz.
        p.   cm.
    Includes index.
    ISBN 0-8376-0142-8 : $34.95
    1. Automobiles, racing--Aerodynamics.   2. Automobiles, Racing--Design and construction.   I. Title.
  TL245.K38 1995
   629.228--dc20   95-34326
                             CIP

Bentley Stock No. GAER

06 05 04 03   11 10 9 8 7

The paper used in this publication is acid free and meets the requirements of the National Standard for Information Sciences-Permanence of Paper for Printed Library Materials. ∞

Race Car Aerodynamics: Designing for Speed, by Joseph Katz Ph.D

The author would like to acknowledge the graphics assistance of the SDSU Media Technology Services.

Manufactured in the United States of America

Front cover: Photo courtesy of F + W, Swiss Federal Aircraft Factory

Back cover: (Photos, from the top) 1992/1993 McLaren MP4/7A Formula One car, courtesy TAG/McLaren; Nissan prototype race car wind tunnel test, courtesy of MIRA; Toyota Celica 1994 Pike's Peak Hill Climb winner, courtesy of Rupert Berrington; Illustration of the Chaparral 2J "fan car" by Brian Hatton

Race Car Aerodynamics
Designing for Speed

How aerodynamics shapes race cars, see Chapter 1.

Using a wind tunnel for surface-flow visualization, see Chapter 3.

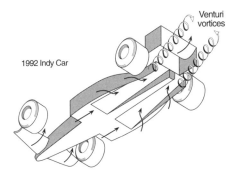

1992 Indy Car

Venturi vortices

Air flow through underbody channels on an open-wheel race car, see Chapter 6.

Significant developments in race-car aerodynamics, see Chapter 7.

CONTENTS

PREFACE

On the surface, automobile racing appears simply as a very popular sport, with its attendent media coverage and commercial sponsorships. But in reality, racing serves as a proving ground for new technology and a battlefield for the giants of the automotive industry.

Although human factors are frequently publicized as the reason behind the success or failure of one racing team or another, engine power, tire adhesion, chassis design, and, recently, aerodynamics probably play a more important role in winning this technology race.

From the historical point of view, post-World-War II automobile racing was initially dominated by developments related to engine technology, and later to tire advancements. Since both technologies were extremely expensive, only the better supported teams could afford large investments.

During the 1960s, race car aerodynamics evolved as an important and relatively inexpensive technology that could place the smaller and less well-funded teams in the winner's circle. As time progressed, race-car aerodynamics became more refined, and today all race cars are tested in expensive wind tunnels as part of a continuous development process.

In spite of the huge progress made by the aerospace industry, the effect of aerodynamics on vehicle performance still seems to be the least understood of the aforementioned technologies. Therefore, after a brief review of the subject of aerodynamics and current vehicles in the first chapter, I explain the elementary aspects of air flow over race cars, so that the reader can later correlate between a race car shape and the corresponding aerodynamic effects influencing vehicle performance. I dedicate an entire chapter to vehicle dynamics and performance to clearly explain the tremendous increases in cornering speeds due to aerodynamic downforce, and to clarify the misconception that aerodynamics is important only for drag reduction.

This book is intended to appeal to a wide range of enthusiasts, from racing fans who want to know why certain devices appear on their favorite team car, to well established designers who will appreciate the overall view of this text and the supporting data. The technical information is sufficiently descriptive for the nontechnical reader, but also includes a wide enough data-base which may be useful, even to professionals, when rapid preliminary information is sought.

The subject is chronologically developed, and it is recommended to start with Chapter 2 and continue sequentially—even though it is tempting to begin with Chapter 6, which includes the largest body of "classified" information. The reader without a strong technical background is urged to read carefully beginning with Chapter 1, paying careful attention to terms such as pressure distribution (and coefficient) which will be used extensively later to diagnose the aerodynamic features of various vehicles.

Throughout this text I have made an effort to use a minimum number of equations so that non-engineers won't be scared away and yet can grasp the basic essentials of the field. The supporting diagrams are presented in an easy-to-understand fashion, but contain information that is vital to novice racing engineers and may even prove helpful to the professional designer.

San Diego, CA

1 AERODYNAMICS AND RACE CARS

THE IMPACT OF AERODYNAMICS ON VEHICLE SHAPE

Let us start the discussion on vehicle shape and aerodynamics by comparing the two race cars in Fig. 1.1 and 1.2. Both are aimed at doing the same thing: winning the biggest race of all, the Indy 500. In spite of the fact that the two cars were designed quite a few years apart, the question remains: why do they differ so much in external appearance?

One possible answer is the increased importance paid to aerodynamic streamlining details in the later car. But a closer examination of the 1916 race car with its tapering boat-tail reveals that even at the dawn of the century aerodynamic drag reduction was a primary concern.

Fig. 1-1. *The 1993 Marlboro Penske PC22 Indy car, which won the Indy 500 in 1993. Courtesy of Marlboro Racing.*

Fig. 1-2. *The 1916 Peugeot, winner of that year's Indy 500 race. Courtesy of Peugeot Motors of America.*

1

Streamlining would seem to be important—after all, we want the car to move more easily through the air (less drag = faster)—but the most dominant reason behind the large difference in the appearance of the more recently designed multiwinged race car is the focus on using its body and wings to create *aerodynamic downforce*. This raises the question of why aerodynamic downforce is needed. But before answering that question let us convince ourselves that aerodynamic loads are significant and survey some of the terms frequently used when speaking about the aerodynamics of a moving vehicle.

It may seem that the loads created by the motion of air are unimportant, especially within the speed range encountered by automobiles. However, you only have to extend your hand out of a car's side window to feel the serious forces exerted by air. And we all have heard about the disastrous effects of the winds in tornadoes or hurricanes. Furthermore, a short glance at the sky reveals that simple airplane wings lift hundreds of tons of cargo and passengers while riding on air alone; those powerful jet engines provide *only* the thrust needed to overcome the airplane's drag.

To understand how such large aerodynamic forces can be created, a typical cross section of a wing is shown in Fig. 1.3. For the sake of the discussion, let us assume that it moves from right to left. Because of the shape and angle of this airfoil section, the air will move faster on the upper surface than on the lower one. As it will be explained later in Chapter 2, this speed difference creates a low pressure (suction) on the upper surface and a higher pressure on the lower one. The result of this pressure difference is the force that *lifts* an airplane or your neighborhood bird.

Fig. 1-3. The low pressure on the upper side and the higher pressure on the lower side of this airfoil add up to the lift force. Of course when used on a race car, the airfoil is inverted.

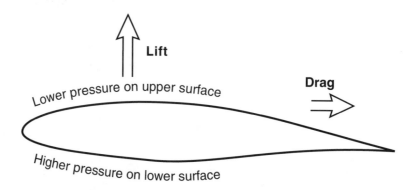

Nothing in life comes free, and when wings generate lift they also create *drag*, which is the force that resists the motion. The drag is usually much smaller than the lift, and it can be reduced by streamlining the vehicle (having a smooth external surface). Of course any improvement in a vehicle's drag leads to potential improvements in fuel economy, which is why drag is quite important to the passenger car industry.

The effect of streamlining on drag reduction can be demonstrated by using the same visual aid my teachers used many years ago. Fig. 1.4 shows the cross section of a long circular rod (depicted by the little circle) which has the same drag as a much thicker (up to 10 times) and larger airfoil. (This is the reason why the suspension members (e.g., A-arms) on many race cars have streamlined sections and not the more simple circular section.)

Fig. 1.3 introduced the lift and drag forces, but in reality a side-force component must be included. Fig. 1.5 depicts these important aerodynamic forces as

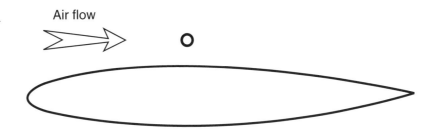

Fig. 1-4. *This small cylinder and much larger airfoil have the same aerodynamic drag. The cylinder's drag can be reduced almost ten times by covering it with a streamlined shape.*

they apply to a moving vehicle. The force which resists the motion and points backward is the drag. The second force component, which points upward, is the lift. It is mostly unnoticed by the everyday driver, but those who have experienced very high-speed driving may have noticed that at that speed more attention is needed to keep the car traveling along a straight line. This instability is usually caused by lift, which on passenger vehicles will usually be larger on the rear wheels than on the front ones. The third force, the side force (positive to the right), is important too, but with relatively low levels of side winds this component of the aerodynamic load is usually small.

For a race car, the next logical step would be to reduce drag and lift or even create a negative lift (downforce). In race car design, drag reduction is secondary. It is the creation of downforce by aerodynamic means (such as the use of inverted wings) that is extremely important and leads to major improvements in race car performance, especially on tracks with numerous high-speed, unbanked turns. Aerodynamic downforce increases the tires' cornering ability, and the faster a car turns the sooner it will see the checkered flag. The significance of aerodynamic downforce to race cars, and the increase in its implementations in recent years, is demonstrated in the next section.

Fig. 1-5. *The directions used to identify the three components of aerodynamic force.*

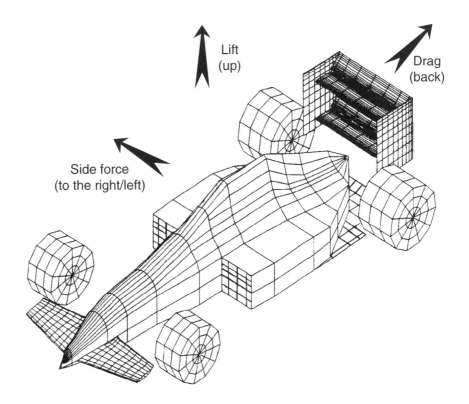

AERODYNAMIC DOWNFORCE AND PERFORMANCE

In a car, driving, braking, and cornering forces are created at the contact patch between the tire and the road. These friction-like forces are strongly affected by the vertical force applied on the tires and are limited by some maximum friction coefficient. For example, we can turn up to a given maximum speed, but when we exceed this speed the car will slide. This is a result of exceeding the limit of tire adhesion (friction coefficient).

Now, if we could increase the normal tire force (and maximum friction) by pushing the tire more against the road, then the cornering force could be increased, too, without the risk of sliding. One way to do this is to add more weight to the car. But this won't work because an increase in the car's mass will affect acceleration and the force needed to turn the car, at the same rate.

Aerodynamic downforce, however, increases loads on the tires *without increasing the vehicle's weight*! The result is increased cornering ability with no weight penalty, which gives a reduction in lap times. The most amazing aspect of the importance of aerodynamic downforce is that it was observed by the race car engineering community only toward the end of the 1960s.

Since the early days of the automobile and of motor racing, engine, tire, and suspension technology have gradually developed. In most of these disciplines the advances were reasonably gradual, leading to increased race car performance, higher speeds, and lower lap times. This trend is demonstrated by Fig. 1.6, which shows the history of the one-lap record speed at the Indianapolis Speedway. The continuing trend indicates the gradual improvements in the various technological aspects of race car design. Our interest is focused on the sharp change in the slope of this curve toward the late 1960s, which can be partially attributed to the aerodynamic experimentations of that era (the other aspect was the similarly rapid development in tire technology).

The biggest jump in speed occurred in 1972 with the first efficient use of front and rear wings, in a manner quite similar to the wings shown in Fig. 1.1. Interestingly, the strong influence of aerodynamics on lap-speed was immediately recognized by the racing-sanctioning organizations, and many of the at-

Fig. 1-6. Variation of the one-lap record speed at the Indianapolis Speedway.

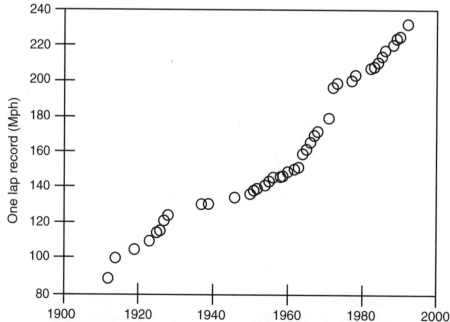

tempts to reduce racing speeds were based on placing limits on the use and size of aerodynamic devices such as inverted wings.

As mentioned, one of the most important benefits of aerodynamic downforce is the increase in cornering speed. To demonstrate this trend, observe the two curves in Fig. 1.7. The units compare the maximum cornering capability of race cars to a modern sports car (a production 1993 Chevrolet Corvette has a relative cornering speed of 1). The gradual increase indicated by the solid line is a result of the continuous improvements in tire technology. This is the level of cornering available for vehicles without aerodynamic downforce (such as production sports cars). The broken line represents the trends in the performance of the most advanced vehicles, including F-1, Indy, and prototype race cars. The huge increase in the cornering capability in the 1970s seems to be a result of using inverted wings. This trend accelerated towards the end of the 1970s, with the introduction of the ground effect principle, which used the car body itself to create additional downforce.

In addition to improved cornering speeds, aerodynamics have dramatically improved vehicle stability and high-speed braking as well, which again lead to faster lap times. This is even more impressive when you consider that aerodynamic drag increases with the addition of wings, reducing straightaway speeds (which suggests that the level of downforce and drag should be carefully tailored to each race track). Drag reduction is only the primary concern in such vehicles as record-breaking streamliners or fuel-efficient vehicles.

Fig. 1-7. *Trends showing the increase of the maximum cornering acceleration over the past years for race cars with and without aerodynamic downforce.*

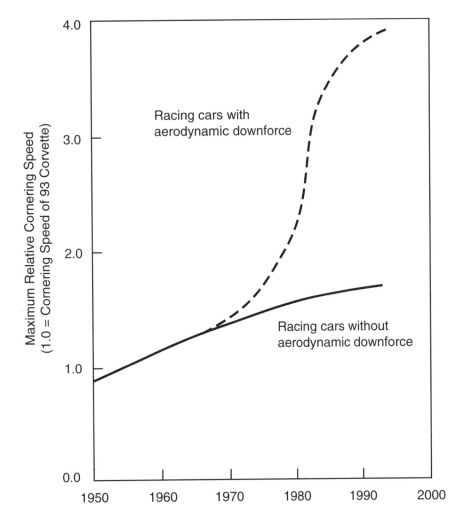

CREATING AND MEASURING AERODYNAMIC FORCES

Now, that we have established that tire and vehicle performance can be improved considerably by having downforce on the tires, and that at higher speed quite large aerodynamic loads can be created, let us investigate the options for generating aerodynamic downforce.

The first and most obvious approach is to use airplane-like wings, inverted of course, to create downforce instead of lift. Indeed, wings are probably the most noticeable difference between the two cars of Fig. 1.1 and 1.2. Such inverted wings can be found throughout the whole spectrum of automobile racing. Typical front and rear wings of open-wheel race cars are shown in Fig. 1.8 and 1.9.

Fig. 1-8. *Typical application of an inverted wing, behind the rear axle (1986 Zakspeed F-1 car).*

Another option is to generate downforce by altering the shape of the car's body. The many spoilers, air-dams, etc., appearing on production sports cars are a clear proof of this concept. As an example, a rear-deck mounted spoiler is shown in Fig. 1.10. It is a very efficient way to reduce the lift on the rear wheels. An interesting development in the effort to use the vehicle's body to create aerodynamic benefits occurred when race car engineers in the late 1970s paid attention to the then well-known fact (within the aeronautical community) that the lift of a wing increases with ground proximity.

This effect is shown in Fig. 1.11, and it becomes noticeable when the ground clearance is less than one chord length (the distance from the leading edge to the trailing edge) of an airfoil, which is clearly the case in Fig. 1.9. Interestingly this "Ground Effect" works both for wings lifting upward, such as airplane wings, and for inverted race car wings creating downforce. The important point is that this logic leads to an effort to use the race car's body to create downforce. As a results, the undertray of race cars became a smooth surface, mimicking a wing shape.

The next logical question is why don't race cars resemble smooth wing-like streamlined bodies. The answer lies in the regulations forcing sometimes

Fig. 1-9. An inverted wing mounted on the nose cone of a 1993 open-wheel Indy car.

Fig. 1-10. Rear spoiler mounted on the rear deck of a sedan-based race car (1993 SCCA Trans-Am). Richard Dole photo.

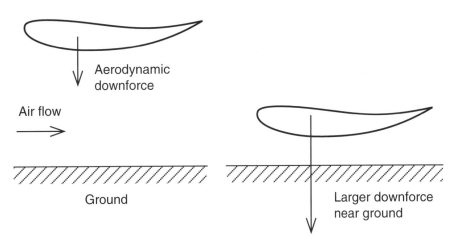

Fig. 1-11. Schematic description of the "ground effect" that increases the aerodynamic lift of wings when placed near the ground (the effect "works" for inverted wings, as well).

quite arbitrary limitations on car shape. As an example, many race-car rules require a flat lower surface. Only a very few allow contouring to exploit the benefits of ground effect. Indy car regulations allow a limited degree of such contouring and the underpan of a 1993 Indy car is shown in Fig. 1.12. It is difficult to recognize the inverted airfoil shape in this underbody panel, and because of the gearbox and other limitations the term *underbody tunnels* is probably more appropriate. Fig. 1.13 shows how these tunnels are integrated into body designs. Basically, these two tunnels form a longitudinal diffuser which is canted upward, toward the tail of the car. The similarity to an inverted airfoil is visible only in a side view, when imagining a longitudinal cut at the center of these tunnels.

Fig. 1-12. The underbody panel of a 1993 Indy car. Note the two tunnels under the two sidepods.

Fig. 1-13. Schematic description of how underbody tunnels can be integrated into the design of enclosed-wheel and open-wheel race cars.

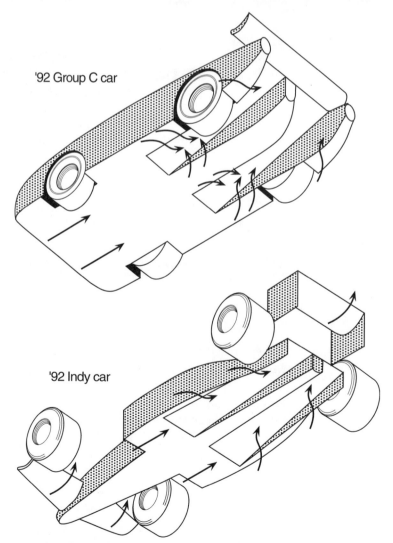

'92 Group C car

'92 Indy car

The next question is how to measure aerodynamic performance. This is very important, since most designers would like to have quite a close estimate on the aerodynamic loads (downforce and drag) before a vehicle is built (and sponsorship money spent). The most common location where aerodynamic evaluation is performed is in sophisticated and costly wind tunnels, both during the initial development of new cars and during the constant refinement of existing race cars.

A wind tunnel is a long tunnel through which the air is moved by large fans. Its advantage is that the expensive instrumentation and data acquisition is housed in a permanent facility (not on a moving vehicle), and that it is a controlled environment where airspeed, flow-direction, temperature, and other variables are not influenced by the outdoor weather.

As an example, Fig. 1.14 shows a 40%-scale race car being tested in the Ohio State University wind tunnel. The car is placed at the test section where the air flow direction and speed are highly uniform. This section is usually far from the fans to avoid the pulsation and swirl caused by the rotating blades. The wheels are placed on a rolling belt to simulate the moving ground, and the aerodynamic lift and drag are measured by a sensitive balance at the lower end of the long rod (or sting) holding the model from above.

Fig. 1-14. A 40%-scale model of an Indy car, as mounted above the moving ground in the Ohio State university wind tunnel. Courtesy of J. D. Lee and the Ohio State University.

When testing full-scale vehicles in a wind tunnel, as shown in Fig. 1.15, then the car can be driven into the test section where its wheels are placed on scales measuring the aerodynamic loads. The smoke traces are used to identify the direction of the airflow and to examine where these lines separate from the vehicle's body. If the flow moves mostly attached to the vehicle body, then the drag is usually lower.

Wind-tunnel testing of automobiles is quite a new angle in the well-matured aerodynamic testing environment of air- or sea-born craft. Until the late 1970s wind tunnels were highly guarded, typically defense-oriented laboratories and as such were extremely expensive to operate—even for some of the smaller airplane manufacturers. The oil crisis of the 1970s forced some of the larger automotive companies to build large wind tunnels which were primarily aimed at improving the fuel efficiency of production automobiles. A full-scale facility may have a larger initial cost, but the ability to test actual vehicles coming off the assembly line was and still is very attractive.

Fig. 1-15. The highly streamlined aerodynamic research vehicle of VW (ARVW), tested in the full-scale wind tunnel. Smoke traces are used to visualize the streamlines near the vehicle, which has a very low drag coefficient (defined in the next chapter) of $C_D = 0.15$. Courtesy of Volkswagen AG.

In regards to race cars, the biggest problem was that before the 1980s almost all of the existing large-scale wind tunnels (including airplane and automotive ones) were not quite suitable for race car application, primarily because of the cars' low ride height and the ground-effect designs. This led to a rapid increase in the number of purpose-built race car wind tunnels with elaborate moving-ground simulation. By the beginning of the 1990s it became almost a standard practice for each race car builder to own a wind tunnel capable of testing at least 1/4-scale models. The outcome of this development was the escalating cost of racing, which is probably one of the reasons behind the recent large cutbacks in all forms of racing.

HOW AERODYNAMICS SHAPES RACE CARS

In this section I will concentrate on the impact of aerodynamics on the external geometry of several representative vehicles. I'll start with one of the most logical forms of racing, at least from the automobile manufacturers' point of view, which is passenger car–based racing. These types of race cars are usually a direct derivative of similar production sports cars and in many leagues the level of modifications needed to create a race-worthy vehicle is quite limited. Since most production cars have positive lift, the aerodynamic modifications are aimed at reducing this lift, especially on the rear axle. The Ford Falcon race car in Fig. 1.16 is a representative example. It strongly resembles the production sedan, and the aerodynamic modifications are limited to front (chin) spoil-

Fig. 1-16. The 1993 production-car based Ford Falcon race car. Courtesy of Peter Gillitzer, Ford Motorsport of Australia.

ers, lowered body panels between the two wheels that form a skirt, and a full-span rear wing. One of the major limitations (from the aerodynamic point of view) is that the car's lower surface stays in its stock form, filled with exhaust plumbing, drive gear, etc. This limits the smooth flow of air under the car, and most ideas about using the car's body for ground effect should be abandoned.

In some forms of sedan racing, contouring of the lower surface is allowed, and in that case considerable gains in the level of downforce can be achieved. Such is the case for the IMSA GTS category, and these race cars, such as in Fig. 1.17, are pure racing machines with smooth aerodynamic underpanels (creating moderate levels of downforce) in spite of their sedan-ish look.

Fig. 1-17. *The 1993 Ford Mustang, IMSA GTS race car in the 24 Hours at Daytona. The car resembles a production car but hardly shares any mechanical part of it. Richard Dole photo.*

NASCAR stock cars are pure racing machines as well, but the outer body contours are usually very close to the production sedans their shape is based upon. Engine regulations are more strict to limit the cost of the sport, but the large output of these engines can propel these cars over 300 km/hr. Aerodynamics could play an important role in setting the performance envelope for these cars, but regulations aimed at keeping development cost down usually allow only a small rear-deck spoiler and some other minor modifications. Also, a quite common spectacle in stock car racing is drafting, when one vehicle follows closely the one ahead, as shown in Fig. 1.18. Because of the wake of the leading car, the one in the back experiences less aerodynamic drag and can go faster with greater ease and with better fuel economy.

The next type of race car that evolved from the production sports car-based concept is the prototype racer. In this form of racing the rules are quite relaxed and most aerodynamic modifications are allowed. An example is the Nissan

Fig. 1-18. *Two NASCAR stockers in a drafting situation. Don Alexander photo.*

Fig. 1-19. *The Nissan NPT-90, prototype race car (1992 Road America). Dennis Ashlock photo.*

NPT-90, shown in Fig. 1.19, that raced in the early 1990s. From the aerodynamic perspective, such race cars will have the largest levels of downforce since ground-effect-type body work is allowed along with large negative lift wings. Because of the large downforce the drag of such vehicles is sometimes twice as much as of similar size sedans. However, these vehicles are still much more efficient in terms of lift/drag ratio than open-wheel race cars (such as Indy or F-1). Most of the aerodynamic development on these cars is devoted to the rear wings and the body's upper and lower surfaces (and the latter, of course, is not visible to either the spectators or the competition).

A somewhat simpler form of enclosed-wheel race car (both for Le Mans and for IMSA) evolved in 1993/4 in an effort to reduce the cost of racing, especially aerodynamic development. Fig. 1.20 depicts one of the earliest designs of the WSC (World Sports Car) class, the Ferrari 333 SP, which dominated the 1994 IMSA season in the US. In this type of race car the underbody surface is flat, so that the aerodynamic trickery will be both cheaper and visible to the competition (and differences between the cars will be smaller—thus emphasizing the driver instead of sophisticated engineering trickery).

Another generic form of race car can be termed as open-wheel. The origins of such cars can be traced back to the early days of motoring, when the car con-

Fig. 1-20. *A 1994 open cockpit IMSA WSC racer, the V12 Ferrari 333 SP. Courtesy of Ferrari North America, Inc.*

sisted of a central streamlined body with four wheels, spread apart. One interesting example to start with is the dragster, shown in Fig. 1.21. There are some efforts to streamline the central body, but the large wheels are the primary contributors to aerodynamic drag. The large rear wing helps to push the driving wheels against the pavement to increase traction. Some of these dragsters can achieve speeds of over 300 mph (482 km/hr) and the downforce of the rear wing at these speeds can exceed two metric tons!

Fig. 1-21. A 1993 Top Fuel Dragster capable of reaching speeds in the neighborhood of 300 mph. Courtesy of Doug Herbert Racing, Les Welch photo.

The most popular form of open-wheel race cars (and of race cars in general) is Indy and Formula One, shown in Figs. 1.22 and 1.23. The quest for aerodynamic downforce is the only reason behind the use of the multiple array of wings on these cars. Again, their aerodynamic drag is usually quite high because of the four exposed wheels, and the primary difference in their appearance is a result of the regulations governing these two forms of racing.

Fig. 1-22. The 1993 Lola Indy car (with Nigel Mansell at the wheel) in a high downforce configuration. Richard Dole photo.

Fig. 1-23. The 1993 Benetton-Ford F-1 car with its distinctive raised front wing. Richard Dole photo.

In the case of Indy cars, the use of underbody tunnels is allowed, but they are limited to only one rear wing with quite restrictive dimensions. For F-1 cars, a flat bottom is mandatory, but two or even three rear wings of various sizes can be used. Of course one loop-hole in the regulations (which did not state clearly that the bottom of the body behind the rear axle should stay flat) allowed the addition of ground-effect tunnels (or venturis), which were banned specifically in mid-1994. In spite of the regulatory advantage that Indy cars had over F-1 cars, both type of cars can create quite large levels of downforce.

Comparing Fig. 1.22 with earlier Fig. 1.1 shows how much aerodynamic features can change from one circuit to another. For races with very high straight-away speeds and banked turns, low aerodynamic drag with moderate levels of downforce is required (as in case of the speedway configuration shown in Fig. 1.1). For twisty road courses with high-speed unbanked turns, a high downforce setting is required, as the much larger wings shown in Fig. 1.23 indicate.

As a last example of the application of aerodynamics to race cars, let's look at off-road racing. In general, off-road racing used to be synonymous with pure fun and low budget. Aerodynamics was not the primary consideration in these low-speed races where the rocky terrain and the gravel and sand on the twisty roads were the primary foes. However, even in this field, aerodynamics can strongly influence performance, as in the case of the record-breaking Toyota Celica entry in the 1994 Pikes Peak hill-climb race, shown in Fig. 1.24. This car had all the tricks of ground effect as well as a large and efficient rear wing, creating levels of downforce similar to F-1 or Indy cars of the same era! So, even if aerodynamics seems to be less important in a certain form of racing, somebody, somewhere will initiate this technology race, leading to escalating costs of staying competitive.

Fig. 1-24. This 1994 Toyota Celica broke the speed record in the 1994 Pikes Peak hill climb, using the most current aerodynamics to push its wheels down against the road. Rupert Berrington photo.

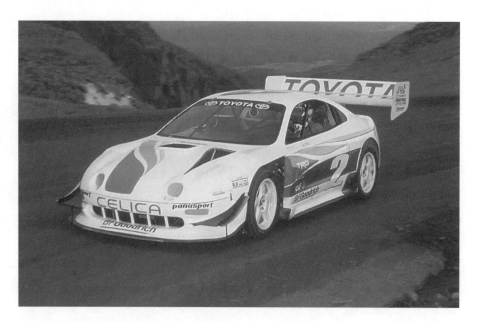

THE IMPACT OF RACING AERODYNAMICS ON PRODUCTION CARS

Before concluding this introductory chapter, one more question needs to be addressed, the so-called "technology transfer" between the technological showcase of racing and off-the-shelf production cars. The answer is not simple, since in many forms of racing the first impression is that race cars and race tracks are basically a huge advertising billboard for the fashion, tobacco, beer, or fine watch industry, and those involved believe that motor racing is a sport on its own. The reality, however, is that without the silent support of the auto makers the survival of the sport is not ensured and its successful existence depends on good working relations with the auto makers and on good sales in their showrooms.

Instead of arguing about the bilateral relation of automobile and race-car designers, let us show that there are indications that there is a technology transfer from race cars to production cars, focusing our attention on aerodynamic aspects only. The following examples attempt to represent a fairly wide spectrum of road vehicles and were selected quite arbitrarily. If your favorite automobile is not represented here, be assured that in the following chapters, most aerodynamic features of both race and production cars will be covered.

Let us start the discussion with an unexpected example: the pickup truck. These vehicles are growing in popularity, reaching new sales records each year, and there are strong signs that pickup truck racing is around the corner. As speed and performance increases, so does the importance of aerodynamics.

Fig. 1-25. *The pickup truck—a highly popular and practical mode of transportation in the mid-1990s. This figure shows one of the popular entries in that segment, the 1995 Dodge pickup truck. Courtesy Chrysler Corporation.*

One typical example of this group is the 1995 Dodge Ram truck, shown in Fig. 1.25. Note the rounded nose, which in addition to improving its appearance also helps to reduce its front drag. The problem with most pickup trucks, though, is the large base drag created by the cabin and the tailgate. The drag coefficient[1] of this Dodge Ram is about $C_D = 0.47$, which can be improved by dropping the tailgate or even by covering the bed. Some aftermarket products are aimed at improvements in this area and nets replacing the tailgate can create noticeable effects. The tailgate itself can also be turned into an airfoil, and when rotated horizontally can add to the rear downforce and at the same time reduce drag.

---

1. The drag coefficient, C_D, will be defined in the next chapter.

The next example is a typical entry-level commuter with a racy image. The 1995 Dodge Neon, shown in Fig. 1.26, may be considered "small" in the U.S., but it is certainly large (with frontal area of 1.91 m^2) compared to the subcompacts found in Europe or Japan. Since a racing image usually helps with some of the younger, first-time new car buyers, the manufacturer must encourage such activities. Indeed, Fig. 1.26 shows the racing version of the Neon, which is very close in all aspects to the showroom product.

Fig. 1-26. The compact commuter car does not necessarily need to be boring. The Neon Challenge race car very closely resembles the same Neon you could see at your neighborhood dealer's showroom. Courtesy of Chrysler Corporation.

To ensure a race-worthy automobile the aerodynamic balance and coefficients must be evaluated. In general, good fuel economy requires low drag coefficient. Therefore, this Neon sports a low value of $C_D = 0.336$, which was recorded in the Lockheed Georgia wind tunnel. In addition, high-speed stability requires as little aerodynamic lift as possible, and the same wind tunnel experiments showed a total lift coefficient[1] of $C_L = 0.197$. More important is the front/rear lift ratio. If this ratio is close to one (actually should be close to the front/rear weight distribution), then the balance of the car won't change much with increasing speed. In the case of the Neon, the wind tunnel tests showed a front lift of $C_{Lf} = 0.097$ and rear lift of $C_{Lr} = 0.100$, which is about as close as it can get to an even distribution.

The BMW M3 model shown in Fig. 1.27 looks like a sedan but owes many of its refinements to lessons learned while racing BMWs in the various European touring series. In fact, many details such as the deep front spoiler and sculpted side skirts were incorporated into the production vehicle so that they could be used when racing these cars. The actual touring car looks strikingly similar, apart from a small rear wing, allowed in the rules (as shown in the lower part of the Figure).

Lift and drag coefficients for the two versions of the BMW M3 are given in Table 1.1. The aerodynamic treatment to the racing version not only reduced drag, but also reduced lift to a near zero level.

Sports cars obviously must possess a racy image, and most manufacturers will support some kind of racing involvement for this reason. In most cases, two seats will suffice, and occasionally two small child seats can be found in the back (hence the 2+2 term). There is a whole range of such vehicles offered; however, our next example, the RX-7, can easily be called an "affordable exot-

---

1. The lift coefficient, C_L, is also defined in the next chapter. Lift can be further divided to front axle lift, C_{Lf}, and rear axle lift, C_{Lr}.

Fig. 1-27. *Top: The race-inspired BMW M3 sports sedan. Bottom: The actual car raced in the 1994 FIA Supertouring Series. Many refinements learned on the race track were incorporated into the production version. Courtesy of BMW of North America, Inc. (top) and BMW AG (bottom).*

Table 1.1 Aerodynamic Coefficients of BMW M3

	Baseline M3	1994 FIA Supertouring
C_D , drag coefficient	0.31	0.30
C_{Lf} , lift coefficient, front	0.214	0.099
C_{Lr} , lift coefficient, rear	0.126	0.006

ic" (that is, you can afford it without selling your home and mortgaging your future income).

The cars in this market segment are mass-produced but their quality and performance match or exceed those of the far more expensive real exotics. The RX-7 is the only vehicle in the 1990s offered with the rotary Wankel engine and the sportier version is shown in Fig. 1.28. It has a long history of racing in a variety of events and its designers clearly understood what is needed for a winning configuration. Thus, the car has a small frontal area (of 1.79 m^2) to achieve low aerodynamic drag. The RX-7 was tested extensively in the MAZDA wind tunnel and Fig. 1.29 depicts the streamlines along the symmetry plane. The aerodynamic coefficients for the two models offered in 1995 are presented in Table 1.2.

Fig. 1-28. *The enthusi-ast-oriented R-2 package of the RX-7 sports car, showing the rear spoiler, which actually increases the drag of the vehicle. Courtesy of MAZDA Information Bureau.*

Fig. 1-29. *Extensive wind tunnel investigations led to the development of the 1993 RX-7 sports car. This photo shows the attached flow streamlines near the car in the MAZDA full-scale wind tunnel. Courtesy of MAZDA Information Bureau.*

Table 1.2 Aerodynamic Coefficients of 1995 Mazda RX-7

	Baseline RX-7	RX-7 R-2
C_D , drag coefficient	0.29	0.31
C_{Lf} , lift coefficient, front	0.16	0.10
C_{Lr} , lift coefficient, rear	0.08	0.08

The sportier looking R-2 package includes a rear spoiler and a front air dam. The latter is responsible for the reduction of the front lift which is essential for high-speed stability. The rear spoiler is more of a fashion statement than a real wing. Of course the 1991 IMSA GTO champion RX-7 (see later chapter 7) had one of the most efficient rear wing designs, but the technology-transfer avenue from racing to production was clogged in this case!

By now it is quite clear that as we proceed with this discussion the showroom price of the cars is increasing. Indeed the Porsche 911, a derivative of which is shown in Fig. 1.30, does not come cheap. To this car's credit we must admit that in spite of the fact that its original design dates back to the early fifties and that it still has a rear engine configuration, it is one of the most successful sports cars. It has raced in many classes such as IMSA, GTU, and LeMans. Through evolutionary refinements its aerodynamic coefficients were reduced to an acceptable range, while its drag coefficient is in the neighborhood of $C_D =$ 0.38–0.4. The curved streamlines in Fig. 1.31 around the roofline indicate that the vehicle generates lift. This is reduced in most of the recent 911s by a spoiler, similar to the one developed for racing. The streamlines in this figure also indicate that the airflow stays attached at the back of the vehicle, which is the reason for the lower than expected drag coefficient.

Fig. 1-30. Porsche 911-based cars were entered in many forms of racing. Here we see a GTU version in the 1993 24 Hours of Daytona. Courtesy of Richard Dole.

Fig. 1-31. One of the all-time favorite sports cars, the Porsche 911. Its original shape dates many years back and yet is still popular with the fans. In this photo one of the latest derivatives is shown in the wind tunnel with smoke traces around its center line. Courtesy of Porsche AG.

The word "exotic" was used before in this discussion, but a true exotic automobile (usually followed by the adjective *Italian*) is typically unaffordable and its production is limited. One true exotic is the new 1995 Ferrari F355, shown in Fig. 1.32. Ferrari's racing heritage is indisputable, and its racing experience is clearly transferred to its production automobiles. The examples in this chapter indicate that most passenger cars will have aerodynamic lift but only serious race cars have true downforce. However, the designers of the F355 wanted true downforce, which indicates that this car is designed for *speed*! In order to preserve the smooth styling of the car, no external aerodynamic aids such as

Fig. 1-32. *The 1995 Ferrari F355 exoticar. Particular attention is given to high-speed stability and handling, so that all of the 375 HP of the engine can be used safely by the novice customer. Courtesy of Ferrari North America, Inc.*

large wings were used. Therefore, apart from the small rear spoiler, most of the downforce is obtained by the underbody diffusers.

The recognition by Ferrari that the entire underbody requires as much attention as the upper surface is an industry first (Citroen, Jaguar, Saab, VW, and Audi, among others, have made limited use of underbody spoilers to primarily redirect air flow) and a major step toward improving aerodynamic performance of production cars. The smooth underbody and the venturis are shown in Fig. 1.33, and Ferrari claims that the important front/rear downforce ratio is independent of ground clearance. No official aerodynamic data was available; however, the 1995 sales brochure suggests that the vehicle produces about 170 kg of downforce at 290 km/hr (claimed top speed is 295 km/hr). This roughly translates to a lift coefficient of about $C_L = -0.24$, which is quite an achievement for a production sports car without large, visible aerodynamic aids such as wings.

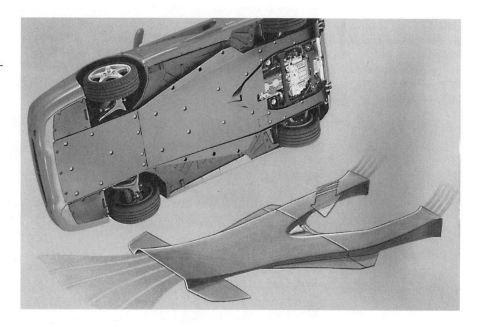

Fig. 1-33. *The smooth underbody of the 1995 Ferrari F355 with built-in diffusers that exit under the exhaust pipes. Courtesy of Ferrari North America, Inc.*

To conclude this section let us look at one of the most recent "ultimate" sports cars, which was designed by one of the most successful Formula One teams. Thus the name F-1 attached to McLaren's dreamcar should not come as a surprise. This is the best example of using racing experience in designing a road-going automobile. Even more important is the fact that its designer, Gordon Murray, tried to incorporate numerous aerodynamic innovations previously seen only on real race cars.

The vehicle has a quite low drag coefficient of $C_D = 0.32$, which is even more remarkable considering the active downforce devices used. These devices consist of two electric fans that assist air flow across the underbody diffuser. This "active" approach was used before by Murray, on his Brabham BT46 fan-car which won the 1978 Swedish GP (see Chapter 7). Under normal conditions, the downforce distribution is similar to the weight distribution (the centers of gravity and pressure coincide), which keeps the car balance unchanged with increasing speed. A target downforce of 160 lb at 150 mph was set by McLaren and if this target is met, then the lift coefficient should be near $C_L = -0.15$. Another very interesting aerodynamic feature of this car is the deployment of a rear deck spoiler during braking (not visible in Fig. 1. 34). This not only helps boost rear-brake cooling but also increases the downforce on the rear axle, reducing the effects of the forward weight transfer and resulting in major improvements in high-speed braking.

Because of the strong racing roots of the F-1 it was only natural that a racing version follow. The McLaren F-1 GTR, which is the racing version of this automobile, is shown in Fig. 1.35. The road-going version actually had to be detuned in order to meet racing regulations, by using engine intake restrictors and by eliminating all of the active aerodynamic wizardry. The car is scheduled

Fig. 1-34. *F-1 by McLaren. A three-seat road-going supercar from the stables of the McLaren Formula One team. Courtesy of McLaren Cars Ltd.*

Fig. 1-35. *McLaren F1 GTR race car, which had to be detuned to meet GT racing regulations. Courtesy of McLaren Cars Ltd.*

to participate in numerous GT and endurance races (and indeed, the car dominated the 1995 LeMans event). In order to regain the lost downforce a large rear wing was added, and the flat underside is positioned at rake (the rear is raised compared to the nose). GT racing regulations disallow the underbody diffusers used on the production car. Consequently, aerodynamic drag is increased somewhat, but the resulting downforce is on par with other LeMans competitors. A downforce of 600 kg was expected at about 350 km/hr (see Racecar Engineering, Vol. 4, No. 5, 1995, p. 8), which translates to a lift coefficient of almost $C_L = -0.6$.

In conclusion, we have seen throughout this chapter that aerodynamics is becoming an important factor in shaping race cars, and that many innovations tested first on the race tracks find their way back onto your daily driver. As a result of this aerodynamic research the stability of our automobiles has improved along with other less noticeable improvements such as less wind noise, less dirt deposition, and improved ventilation and cooling.

THE FOLLOWING CHAPTERS

Now that we have established in our minds the importance of aerodynamics to all forms of automobile racing, we must clarify a few things about the related science called *Aerodynamics*. While it would be very rewarding to be able to immediately discuss the various aerodynamic treatments found on race cars and their purpose and function, we must first devote some of the early chapters to explaining the basic terms and research tools used in this fascinating branch of science.

Remember, though, that this field is quite unpredictable (called *nonlinear* by the mathematicians), especially when the vehicle is not highly streamlined and the air flow doesn't follow exactly the curved shape of the vehicle (we shall later call this *flow separation*). The logic of this book is based on the concept of a data-base, where the author has made an effort to systematically collect, organize, and present the current level of knowledge in this field. Because of the unpredictable nature of this field, many of the details (especially in the earlier chapters) should be viewed as a presentation of observed facts—they cannot always be linked directly and immediately to a practical objective or question such as: how will this increase the downforce on a particular vehicle? However, as we gradually learn about the various types of flow fields, then we can face and hopefully understand the logic behind many of the aerodynamic details of actual race cars that are presented later.

2 AERODYNAMIC FORCES AND TERMS

INTRODUCTION

The objective of this chapter is to familiarize yourself with the basic phenomena of aerodynamics and eventually understand the mechanisms that create aerodynamic forces on a moving car. If you are mathematically inclined, a limited number of equations will be presented to explain some of the basic coefficients frequently used in the popular literature.

The chapter begins with a description of the friction-like forces that act parallel to the vehicle surface and contribute to vehicle drag. In addition to this friction-type force there is another mechanism that creates forces in the moving air. It is called *pressure*. Any time air moves around a body the pressure changes slightly. This change creates an uneven pressure distribution on the body, and when its effect is added up it contributes to vehicle drag and lift.

I will also review the Bernoulli equation, which allows us to calculate the pressure when the airspeed is known. This equation also states that aerodynamic loads increase with the square of speed, that is, when a vehicle's speed doubles, its drag force will increase fourfold.

The next task is to understand how the shape of a vehicle changes the airspeed near its surface so that you can solve the puzzle connecting vehicle shape to airspeed, friction, and pressure loads (and lift and drag).

Armed with the basic and essential knowledge of this chapter, you can familiarize yourself with most frequently used buzz words in this field. After reading some of the following chapters you should be able to form your own opinion about the virtues of certain aerodynamic gizmos appearing on race cars.

BASIC TERMINOLOGY

Before embarking on a discussion about the aerodynamics of race cars or even of simple wings, I must explain some of the most basic terms in the professional jargon. I'll start with the observation that, due to a vehicle's forward motion, otherwise still air is set into motion. In order to visualize this air motion, I must discuss the resulting airflow directions, the magnitude of velocity and pressure fields, and a few other basic terms. These basics will establish the relation between airspeed and pressure. Understanding the pressure distribution over a vehicle's body is, of course, one of the primary objectives of this discussion since the collective effect of the small differences in the pressure around the vehicle's body are responsible for aerodynamic loads such as lift and drag.

Some patience and dedication is needed for the next few sections because an initial "load" of definition is required before we can implement our newly acquired knowledge. Beyond this initial phase we can better relate to the new information and relate its significance to the main scope: the effect on vehicle performance.

Streamlines, Attached and Separated Flows

Let us begin with one of the simplest definitions. It is related to the frequently shown smoke traces in the airflow near cars being tested in wind tunnels. These **streamlines** are the curves associated with a pictorial description of a fluid[1] motion. If our vehicle is moving forward at a steady speed, the flow is then called steady-state flow. In this case the air particles will move along the streamlines (lines which are parallel to the local velocity direction).

Fig. 2.1 demonstrates the shape of such streamlines as formed near an airfoil. Flow visualization of the streamlines can be obtained in a wind tunnel by injecting smoke or, in a water tunnel (which is usually used with smaller-scale models), by the injection of colored dye. However, if the injected fluid has different density than the fluid, it may not follow the streamlines exactly. Therefore, the coloring material has to be selected very carefully, and in the case of automotive wind tunnel testing, the injection of smoke (with fairly close density to air) is widely used.

Fig. 2-1. *Streamlines in a steady-state flow over an airfoil.*

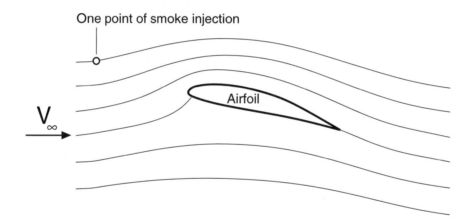

A reasonably dense set of streamlines, such as in Fig. 2.1, can be obtained by injecting the dying material at a number of locations ahead of the model. If we inject the smoke at one point only (as shown by the arrow in Fig. 2.1), then only one streamline will be visualized (in this case the upper streamline).

By observing several streamline traces in the flow (as in Fig. 2.2), it is possible to see if the flow follows the vehicle's body shape close to its surface. When the streamlines near the solid surface follow exactly the shape of the body (as in the upper portion of Fig. 2.3) the flow is considered to be **attached**. If the flow does not follow the shape of the surface (as seen behind the vehicle in Fig. 2.2 and in the lower part of Fig. 2.3) then the flow is considered detached or **separated**. Usually such separated flows behind the vehicle will result in an unsteady wake flow, which can be felt up to large distances behind the vehicle. As we shall see later, having attached flow fields is extremely important in reducing aerodynamic drag and/or increasing downforce.

---

1. Both liquid or gas (air) flows are possible, and we can refer to both by the generic term *fluid flow.*

Fig. 2-2. Visualization of streamlines (by smoke injection) during a wind-tunnel test. Courtesy of Volkswagen AG.

Fig. 2-3. Attached flow over a streamlined car (A), and the locally separated flow behind a more realistic automobile shape (B).

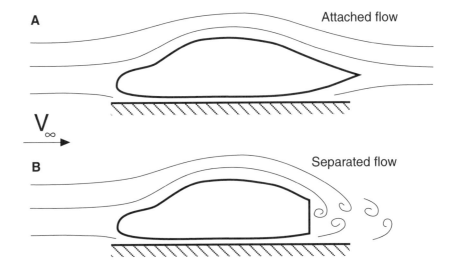

Velocity Distribution

When a vehicle moves through still air (forgetting about winds for a moment), then its shape disturbs the air particles so that their velocity is not equal at all points in the flow. In order to describe the magnitude of velocity of air particles passing an object, velocity-distribution diagrams (or velocity profiles) are used. To illustrate the velocity distribution on a flat plate, consider a constant-velocity free stream flow as shown in Fig. 2.4.[1] A flat plate is inserted into the flow parallel to the streamlines.

The flat plate introduces a disturbance, even if the plate is parallel to the flow direction (and to the local streamlines). This disturbance can be visualized by injecting smoke along a vertical grid at a given moment. After a short while (say 1 sec) we can record the location of the injected particles, and by connecting these points with the points of injection, create a visual description of the magnitude of the velocity (as shown at the right hand side of the plate). This diagram usually describes the change in the fluid velocity along a vertical line (ordinate z) and the magnitude of the velocity (V) is plotted parallel to the abscissa (free stream direction) of this diagram. Thus, this diagram describes the **velocity distribution** on the upper surface of the plate, along the line connecting the points of particle injection.

---

1. This flow is usually called a constant-velocity free stream, V_∞, which is the velocity observed by the driver of a vehicle (which is equal to the vehicle's speed). The notation V is the local velocity, caused by the motion of the body.

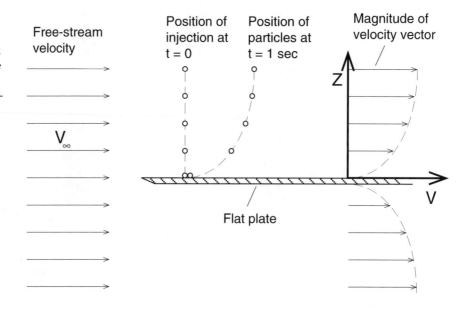

Fig. 2-4. *Side view of the velocity distribution near a flat plate in a free stream, V_∞ (velocity profile on the upper surface is described by the V vs z graph).*

Now, leaving momentarily the discussion about the basic definitions, we can observe a couple of interesting features in Fig. 2.4. First, the air velocity near the surface comes to a halt! This is known as the "no-slip condition." The fluid particles touching the body will stick to the surface; they have no relative velocity. Farther away from the solid body the velocity increases, until it equals the local free-stream value. This thin boundary is termed the **boundary layer** and will be discussed with more details later.

Perhaps you can "feel" that stopping the flow near the surface leads to friction drag, which is indeed one significant contribution to vehicle drag. For a car moving at 100 km/hr, the boundary layer may be a few mm thick near the front and several cm thick near the roof. Also note that in the case of the flat plate, such a boundary layer develops on both the upper and the lower surfaces.

Flows: Laminar and Turbulent

Let us return to the free-stream flow described at the left hand side of Fig. 2.4, but this time assume that the flat plate is not there. If we follow the traces made by several particles in the fluid we would expect to see parallel lines as shown in the upper part of Fig. 2.5. If, indeed, these lines are parallel and follow the direction of the average velocity, and the motion of the fluid seems to be "well organized," then this flow is called **laminar**. On the other hand it is possible to have the same average speed in the flow, but in addition to this average speed the fluid particles will momentarily move in the other direction. The fluid is then called **turbulent** (even though the average velocity could be the same for both the laminar and turbulent flows).

Knowing whether the flow is laminar or turbulent is very important for race car engineers since features such as flow separation and vehicle drag or lift can change dramatically between these two flows. Usually when an automobile travels in an undisturbed environment, the prevailing flow can be considered laminar. However, conditions such as winds (that interact with buildings, vegetation, etc.) or the motion of other vehicles can cause the flow to become turbulent. Furthermore, even if the flow is initially laminar, it may turn turbulent (near the vehicle) due to the disturbance created by the vehicle itself.

Laminar flow

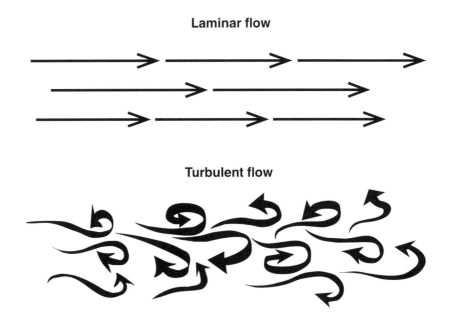

Turbulent flow

Fig. 2-5. *Fluid particle traces in laminar and in turbulent flow.*

Fluid Properties

The loads exerted on a vehicle moving through air, or on a scaled-down model in a water tunnel, depend on the properties of the fluid material (e.g., temperature, pressure, density, viscosity, etc.) Assuming that the reader is familiar with terms such as temperature and pressure, we shall mention here fluid density and viscosity only. Density (mass per unit volume) is familiar to all of us, and we all know that a steel bar is heavier than a wooden one of the same size. When using our equations the density is designated by the greek symbol rho, ρ. Viscosity is, in a very generic sense, a measure of fluid resistance to motion (similar to friction), and is designated by the Greek symbol μ.

The effect of viscosity in a fluid can be demonstrated by the simple example shown in Fig. 2.6 (following the analogy to dry friction) where a viscous fluid is placed between two parallel, solid surfaces. The lower surface is stationary, while the upper one is moving to the right at a constant speed. The fluid particles near the two walls tend to stick to the solid surface and maintain a zero relative velocity (this is the previously mentioned no-slip condition).

Fig. 2-6. *Velocity distribution between two parallel plates, caused by the motion of the upper plate. The lower plate is stationary, and the upper one is moved by the force F at a constant speed V_∞.*

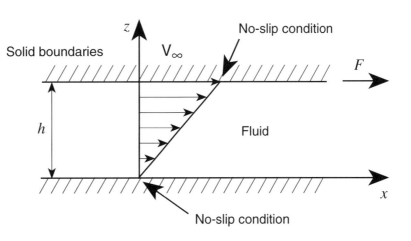

Fluid Viscosity The property called viscosity can be described by using the experiment shown in Fig. 2.6. Here the upper surface is moved by a shear force F at a speed V_∞. The fluid fills the gap between this moving surface and the lower stationary surface. The motion of the fluid is caused by the motion of the upper surface, since the particles adjacent to it must move at the same speed (recall the no-slip condition). For the same reason, the particles adjacent to the lower surface won't move, but the speed of the rest of the fluid will increase gradually toward the moving surface. The magnitude of the shear force F can be connected to the speed of the upper plate and to the viscosity of the fluid by the relation:

Eq. 2.1

$$\frac{F}{A} = \mu \frac{V_\infty}{h}$$

Here μ (pronounced mu) is the coefficient of viscosity and A is the area of the upper surface. It is clear now that for a fluid with higher viscosity (e.g., when motor oil is compared to water), the shear force F will increase.

As an example, assume that the upper plate with an area of $A = 1 m^2$ is being pulled at a speed of $5 m/s$. The fluid between the two surfaces is water, and the separation distance is 0.02 m. Taking the value of the viscosity coefficient μ from Table 2.1 we can calculate the force F required to pull the plate as:

$$F = \mu \left(\frac{V_\infty}{h} \right) A = 1.0 \times 10^{-3} \times \frac{5}{0.02} \times 1 = 0.25 N$$

As the upper surface moves relative to the lower one, the fluid is sheared, and the molecules are forced to move relative to each other. The resistance of the fluid to shear results in the force F which must be applied to the moving surface in order to sustain motion. Because of the no-slip condition the velocity distribution between the walls (in the absence of a pressure field) is linear, as shown in Fig. 2-6. Thus, to an observer standing on the lower surface, the fluid velocity seems to be zero on the stationary surface and equal to the velocity of the plate on the upper surface. This simple experiment can also help to define viscosity by simply measuring the **shear force** required to pull the upper plate, as described in Eq. 2.1. It is also clear that when viscosity increases, the shear force (that causes the friction drag) will increase too.

The values for the density and viscosity of three common fluids are listed in Table 2.1. Because of our interest in automotive aerodynamics we shall focus later on the properties of air only, but for the purpose of comparison the density and viscosity of water and oil are listed as well. Since the density and viscosity of fluids depend on other conditions such as temperature and pressure, the values in the following table are given approximately for atmospheric pressure at a temperature of 20° C.

One obvious conclusion from this table is that the density and viscosity of air are small compared to other fluids. However, at higher speeds noticeable aerodynamic loads can be generated in spite of the seemingly negligible magnitudes of the properties.

Table 2.1 Density and Viscosity of Air and Water (at 20° C, 1 *atm*)

	$\rho\,[kg/m^3]$	$\mu\,[N\sec/m^2]$
Air	1.22	1.8×10^{-5}
Water	1000	1.0×10^{-3}
SAE 30 Motor oil	919	4.0×10^{-1}

The Reynolds Number   At this point we can define one of the most frequently used nondimensional numbers; the **Reynolds number**, named after the famous 19th-century British fluid dynamicist, Osborne Reynolds (1842-1912). For our purpose the Reynolds number represents scaling effects, and can be used to quantify the product of speed versus time. Its importance becomes evident when comparing test results from different model scales or different speeds. Also, knowing the magnitude of the Reynolds number can indicate if the flow is mostly laminar or turbulent (with increasing speed the flow becomes more turbulent).

The Reynolds Number   The Reynolds number, when used in the field of race car aerodynamics, can quantify the product of speed times size. For example, the Reynolds number (Re) of a quarter-scale race car model tested at actual speeds is still 1/4 of the full-size car Re number. The implementation will be clarified later. More precisely, the Re number represents the ratio between inertial and viscous (friction) forces created in the air and is defined by the following formula:

Eq. 2.2

$$Re = \frac{\rho VL}{\mu}$$

Here ρ (pronounced rho) is the fluid density, μ is the viscosity, V represents the velocity, and L is some characteristic length (of the vehicle, for example). Engineers sometimes define a representative Reynolds number for a particular test (and then they use the car length or a wing's chord for L) or they may define a *local* Reynolds number which varies with the local distance (and then L stands for the local distance from the plate leading edge, as in Fig. 2.4, or for the distance behind a vehicle's nose).

An important feature of this number is that it is nondimensional, that is, the units cancel out (even if we use British, US, or European units). For a typical numerical value of the Reynolds number we can assume a car length of 4 m and a speed of 30 m/sec, and use the properties of air from Table 2.1, thus;

$$Re_L = 1.22\times30\times4/(1.8\times10^{-5}) = 8.1\times10^6$$

The subscript L, signifies that the Reynolds number is based on the length of the vehicle, L.

For example, for Reynolds number values (based on the car length) of less than 10^5 the flow over wings will be laminar and the drag and lift obtained at this range may be considerably different than at the higher values of the Reynolds number. Returning to the case of a race car piercing its way through air (with very small viscosity) we find that the Reynolds number will be on the order of several millions. But if the same vehicle moves through a highly viscous fluid such as motor oil then the Reynolds number will be far less.

The punch line here is that some small-scale testing (e.g., 1/5 scale) conducted at low speeds (e.g., at 100 km/hr) may drop the Reynolds number below 2×10^5 and then the results of expensive wind tunnel testing may not be fully applicable to the actual car! (More details about the significance of the Reynolds number can be found later.)

Another interesting feature of the Reynolds number is that two different flows can be considered similar if their Reynolds numbers are the same. A possible implementation of this principle may apply when exchanging water tunnel for wind tunnel testing, or vice versa. Typical gains are in reduced model size, or in lower test speeds. For example, the ratio of viscosity/density in air is about 15 times larger than in water; therefore, in a water tow tank much slower speeds can be used to test the model at the same Reynolds number (and this has been done but seems not to be very practical for automobile testing). A more practical application of this principle would be to test a 1/15-scale submarine model in a wind tunnel at true water-speed conditions. Usually it is better to increase the speed in the wind tunnel and then even a smaller scale model can be tested.

THE BOUNDARY LAYER

The concept of a boundary layer can be described by considering the flow past a two-dimensional flat plate submerged in a uniform stream, similar to the one shown in Fig. 2.4. As mentioned earlier, because of fluid viscosity, the velocity on the surface of the stationary plate becomes zero, while a thin layer exists where the velocity parallel to the plate gradually reaches the outer velocity V_0 (here V_0 denotes the velocity outside the boundary layer and for the case of the flat plate, it is equal to the free stream velocity, $V_0 = V_\infty$).

This layer of rapid change in the tangential velocity (shown schematically by the velocity profile in Fig. 2.4) is called the **boundary layer**, and its thickness δ (delta) *increases* with the distance along the plate. The boundary layer exists on more complicated shapes, as well, (e.g., the automobile shown in Fig. 2.7). A typical velocity profile within this layer is described by the inset on this figure.

The thickness of this boundary layer is only several mm at the front of a car traveling at 100 km/hr, and can be several cm thick toward the back of a streamlined car. As you will see, a thicker boundary layer creates more viscous friction drag. Furthermore, a too steep increase in this thickness can lead to flow separation, resulting in additional drag and a loss in the downforce created by a race car's wings.

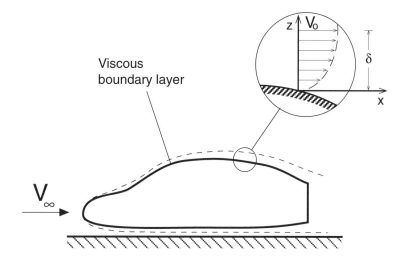

Fig. 2-7. Boundary layer near a vehicle's surface, and typical velocity distribution within this layer.

Viscous boundary layer

Some Features of the Boundary Layer

Now we are in a position when we can use some of the earlier definitions to better understand the development and the importance of the boundary layer. In reality the boundary layer can be laminar or turbulent. It usually begins as a laminar boundary layer which gradually becomes turbulent. This is shown schematically, for the case of the flat plate, in Fig. 2.8. In principle, in an undisturbed flow, the boundary layer is initially laminar, but as the local distance L (and the corresponding *local* Reynolds number) increases, the flow becomes turbulent. The region where this change takes place is called the region of transition. As Fig. 2.8 shows, due to the fluctuating turbulent velocity components, the turbulent boundary layer is thicker. Therefore, the momentum loss in this boundary layer is larger and the turbulent (surface) friction is expected to be larger (and so is the vehicle's drag).

At this point we can define a skin-friction coefficient. This number is really a measure of the skin friction on a vehicle's surface, which directly relates to friction drag. The primary reason that engineers use the nondimensional friction coefficient is because of its wider appeal (i.e., independent of engineering units).

Fig. 2-8. Variation of the boundary layer thickness along a flat plate. Note the velocity distribution inside the boundary layer and its increase in thickness during the transition from laminar to turbulent flow.

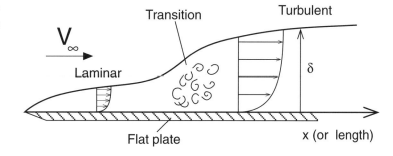

The Skin-Friction Coefficient

The skin-friction coefficient C_f is a nondimensional number (independent of units) indicating the level of friction between the vehicle surface and the air. It is defined as:

Eq. 2.3

$$C_f = \frac{\tau}{\frac{1}{2}\rho V_\infty^2}$$

where τ is the surface shear force per unit surface (friction resistance) and it is nondimensionalized by the quantity $\frac{1}{2}\rho V_\infty^2$ (called the *dynamic pressure*) so that the numerical value of C_f will be (almost) independent of speed.

For example, if the friction coefficient is $C_f = 0.002$ (from Fig. 2.9) and the air moves over the plate at a speed of 30 m/sec (108 km/hr) then the shear force per unit area $(1 m^2)$ is:

$$\tau = C_f \left(\tfrac{1}{2}\rho V_\infty^2\right) = 0.002 \times \frac{1}{2} \times 1.22 \times 30^2 = 1.098\,N/m^2$$

and the density of air was taken from Table 2.1.

Now, in terms of the effect of speed on friction, note that the boundary layer thickness decreases as airspeed increases. This is due to the larger momentum (the product of mass times velocity) of the free stream compared to the loss of momentum caused by the viscosity near the solid surface. Therefore, the friction coefficient (that contributes to the vehicle's drag) will be reduced with increased flow speed. This trend is reinforced by the typical experimental skin friction results in Fig. 2.9, for the case of a flat plate submerged in a parallel flow.

Fig. 2-9. Skin-friction coefficient C_f values on a flat plate, placed parallel to the flow, for laminar and turbulent boundary layers, versus the Reynolds number.

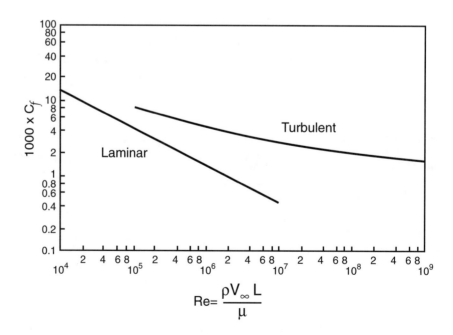

Note that instead of a speed scale on the abscissa, fluid dynamicists like to use the Reynolds number, so that this diagram will have a wider application. The interesting observations on this figure are that there are two separate curves: one for laminar and one for turbulent flow, and that both decrease with increased Reynolds number. Furthermore, for a large range of the Reynolds number, both turbulent and laminar flows are possible. In these cases the friction in laminar flow is considerably lower (sometimes 4 to 5 times less) which means that for the purpose of drag reduction, *laminar* flow is preferred.

Before proceeding to the next topic we can draw a few important conclusions about the boundary layer:

- Boundary layer thickness is larger for turbulent than for laminar boundary layers.
- The skin friction coefficient becomes smaller with increased Reynolds number (mainly for laminar flow).
- At a certain Reynolds number range both laminar and turbulent boundary layers are possible. The nature of the actual boundary layer for a particular case depends on flow disturbances, surface roughness, etc.
- The skin friction coefficient is considerably larger for the turbulent boundary layer (larger skin friction results in larger friction drag).
- Because of the momentum transfer normal (perpendicular) to the direction of the average speed, in the case of a turbulent boundary layer, flow separations will be delayed somewhat compared to a laminar boundary layer. This is an important and indirect conclusion, but in many automotive applications it forces us to prefer turbulent boundary layers in order to delay flow separation.

The outcome of the above conclusions, with race cars in mind, is that for low drag, large regions of thin, laminar boundary layers must be maintained (and transition delayed). However, in cases where flow separation is likely, as at the aft section of the car or on highly cambered (curved) wings, it is better to have a turbulent boundary layer (with some drag penalty) but avoid painful flow separations (leading to the loss of downforce).

Transition and Laminar Bubble

If we limit the present discussion to automobile-related aerodynamics, then the order of magnitude of the Reynolds number is about 10^7, and based on Fig. 2.9 large regions of laminar boundary layers are possible. As mentioned in the previous paragraph, such a laminar boundary layer is desirable if we want to reduce drag due to skin friction. But if surface curvature is high the flow may separate, and this drag advantage may be lost.

A typical case is demonstrated in Fig. 2.10, where the boundary layer on a streamlined hood is initially laminar. However, due to the large curvature of the upper surface the laminar boundary layer separates initially, then reattaches later (remember from the discussion of Fig. 2.3 that attached flow is preferred). The reattachment is usually a result of the boundary layer turning turbulent due to this disturbance, and due to the larger momentum transfer in the turbulent flow, the separation is delayed (or avoided). This early flow separation is called a *laminar separation*, and the enclosed streamlines (where reversed flow exists) are called a *laminar bubble*. There are three reasons to mention this phenomenon:

First, the laminar bubble area is sensitive; the flow may separate entirely without a reattachment, resulting in a considerable drag increase.

Fig. 2-10. Schematic description of the laminar bubble and the transition from laminar to turbulent boundary layer.

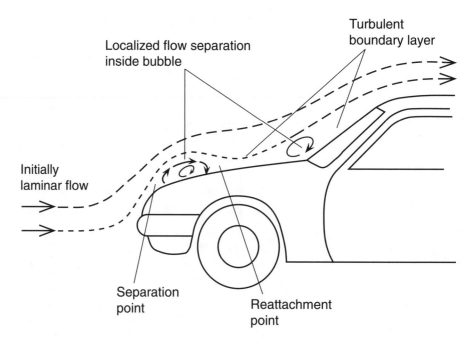

Second, the laminar bubble appears in the low Reynolds number range $(10^4 - 0.2 \times 10^6)$ and may disappear as the vehicle speed is increased. This may cause severe discrepancies in flow visualizations and aerodynamic data when comparisons are made over a wide speed range. This becomes even more pronounced when small scale wind tunnel models are used to develop a high-speed, full-scale vehicle (i.e., a race car).

Last, it is possible to force transition (from laminar to turbulent flow) within the boundary layer by introducing disturbances. Engineers call this: "tripping of the boundary layer," and it can be done by using small vortex generators (little wedges the height of the boundary layer) or even by placing a strip of coarse sanding paper on the desirable transition line. Since turbulent boundary layer has a tendency to stay attached longer, some drag benefits due to a reduction in separated flow can be gained by using this technique.

BERNOULLI'S EQUATION FOR PRESSURE

The shape of a moving vehicle causes the airflow to change both direction and speed. This movement of the airflow near the body creates a velocity distribution which in turn creates the aerodynamic loads acting on the vehicle. These loads, in general, can be divided into two major contributors. The first is the shear (skin friction) force, resulting from the viscous boundary layer (described by Eqs. 2.1 and 2.3), which acts tangentially to the surface and contributes to drag. The second force is pressure, and it acts normal (perpendicular) to the surface and contributes to both lift and drag (so vehicle downforce is really the added effect of the pressure distribution).

Note that the pressure force is caused primarily by the velocity *outside* the boundary layer, such as the V_0 shown in Fig. 2.7 (the velocity at the bottom of the boundary layer is zero).

Bernoulli's Equation   The Bernoulli equation describes the relation between air-speed and pressure. The formula can be applied to streamlines such as those described in Figs. 2.1 or 2.2. Along any point on a streamline the relation between the local static pressure p, density ρ, and velocity V is:

Eq. 2.4
$$\frac{p}{\rho} + \frac{V^2}{2} = \text{Constant}$$

The value of the constant is really unimportant because the equation will be used only to compare the velocity and pressure between two points in the flow (see next equation). In case of attached, smooth, and constant density flows the equation can be used for any point in the field (and not on a streamline only). To clarify these limitations and for additional information about the applicability of the Bernoulli equation, see Ref. 2.1, pp. 156–160, or Ref. 2.2, pp. 32–35.

Application of Bernoulli's Equation

In order to understand the importance of this equation, let us consider the flow over a vehicle moving forward at a speed of V_∞, as shown in Fig. 2.11. Note that a passenger inside the vehicle observes the free stream moving towards him at a speed of V_∞, too. Because the vehicle deforms the local streamlines, the velocity increases near the body. We can write Eq. 2.4 for a point far ahead of the vehicle (e.g at any of the three points shown at infinity, ∞, at the left hand side of the figure) and for a second point on the body (e.g., at point A). Since the constant of Eq. 2.4 is the same for those two points we can write

Eq. 2.5
$$\frac{p_A}{\rho} + \frac{V_A^2}{2} = \frac{p_\infty}{\rho} + \frac{V_\infty^2}{2}$$

and the subscript, A, represents the quantities measured at point A. So, in principle, if we know the ambient pressure p_∞, vehicle speed V_∞, and static pressure p_A near the vehicle's surface, then, based on this equation, we can calculate the local air speed V_A.

To demonstrate the application of this equation let us select another interesting point in the flow, where velocity comes to a complete halt on the moving vehicle (zero velocity), as in the case of an enclosed cavity created at the front of the car (point B, in Fig. 2.11). Now if we write this equation for the points ∞ and B we get

Eq. 2.6
$$\frac{p_B}{\rho} = \frac{p_\infty}{\rho} + \frac{V_\infty^2}{2}$$

since the velocity $V_B = 0$. Suppose our vehicle travels at a speed of 30 m/sec; based on this equation and on the value of the air density (taken from Table 2.1), the pressure at point B will be higher than the ambient pressure p_∞ by:

$$p_B - p_\infty = \frac{\rho}{2}V_\infty^2 = \frac{1}{2}1.22 \times 30^2 = 549\frac{N}{m^2} = 0.0055\,atm$$

(Note that $1\,atm = 101325\frac{N}{m^2}$.)

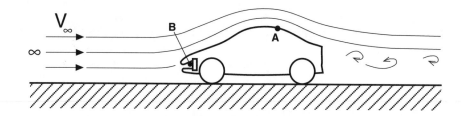

Fig. 2-11. *Terminology used to describe the application of the Bernoulli equation.*

Both contributors to loads depend on the velocity near the vehicle surface (outside the boundary layer), which is the result of the body's shape. In order to fully understand the origin of aerodynamic loads we must be able to connect a vehicle's geometry to the resulting velocity field. An attempt to describe this relation between the body shape and corresponding airspeed will be presented later. But first, we must complete the discussion about the pressure and establish the relation between it and the local velocity, so that the contribution of pressure distribution to the total aerodynamic loads can be added.

This relation was established by Daniel Bernoulli (Dutch/Swiss mathematician, 1700–1782) with his equation, which states in effect, that if airspeed varies as it flows around an object, then the pressure will change in an inverse proportion to the square of the airspeed. In other words, as the air flows faster around the vehicle, the pressure will be reduced. The algebraic formulation of Bernuolli's equation is given in Eqs. 2.4–2.6, along with some typical applications.

An important conclusion that can be drawn from Bernoulli's formula is that in order to create downforce on a vehicle, we must create faster flow on the lower surface than on the upper one. This, in turn, will create lower pressure on the lower surface, resulting in downforce. Of course, an inverted wing works exactly on this principle. Also, using the Bernoulli equation, the speed of a vehicle can be calculated simply by measuring pressures. This led to the development of various flow measuring apparatuses and two of the most common devices, based on this principle: the pitot tube and the venturi tube.

The Pitot Tube

The principle introduced by Bernoulli's equation allows us to measure speed at a point in the flow by simply measuring pressure. The device utilizing this principle is called the **pitot tube**, and was named after Henry Pitot (1695-1771), a French hydraulic engineer who invented this device to measure river flows. The basic apparatus is described schematically in Fig. 2.12, and consists of two concentric tubes. The inner tube measures at its tip the higher, total pressure, which increases as flow speed increases. The holes surrounding the outer tube measure the static pressure which should be equal to the undisturbed pressure which is not affected by the vehicle's speed. The difference between the pressure in the two concentric tubes varies with the square of the speed. This difference can be measured and connected to a display that shows the speed of the air stream.

Pitot tubes are widely used on airplanes and in wind tunnels to measure airspeed. For best accuracy, the flow must not be disturbed by the moving vehicle. Therefore pitot tubes are frequently mounted on long rods extending ahead of an airplane or race car nose.

Pitot tube

Fig. 2-12. *The pitot tube.*

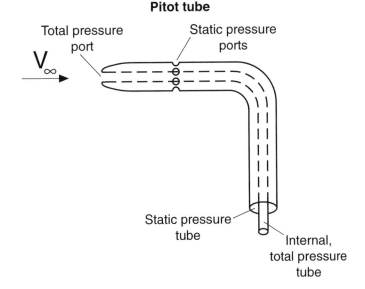

How the Pitot Tube Works The basic pitot tube consists of two concentric tubes, as shown by Fig. 2.12. The far-field, undisturbed static pressure p_∞, is the prevailing ambient pressure which can be measured far from the vehicle or at the sides of a thin long tube placed parallel to the stream (thus not disturbing the flow). This pressure is picked up at the sides of the outer tubes, as indicated on the figure. The second pressure is called the total pressure p_{tot}, and is picked up at a point of zero velocity (as in point B in Fig. 2.11, or at the front tip of the inner tube on the pitot tube). This point of zero velocity is usually called a *stagnation point*, and p_{tot} is also called the *stagnation pressure*.

Using the Bernoulli equation, Eq. 2.6, and multiplying by ρ, we can write

Eq. 2.7
$$p_{tot} - p_\infty = \frac{\rho}{2} V_\infty^2$$

Thus, by measuring the pressure difference between the two tubes and knowing the air density it is possible to find the speed of the free stream V_∞ (or the vehicle's velocity). The calculation of speed with this equation and the use of the engineering units are exactly the same as in the example following Eq. 2.6. Incidentally, sometimes the right-hand side term in Eq. 2.7 ($\frac{\rho}{2} V_\infty^2$) is called the *dynamic pressure*, and therefore we can say that:

Eq. 2.8   total pressure = static pressure + dynamic pressure.

The Venturi Tube

Another device that can be used to measure fluid flow (or velocity) is the **venturi** tube (or meter), named after the Italian physicist G. B. Venturi (1746–1822), who was the first to investigate its operating principles in 1791. You may have heard this term in context with carburetor venturis, or the underbody tunnels found on several types of race cars.

The venturi meter consists of a tube with a narrowed center section as shown in Fig. 2.13. In operation, the air (or water) flow moves faster through the narrow section, as explained in Eq. 2.9. By using Bernoulli's equation, you can see that the pressure in the narrow section will be lower than at the mouth of the venturi. This is shown schematically by the lower diagram that describes the pressure variation along the tube. The proportion of the change in pressure can therefore be directly related to the change in flow velocity, so by measuring the pressure difference the flow rate can be known as well.

To measure the pressure difference, a thinner tube is connected as shown in the figure and filled partially with (sometimes heavier) liquid. The pressure

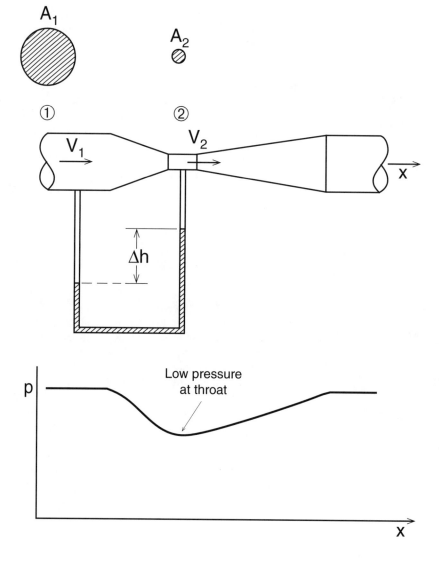

Fig. 2-13. The venturi tube and the thinner tubes used to show the pressure difference (indicated by the difference in height of the liquid columns). The variation of the average pressure in the fluid flowing through the venturi tube are shown by the lower diagram.

difference between the wide and narrow sections of the venturi causes the fluid to rise in the lower pressure side of the tube. The movement of the fluid can be directly related (and calibrated) to the velocity inside the venturi.

In general, the pressure difference (and signal) created by a venturi meter is smaller than the signal from a pitot tube. This makes the venturi meter less desirable for measuring external airspeeds, and in actual practice venturi meters are used primarily to measure liquid flow rates in pipes. However, the term *venturi* was attached to the underbody tunnels found on several types of race cars, in spite of the distant similarity. I hope this section clarifies the origins of this frequently misused term.

How the Venturi Tube Works

The venturi meter consist of a converging-diverging section as shown in Fig. 2.13. If the pipeline inlet area is A_1 , and the throat area of the venturi is A_2 , then in the case of an incompressible fluid such as water, the flow will move faster through the narrow section. The flow rate at the large section, say during one second, is $\rho_1 V_1 A_1$, and similarly at the narrow section is $\rho V_2 A_2$. We can now apply one of nature's rules, the conservation of mass, and state that the flow rate in the throat is equal to the flow rate in the pipeline:

Eq. 2.9

$$V_1 / A_1 = V_2 / A_2$$

where we have assumed a constant density and dropped ρ from both sides of the equation. The significance of this equation is that it indicates that the velocity must be higher at the throat. To continue, we can write Eq. 2.5 for points 1 and 2 along the tube:

$$\frac{p_1}{\rho} + \frac{V_1^2}{2} = \frac{p_2}{\rho} + \frac{V_2^2}{2}$$

And using basic algebraic substitutions, we can solve those two equations for V_1 :

Eq. 2.10

$$V_1 = \sqrt{\frac{2(p_1 - p_2)}{\rho \left[\left(\dfrac{A_1}{A_2} \right)^2 - 1 \right]}}$$

Since the velocity is higher at the throat, the pressure there will be lower, and the pressure difference $p_1 - p_2$ can be calibrated to measure flow rates inside the tube. In practice we can use the liquid column height Δh in the thin tube, instead of the pressure difference, by using our high-school knowledge that $\rho_1 g \Delta h = p_1 - p_2$, where ρ_1 is the density of the liquid in the tube and g is the gravitational acceleration. So, Eq. 2.10 can be used to measure the speed inside the tube by reading Δh and by knowing the cross-section area ratio of the venturi tube. Once V_1 is calculated, the flow rate can be calculated as well, by the term $\rho V_1 A_1$.

FLOW OVER BODIES AND THE PRESSURE COEFFICIENT

As we continue to develop the basic terms used in fluid dynamics we have to recall our original objective, which is to measure aerodynamic loads. Knowing the local velocity distribution is enchanting, but in order to evaluate aerodynamic loads we need to know the surface pressure distribution; in actual experiments the measurement of pressure is easier than the direct measurement of velocity. In fact, in most experimental cases the surface static pressure data (e.g., p_A in Fig. 2.11) is obtained by drilling a flush hole on the vehicle's surface, while the overall pressure force on the vehicle can be obtained by integrating (adding up) those pressures over the vehicle's body. In these situations a nondimensional pressure coefficient is used as described in Eqs. 2.11 and 2.12.

The Pressure Coefficient The nondimensional pressure coefficient is directly related to pressure. In order to make it independent of speed it is divided by the dynamic pressure (defined in Eq. 2.7). The equation for C_p is:

Eq. 2.11
$$C_p = \frac{p - p_\infty}{\left(\frac{1}{2}\right)\rho V_\infty^2}$$

and for typical application we can refer back to Fig. 2.11. Here all terms (such as V_∞ or p_∞, except the pressure p), are constant, and the shape of the pressure distribution on the car will be visually unchanged if we use the nondimensional coefficient (instead of the actual pressure).

It is possible to derive the pressure coefficient in terms of the local velocity, by using the relation $p - p_\infty = \frac{1}{2}\rho\,(V_\infty^2 - V^2)$ from Eq. 2.6. Exchanging the numerator with this expression results in the following simpler form for the pressure coefficient:

Eq. 2.12
$$C_p = 1 - \frac{V^2}{V_\infty^2}$$

So, if our car of Fig. 2.11 travels at a speed of V_∞, and the pressure p is measured at point A, then the pressure coefficient can be calculated by using Eq. 2.11. On the other hand if the local velocity V at point A is known, then we can use Eq. 2.12 for the same purpose.

Note that the pressure coefficient, C_p, in spite of its complex appearance, is a measure of the local pressure p (since the other quantities are the same for all the points on the vehicle). Also, the above presentation of the pressure distribution is independent of the vehicle speed, and the pressure distribution on the vehicle in terms of C_p should be the same (at least, in principle) for all speeds (e.g., V_∞ = 100, 150, 200 km/hr, etc.).

In order to become familiar with some typical values of the pressure coefficient let us create a small table. First, at the stagnation point (e. g., point B in Fig. 2.11) where the velocity is zero, we get C_p = 1.0 (see Eq. 2.12). Second, at an undisturbed point, far from the vehicle $p = p_\infty$ we get $C_p = 0$ (or use $V = V_\infty$ in Eq. 2.12). Also, if the local velocity is larger than the free stream velocity (V_∞) then C_p becomes negative. So to summarize these conclusions the following table is presented:

Table 2.2 Typical values of the pressure coefficient (C_p)

Location	Velocity	C_p
Stagnation point	0	1.0
On vehicle	If V less than V_∞	0 to 1.0
On vehicle	If V larger than V_∞	Negative

Thus the typical range of C_p is from +1 (for zero velocity) down to –8 (for a local speed of 3 times V_∞). It is also much easier to use Eq. 2.12, which directly relates the pressure coefficient to the speed.

Pressure Distribution Over Bodies

Now we are ready to observe the influence of a body's shape on the velocity and pressure distribution. Let us start with the hypothetical case of an attached flow over a simple shape such as a hemisphere, for which such data is easily calculated and can be found in a fluid dynamic textbook (e.g., Ref. 2.2, pp. 79–81). These results are summarized in Fig. 2.14 where both the velocity and the pressure are plotted along the hemisphere centerline, where θ measures the angular position on the body. At the front of the hemisphere, near the ground, there is a stagnation point ($V = 0$, and $C_p = 1.0$), and at the top the velocity is the largest and the pressure coefficient is the smallest. Since this body is symmetrical, there will be another stagnation point at the back of the hemisphere. So we can conclude, in very general terms, that the velocity increases with increased thickness (or height) of the body; similarly the pressure decreases, ac-

Fig. 2-14. Velocity and negative pressure coefficient distribution over the centerline of a hemisphere in a free stream V_∞ (θ measures the angular position on the centerline).

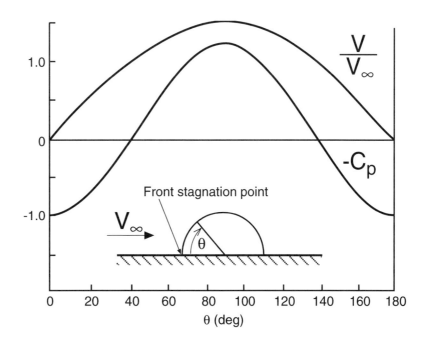

cording to Bernoulli's equation (that is, the general trends in the shape of the velocity and the inverted pressure distributions are the same). For this reason the pressure coefficient appears in Fig. 2.14 with a minus sign, $-C_p$, so that the velocity and pressure could be plotted on the same diagram. In practice and in the following figures, though, the pressure coefficient ordinate will be inverted with the negative values placed upward.

Pressure Distribution on an Automobile Shape

The next step is to understand pressure distributions over automobile-like shapes. At this point, we can also summarize the intuitive knowledge acquired in the previous section: When the flow is turned by a concave surface (as in front of the hemisphere in Fig. 2.14), then the speed slows down and the pressure increases. On the other hand, when the flow turns around a convex surface (as on the upper part of the hemisphere), then the speed increases and the pressure goes down.

Now we can look at Fig. 2.15 and try to see how body shape affects pressure distribution (along the centerline). The basic features of this pressure distribution are still similar to those shown in Fig. 2.14. At the front there is a stagnation point and $C_p = 1.0$, since the surface shape is concave. The flow then accelerates over the hood and C_p becomes negative, since the surface shape can be classified there as convex. At the root of the windshield the flow slows down again (concave) and the pressure increases. The flow reaccelerates over the top of the vehicle (convex), where the lowest pressure is observed. Across the back side of the vehicle the whole sequence is reversed (of course the shape of the

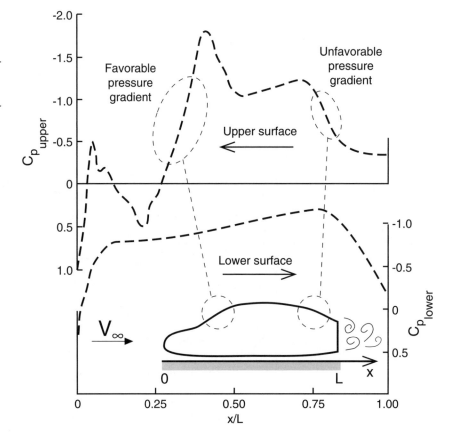

Fig. 2-15. *Distribution of measured pressure coefficient over a two-dimensional automobile shape (Data from: Buchheim, R., and Rohe, H., "Kann die Stromungsberechnung in Zukunft zur Besseren Aerodynamichen Entwicklung von Pkw Beitragen," Verein Deutscher Ingenieure, Berichte, pp. 261–288, 1985).*

front is different from the aft portion of this vehicle). However, the pressure at the back of the vehicle does not reach the $C_p = 1.0$ value, as it was in the attached flow case in Fig. 2.14. This is because the flow separates behind the vehicle.

The pressure distribution on the lower side of the vehicle is shown in this figure as well, and here, too, the pressure at the back does not recover to the stagnation pressure level. As a result of the flow separation, the pressures at the back of the car are lower than at the front (where we get $C_p = 1.0$), which effect creates drag. We shall call this component of the drag force, which results from flow separations, the **form drag**.

Favorable and Unfavorable Pressure Distributions

The importance of pressure distribution is that we can use that information for placing cooling inlets and exits (by making sure that pressure at the exit is lower than at the inlet). Also, based on the pressure distribution we can identify areas on the vehicle where the pressure is decreasing along a streamline. This condition is called **favorable pressure distribution** (or favorable gradient, or slope). One such area is shown near the windshield area on Fig. 2.15. Another area can clearly be seen near the front stagnation point (where the radiator inlet should have been). The opposite pressure distribution near the rear window is called **unfavorable pressure distribution** (or gradient) since the pressure increases along the streamline.[1]

The reason that we have dedicated a full paragraph to explain banal terms such as a positive and a negative slope is the enormous influence that such pressure distributions will have on the nature of the flow. For instance, in a favorable pressure gradient, the flow stays attached longer. Also the boundary layer in undisturbed free streams will stay laminar for longer distances along the body surface. All this results in less friction and form drag. On the other hand, steep unfavorable pressure gradients will initiate flow separations and transition to turbulent boundary layers. By knowing the local speed (e.g., Reynolds number) and the slope of the pressure distribution, certain aerodynamic computational tools can predict the boundary layer behavior (e.g., transition, flow separation, etc.).

Wakes

The discussion on the flow field created by bodies moving through air is incomplete without mentioning the far-field effects caused by this motion. The track of disturbed flow left behind a body moving through an otherwise undisturbed fluid is called a **wake**. Typical examples for wake flows include the vortex wakes visible behind airplanes flying in humid air, or the dust clouds which continue to roll behind a truck, long after it has passed by. In the following examples, let us highlight some of the features of such a wake flow, and establish its relevance to vehicle aerodynamics.

The concept of flow separation behind bluff bodies was introduced as early as Fig. 2.3. This local disturbance in the flow pattern behind the vehicle actually causes a momentum loss (or form drag) which extends far behind the vehicle and is described schematically by Fig. 2.16. Suppose we measure the velocity distribution, at various heights z, in the symmetry plane ahead of the vehicle at point A. Then, if the measurement is taken at a reasonable distance ahead of

1. Don't be confused by the inverted C_p ordinate in Fig. 2.15. Just remember if the curve slopes up then we call it favorable pressure slope (the mathematical term for slope is *gradient*).

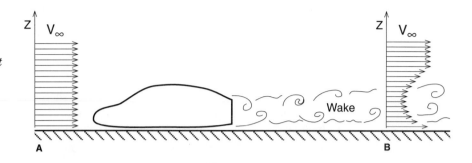

Fig. 2-16. *Wake flow behind a bluff body (with flow separation at the base area).*

the vehicle (e.g., more than one car length) the velocity profile indicates a near uniform velocity distribution. Now, if the same measurement is made behind the vehicle, even at a relatively large distance of 10 to 20 body lengths, then a velocity deficiency will be detected, as shown at point B. If the flow separates behind a bluff body, then such a wake will result, and in the wake area the flow seems to be dragging behind the vehicle. The energy of dragging this wake behind results in drag, whereas an ideal body with a completely attached flow may not have such a wake (and also no form drag).

Because, the flow inside the wake is moving into the vehicle's direction, another vehicle moving closely behind the first one can use the drafting effects of this separated flow. In many forms of racing those effects are noticeable and drafting behind a lead car is common practice in stock-car racing (Fig. 1.18). In forms of racing where high downforce cars are used, usually the wake can spoil part of the downforce on a following car, making it less competitive.

An important aspect of a wake is its time-dependent, periodic nature, as shown in Fig. 2.17. This figure depicts the top view of a typical condition when a motorcycle is moving in the wake of a large truck. Usually, the wake will have a periodic shape where vortices are being shed in an alternating pattern. The vortex direction is fixed by the separated shear layer. To explain this last sentence, let us observe the velocity at the right-hand side of the truck (at point A), outside the wake, where its magnitude is close to the free-stream velocity. At point B, behind the truck, the flow is separated and the velocity relative to the truck is close to zero. Therefore, the vortex forming at the right edge of the truck's rear end will rotate inside. The vortex shed from the left side will rotate in the opposite direction, and the velocity field induced by those alternating vortices in the wake is quite annoying to any motorcycle rider who tries to follow a large truck (especially at higher speeds).

Another frequently found form of wake is the trailing-vortex wake which stretches behind lifting wings. These wakes consist of two counter rotating, concentrated vortices, as shown in Fig. 2.18. They are often observed behind

Fig. 2-17. *Schematic description of the periodic vortex formation in the wake of a large truck.*

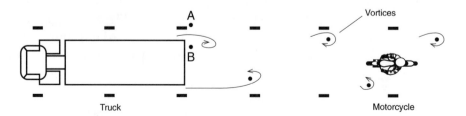

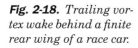

Fig. 2-18. *Trailing vortex wake behind a finite rear wing of a race car.*

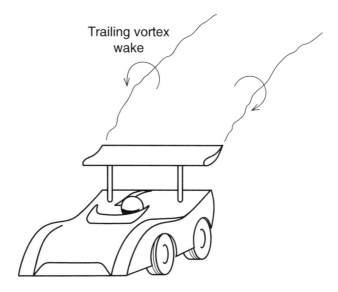

Trailing vortex wake

flying airplanes. These vortices are usually very stable and strong, and can last a large distance behind the wing that created them. The air in the vicinity of those vortex cores circulates around the core. The direction of the rotation for a typical race car rear wing (that creates downforce) is depicted in Fig. 2.18. Consequently, between these two vortices an upwash (flow upward) is induced, whereas outside the vortices an induced downwash (down flow) region exists.

DRAG, LIFT, AND SIDE FORCE

In the previous sections we have seen that there are two basic categories of aerodynamic forces acting on the vehicle. The first is pressure, which acts normal (perpendicular) to the surface and is responsible for a vehicle's lift and part of the drag. The second force is shear force (e.g., friction), which acts parallel to the body's surface and contributes only to drag.

The resultant force due to these contributions can be divided into various components. The most common directions are shown in Fig. 2.19. Based on this coordinate system we can define three force and three moment coefficients, but for simplicity we shall focus on the two most common forces only; namely lift and drag. The side force is important in cases of strong cross winds and when passing. (However, our main topic is related to race cars, and racing people tend to believe that their vehicles are so fast that side wind effects are negligible.)

The direction of the drag force (Fig. 2.19) is parallel to the vehicle's motion and points toward the back of the vehicle (into the x direction); the side force is positive, into the y direction; while the lift acts upward, normal to the ground (into the z direction). Of course, downforce is equal to negative lift and acts into the –z direction.

The basic idea behind defining nondimensional coefficients for lift and drag is that the value of the coefficients will be independent of speed and will be related to the vehicle's shape only. For example, the results of a vehicle's towing experiment, in terms of the total towing force versus speed, are presented in Fig. 2.20. The rolling resistance between the road and the tires is shown by the "x" symbols. This usually changes only a little with increased vehicle speed

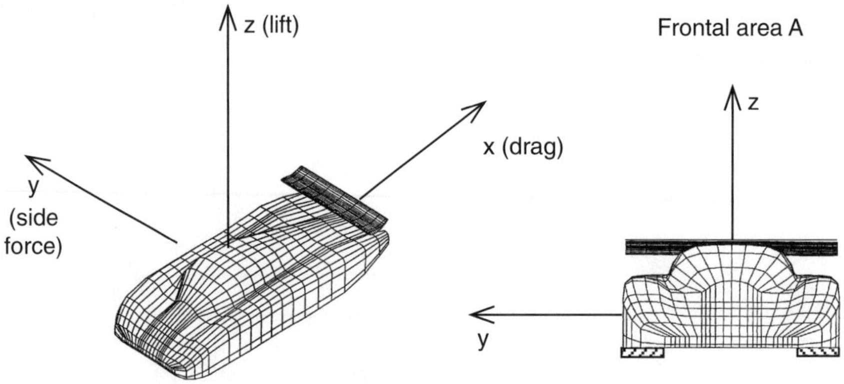

Fig. 2-19. Coordinate system used to define the directions of aerodynamic loads on a vehicle, and the frontal area used to define the force coefficients.

Fig. 2-20. Variation of vehicle total drag and tire rolling resistance versus speed. Reprinted with permission from Ref. 2.3, Copyright ©1985 SAE, Inc.

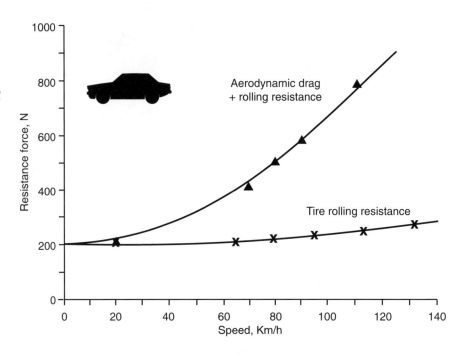

(and this information can be obtained by separate measurements). However, the total resistance, including aerodynamic drag, increases very rapidly and shows a parabolic curve fit (e.g., $D = C \cdot V_\infty^2$ with C being a constant), which indicates that aerodynamic loads increase by the square of speed V_∞. The solid triangular symbols represent the measured data and usually at higher speeds the curve-fit is far better.

Aerodynamic forces are very important (and are huge once the speed goes beyond 200 km/hr), but, more important, if we want to present the data in a nondimensional form, then we must divide the measured forces by the square of the velocity. The exact definitions of the coefficients of aerodynamic lift C_L, drag C_D, and sideforce C_Y are given in the Equation sidebar. The important conclusion is that if we plot the drag in Fig. 2.20 in terms of C_D, the result will be a straight horizontal line indicating no change in the drag coefficient with speed!

The reference area (appearing in the coefficient) used in automotive applications is usually taken as the frontal area shown at the right hand side of Fig. 2.19. In some cases, automobile manufacturers piously measure the accurate frontal shadow of the car while some others (e.g., race car designers) use a fairly liberal definition for their reference area. It is not uncommon to find different aerodynamic coefficient values for the same vehicles, and a deviation on the order of 5% in the data is fairly common. (Of course, as we shall see in the next chapter, force measuring methods, wind tunnel installations, wheel rotation, turbulence levels and model size in the wind tunnel also affect those results.) [1]

The Drag, Lift[1], and Side-Force Coefficients   Fig. 2.20

indicates that aerodynamic drag increases with the square of speed. In order to obtain nondimensional load coefficients we must divide by V_∞^2. As noted earlier, such coefficients will be independent of vehicle speed and will depend on the vehicle shape only. Consequently, the definition of the lift C_L, drag C_D, and sideforce C_Y coefficients is as follows:

Eq. 2.13
$$C_D = \frac{D}{\frac{1}{2}\rho V_\infty^2 A}$$

Eq. 2.14
$$C_L = \frac{L}{\frac{1}{2}\rho V_\infty^2 A}$$

Eq. 2.15
$$C_Y = \frac{Y}{\frac{1}{2}\rho V_\infty^2 A}$$

In practice, lift L, drag D, and side force Y, are divided by the dynamic pressure, which was defined in Eq. 2.7, and by a reference area A. For automotive applications the frontal area is commonly used as the reference area. Also note that sometimes the coefficients are defined, especially in Europe, based on the direction only. In this case C_X, C_Y, and C_Z are used instead of C_D, C_Y, and C_L, respectively.

As an example for using the drag coefficient (assume C_D =0.4) to calculate a vehicle's drag D, at a speed of V_∞ = $30 m/\sec$ we can use the following calculation:

Eq. 2.16
$$D = C_D\left(\frac{1}{2}\rho V_\infty^2 A\right) = 0.4 \times \frac{1}{2} \times 1.22 \times 30^2 \times 1.5 = 329.4 N$$

For the reference area A, a cross-section area = $1.5 m^2$ was used, and air density was taken from Table 2.1.

Typical Values for the Drag and Lift Coefficients

Fig. 2-21 shows the general range of the aerodynamic coefficients for some generic shapes (let us assume that all have the same frontal area, A). In terms of drag coefficient, one of the worst cases is to have a plate perpendicular to the flow; thus we start with a circular plate which has a C_D of about 1.17 and zero lift (due to symmetry). The reason for the large drag is that the circumference

---

1. The letter L often represents lift, but also sometimes length, as in Eq. 2.2. As long as we are aware of this tradition, any future confusion can be avoided!

Fig. 2-21. Typical lift and drag coefficients for several configurations.

			C_L	C_D
1	Circular plate	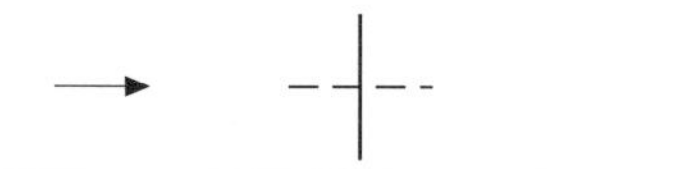	0	1.17
2	Circular cylinder L/D <1	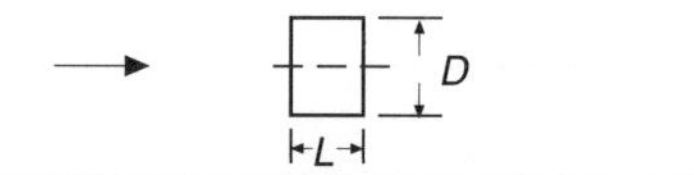	0	1.15
3	Circular cylinder L/D >2	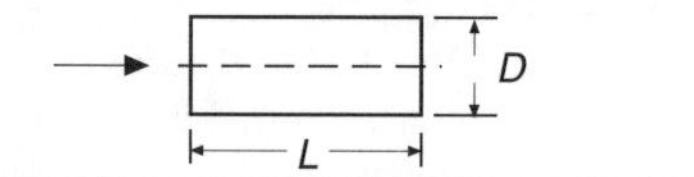	0	0.82
4	Low drag body of revolution	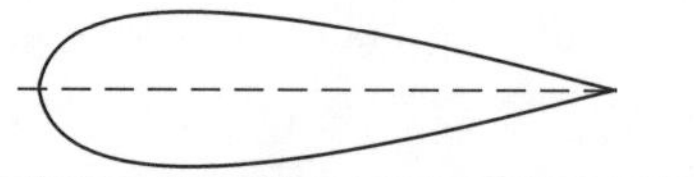	0	0.04
5	Low drag vehicle near the ground	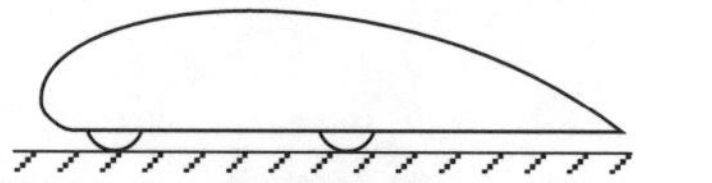	0.18	0.15
6	Generic automobile	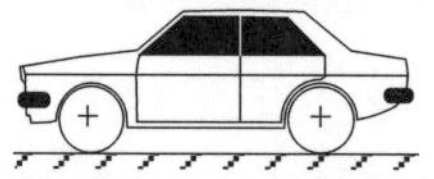	0.32	0.43
7	Prototype race car	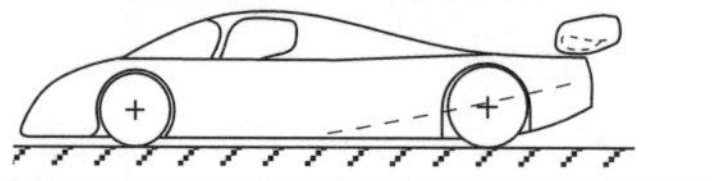	-3.00	0.75

of the zero thickness plate causes a flow separation. By increasing the plate thickness (streamwise length of this cylinder) the flow will have more length to return behind the body, so drag will be reduced, as shown by the two following examples. By streamlining the front and especially the aft section of the cylinder, flow separations can be eliminated entirely, and the drag coefficient falls to the very low range near $C_D = 0.04$.

When trying to develop a streamlined shape for a road vehicle, as shown by the fifth figure, we block much of the flow near the ground and create drag on the wheels and for such generic shapes, C_D of about 0.15 is obtainable. Because of the ground proximity the flow is no longer symmetric and will have larger speed (and lower pressure) near its roofline, which results in positive lift. A practical automobile will have more body details, which in turn will cause local flow separations and increased vehicle drag (the value of 0.43 is representative of 1960–80 boxy designs). Also, the lower surface of these vehicles is far from being smooth (engine, cooling, and suspension parts obscure the flow) and therefore even more lift is created by typical passenger cars (e.g., $C_L \approx 0.32$).

As will be explained later, downforce can improve race car performance, and therefore the designers add wings to create aerodynamic downforce. The last example in Fig. 2-21 shows a generic prototype race car. Lift coefficients in the order of $C_L = -3.00$ are not uncommon. The increased drag of these vehicles is partially a result of induced drag, a penalty that must be payed when using such high-lift finite wings.

There are three very important conclusions that can be drawn from this simple set of examples:

- For a streamlined body (No. 4), without flow separation, the contribution of pressure forces should cancel in the x direction (see Ref. 2.2, Section 8.3.4). Therefore, drag is a result of skin friction only. Thus, by using this simple example we were able to estimate the order of magnitude of the skin-friction effect on the drag force (i.e., $C_D \approx 0.04$).
- Longer bodies can have a lower drag coefficient (within the range of practical automobile geometry).
- Ground proximity can create aerodynamic lift (positive when the flow is limited under the vehicle).

This last observation leads us to further investigate the effect of ground proximity on the flow over bodies. For this purpose let us consider the two generic bodies shown in Fig. 2.22, whose shape is based on elliptic sections (both have the same frontal area and volume), and measure their lift and drag as they approach the ground. These geometries represent two basic automobile styling

Fig. 2-22. *Effect of ground proximity on the aerodynamic lift and drag of two generic ellipsoids (width/height = 1.25, length/height = 3.6, and max. thickness is at 1/3 length). Reprinted with permission from SAE paper 920349, Copyright ©1992 SAE, Inc.*

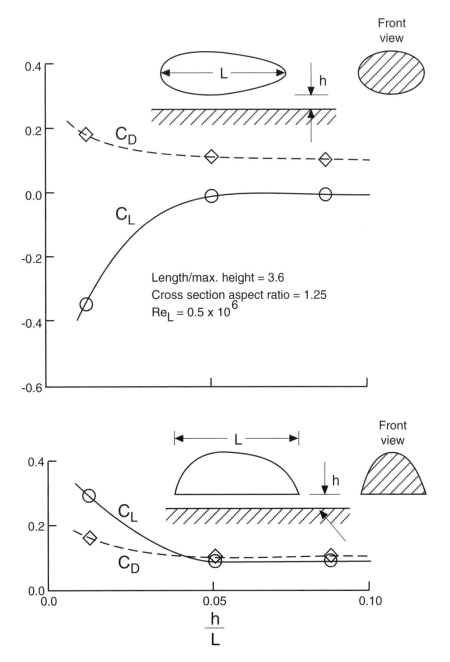

trends observed over the years. In case of the symmetric ellipsoid, decreasing the ground clearance h will cause the flow to accelerate under the body, creating more downforce (remember Bernoulli's equation stating that faster speed results in lower pressure). Of course the drag will increase, too, due to increased flow separation behind the ellipsoid. This trend is reversed in the flow over the semi-ellipsoid because the reduction in ground clearance tends to block the flow under the body (because of the sharp edges surrounding the lower surface). The drag force follows a similar trend to that of the symmetric body, but in this experiment somewhat lower drag values were obtained for the semi-ellipsoid.

Drag and Lift Coefficients of Several Road Vehicles

We can divide road vehicle shapes into two basic aerodynamic categories (based on Fig. 2.22). There are those stylists who make every effort to block the flow under the vehicle and those brave few who try to push as much air as possible under the car. Both styling schools can create reasonably low drag coefficients. However, if high downforce is sought then the latter approach is inevitable. This began to seriously influence race car design in the late 1970s and again in the late 1980s. (Additional information on shaping bodies for increased downforce can be found in Chapter 6.)

Table 2.3 Lift and Drag Coefficients for Several Road Vehicles

	Year/Make	C_D	C_L	Remarks
Sedans	1973 Opel Record	0.47	0.36	Ref. 2.3
	1980 Peugeot 305 GL	0.44	0.44	Ref. 2.4, p. 128
	1986 Subaru XT	0.29–0.31	0.10	Ref. 2.5
Sports cars	Porsche 911 Carrera	0.38–0.39	NA	Ref. 2.6, p. 198
	1982 Camaro Z28	0.37–0.38	NA	Ref. 2.6, p. 198
	1982 Corvette	0.36–0.38	NA	Ref. 2.6, p. 198
Race cars	1990 Mazda GTO (rear deck spoiler)	0.51	−0.44	Ref. 2.7
	1991 Mazda GTO (rear wing)	0.48	−0.53	Ref. 2.7
	1973 Porche 917/30	0.57	−1.04	Ref. 2.8 p. 170
	1985 Generic Prototype	0.74	−1.79	Ref. 2.9
	Generic Porsche 962 C	0.80	−4.80	Ref. 2.10
	1992 Mazda RX-792P	0.70	−3.80	Ref. 2.11
	1992 Nissan P35, C	0.50	−3.00	Say so
	1983 generic F1, no sidepods	1.07	−0.99	Ref. 2.12
	1987 March INDY	1.06	−1.71	Ref. 2.13
	1991 Penske PC20, high downforce	1.11	−3.33	Ref. 2.14
	1991 Penske PC20, speedway	0.740	−2.073	Ref. 2.15
	1992 Galmer G92, high downforce	1.397	−3.688	Ref. 2.15
	1992 Galmer G92, speedway	0.669	−1.953	Ref. 2.15

NA = not available

A limited list of the aerodynamic coefficients is compiled in Table 2.3 to demonstrate the range of these coefficients. The limited list of passenger and sports cars in this table serves primarily to demonstrate the difference between production and pure racing cars (a longer list of passenger car-drag coefficients is provided in Appendix 1). The list of the race cars is limited, too, because such information on actual race cars is very scarce and unavailable in the open literature. Also, Eqs. 2.13–2.15 indicate that the frontal area A is an important factor in determining aerodynamic loads. The list in Appendix 1, therefore, provides the total aerodynamic resistance, $C_D \cdot A$, which accounts for the frontal area as well.

It must be emphasized that the above table only demonstrates the typical range of aerodynamic coefficients. Because of a large variation in the experimental techniques and facilities, a quite large variation in the data can be expected, and two vehicles can be compared fairly only if their coefficients were evaluated in the same facility. For completeness, one may speculate about the extremes of lift and drag, and it's worth mentioning that unofficially, engineers who worked with Porsche and Nissan prototype race cars in the early 1990s claimed to have reached a lift-over-drag ratio of about 6 and lift coefficients on the order of $C_L \approx -5.0$ with some experimental models. In terms of actual race cars, the 1992 Mazda RX-792P is probably the leader in the downforce record race with a *measured* C_L of –3.80, and lift drag ratio of –5.4! The importance of this information is in placing a limit on the value of the downforce, which was available for the race car designers of the early 1990s.

Sources of Drag and Lift

Armed with the elementary fluid dynamic knowledge of this chapter we can take a brief look at some of the basic sources that contribute to aerodynamic lift and drag. The two tables presented in this section show the range for the various force contribution in terms of incremental drag and lift coefficients (ΔC_D and ΔC_L). The numbers quoted here are very general and each class of vehicles will have a separate breakdown of the various contributions listed. Let us start with a generic breakdown of the drag force components.

Table 2.4 Typical Range of the Various Contributions to a Road Vehicle's Aerodynamic Drag

Location	ΔC_D
1. Skin friction	0.04–0.05
2. Cooling drag	0.00–0.06
3. Internal flow, ventilation	0.00–0.05
4. Form drag (flow separations)	0.00–0.45
5. Lift-induced drag	0.00–0.60

We have already established that the contribution of skin friction (due to the boundary layers) is in the range of $\Delta C_D = 0.04 - 0.05$, but the other contribution to drag force requires some additional discussion. Cooling drag is the component created by the loss of cooling-air momentum across the radiators and the internal channels. Most references place this component in the range of $\Delta C_D = 0.02 - 0.06$ (e.g., Ref. 2.6, p.178) but, in principle, using the thrust of the heated cooling flow can reduce this part of the drag to the negative range (and there are many stories about the negative cooling drag of the WW II era, P-51 Mustang, aircraft).

The internal (passenger compartment) flow component can be very small, but some racing regulations require open windows, which can add up to $\Delta C_D = 0.06$ the drag force.

The largest part of the drag on road vehicles is a result of flow separations, especially at the aft section of the vehicle (form drag). The value of zero in this Table relates only to highly streamlined ideal vehicles, but for most practical configurations this component of the drag is responsible for as much as $\Delta C_D = 0.30$. In the case of open-wheel race cars, the drag of the four tires can drive the total drag coefficient over the value of 1.00.

The last item on this list, lift-induced drag, is an inherent result of downforce generating efforts. It is partially due to the added wings and partially due to the body's lift and the effect of these wings on the flow over the vehicle's body (called *interaction*). This drag increases with increased lift force and its nature will be explained in Chapters 4 and 6. On passenger cars this term is usually very small, and the value of $\Delta C_D = 0.60$ applies only to cars with very high lift coefficients (e.g. where $\Delta C_L \approx -3.0$).

Next, let us examine typical sources of aerodynamic lift on a road vehicle. Based on the lower part of Fig. 2.22 one can conclude that most basic automobile shapes will have positive lift in the range of $\Delta C_L = 0.1 - 0.35$. By enhancing the flow under the vehicle, such as by using some underbody channels (sometimes called venturis) the lift can be reduced down to –0.10. This first contribution is a function of the vehicle's shape and listed as the first part of the lift contribution in the following table.

Table 2.5 Typical Range of the Various Contributions to a Road Vehicle's Aerodynamic Lift

Location	ΔC_L
1. Vehicle body	0.35 to (-0.10)
2. Wings	0.00 to (-2.00)
3. Wing/body interaction	0.00 to (-2.00)

The most logical add-on to a vehicle to increase downforce is the inverted wing. Such wings can lift airplanes and therefore can plant cars in the ground, as well. Downforce levels of over one (metric) ton at high speeds on a half-ton vehicle are not rare occurrences; thus the range of $\Delta C_L = 0.0$ to (-2.00) represents the range spanning the various race car leagues.

The wing/body interaction is a result of using the wings in such a way that the body's downforce will increase, too. This interaction can result in forces similar in magnitude to those generated by the wing itself and some examples will be provided in Chapter 6.

SOME RELEVANT LITERATURE

In this short chapter we reviewed the very basics of automobile-related aerodynamics. However, since automobile manufacturers discovered that aerodynamics can sell their products, a considerably large aero-research effort was launched in the 1980s. Consequently, numerous technical articles, conference proceedings, and even books were written on this subject, and the following brief survey may prove useful for seeking additional references.

First, when considering the field of automotive aerodynamics, Refs. 2.6, 2.8, and 2.16 represent a typical cross section of recent publications. While Ref. 2.8 is aimed at the general public, Ref. 2.16 is more focused toward engineering facts, whereas Ref. 2.6 is an excellent collection of real engineering data in this field. Although these publications deal primarily with the aerodynamics of road vehicles, they include some sections on race car-related issues.

For professional engineers, some of the SAE special publications (SP) are useful and they appear each year after the SAE Conference in late February. Some of the noteworthy collections of technical papers in the field can be found in Refs. 2.4 and 2.17–2.19. Within this vast collection of technical articles there is always a small fraction that is race car related.

For those who wish to follow college-level engineering books on the subject of low-speed aerodynamics, it is recommended to begin with an introductory text such as Ref. 2.1. At a more advanced stage Ref. 2.2 can be used: It focuses also on computational methods for airfoils and wings. Finally, if experimental information is sought on the aerodynamic drag or lift of certain configurations, then the excellent data base compiled by S. F. Hoerner is the place to look first. His lifelong collection of this information was published in two separate volumes dealing with drag (Ref. 2.20) and with lift (Ref. 2.21).

SUMMARY

Considerable aerodynamic loads can act on a vehicle moving through the air, and these loads will increase with the square of speed. The most frequently observed loads are drag, which can be related to fuel economy, and lift, which affects a vehicle's handling characteristics.

Near the vehicle's body a thin boundary layer exists where the airspeed is reduced to zero (on the surface). If this boundary layer stays attached to the vehicle (especially at the back), then very low drag coefficients can be obtained, but if the boundary layer separates, then the drag coefficient will usually be much larger.

The boundary layer can be laminar or turbulent; the latter is thicker, generates more friction drag, but this delays flow separation.

The lift of basic body configurations is usually positive if the flow under the body is limited. Negative lift is possible when the flow under the body is increased (or less restricted).

REFERENCES

2.1   Anderson, J. D., *Fundamentals of Aerodynamics*, Second Edition, McGraw-Hill, Inc. 1991.

2.2   Katz, J., and Plotkin, A., *Low-Speed Aerodynamics: From Wing Theory to Panel Methods*, McGraw-Hill Book Co., 1991.

2.3   Fanger-Vexler, S., Katz, J. and Fux, A., "Full-Scale On-Road Study of the Effect of Automobile Shape on Its Aerodynamic Characteristics and Comparison with Small-Scale Wind Tunnel Results," SAE Paper 85-0287, SAE Transactions, Vol. 94, Part 2, pp. 715–726, 1985.

2.4.   Dorgham, M. A., Editor, "Impact of Aerodynamics on Vehicle Design," *Int. J. of Vehicle Design*, Technological Advances in Vehicle Design Series, SP3, 1983.

2.5   Tsukada, T., Sakagami, J., Arai, Y., and Takahara, H., "Aerodynamic Characteristics of Subaru XT," SAE paper No. 86-0216, Feb. 1986.

2.6   Hucho, W. H., 1987, *Aerodynamics of Road Vehicles*, Butterworth and Co. Publishing, Boston.

2.7   Katz, J., and Dykstra, L., "Effect of Passenger Car's Rear Deck Geometry on its Aerodynamic Coefficients," *ASME J. Fluids Eng.*, Vol. 114, No. 2, 1992, pp. 186–190.

2.8   Howard, G., *Automobile Aerodynamics*, Osprey Publishing Limited, London, 1986.

2.9   Katz, J., and Largman, R., "Experimental Study of the Aerodynamic Interaction Between an Enclosed-Wheel Racing-Car and its Rear Wing," *ASME J. of Fluids Engineering*, Vol. 111, No. 2, 1989, pp.154–159.

2.10   Eckert, W., Singer, N., and Vagt, J. D., "The Porsche Wind Tunnel Floor Boundary Layer Control—A Comparison with Road Data and Results from Moving Belt," SAE Paper, No. 920346, Feb. 1992.

2.11   Katz, J., and Dykstra, L., "Application of Computational Methods to the Aerodynamic Development of a Prototype Race Car," SAE Paper, No. 942498, Detroit 1994.

2.12   Katz, J., "Aerodynamic Model for Wing-Generated Down Force on Open-Wheel Racing-Car Configurations," SAE Paper No. 86-0218, Feb. 1986. *SAE Transactions*, Vol. 95, 1986.

2.13   Katz, J. and Dykstra, L., "Study of an Open-Wheel Racing-Car's Rear Wing Aerodynamics," SAE Paper 89-0600, presented at the SAE Int. Conference, Feb. 1989.

2.14   Bennett, N., "Indycar Aerodynamics," *Motorsport Technology*, Vol. 1, No. 1, pp. 6 - 11, 1992.

2.15   Bamsey, I., "Galmer G92 Aerodynamics: MIRA Development," *Race-Car Engineering*, Vol. 2, No. 3, pp.18-23, 1992.

2.16   Scibor-Rylski, A. J., *Road Vehicle Aerodynamics*, Pentech Press Limited London, England, second edition, 1984.

2.17   Stephens, H.S., Editor, *Advances in Road Vehicle Aerodynamics*, BHRA Fluid Engineering, London, 1973.

2.18   Pershing, B., Editor, *Proceedings of the Second Symposium on Aerodynamics of Sports and Competition Automobiles*, Collection of AIAA papers published by Western Periodicals Co., North Hollywood, CA, 1975.

2.19   Sovran, G., Morel, T., and Mason, W. T. Jr., *Aerodynamic Drag Mechanisms of Bluff Bodies and Road Vehicles*, Proceeding of the symposium held at G.M. Research Labs., Sept. 27-28, 1976, 1978 Plenum Press, New York.

2.20   Hoerner, S. F., *Fluid Dynamic Drag*, Hoerner Fluid Dynamics, 1965. Albuquerque, NM.

2.21   Hoerner, S. F., *Fluid Dynamic Lift*, Hoerner Fluid Dynamics, 1985. Albuquerque, NM.

3   Tools of the Trade

Introduction

Assuming that you don't want to test your aero ideas during a race, then you are left with three basic methods to investigate your vehicle's aerodynamic performance: road testing, wind tunnel testing, and, more recently, computations. Each method has its own advantages and disadvantages, and budgeting considerations and the availability of certain testing facilities will dictate which tools will be used for a particular vehicle design and development.

Road testing at first seems to be the easiest way to obtain desirable performance data. But the moment we think about measuring lift, drag, and their front/rear axle distribution we discover the serious difficulties involved—suspension vibration, varying ambient conditions, etc. Of course, while developing a new vehicle there is no actual car to test, so this method cannot be applied in the early design stages. Even later the method is still not attractive since many model changes (changes in body shape, wings, etc.) will require lots of time, while driver performance and ambient conditions may not be repeatable, and track time and vehicle support may be very expensive.

Wind tunnels have the advantage of being a controlled environment, but full-scale testing is usually expensive, and models may not be available (or built yet). On the other hand, small-scale models and their testing may not duplicate exactly full-scale conditions. Furthermore, the wind tunnel's walls and stationary floor introduce additional problems that may result in data that is substantially different from race track data.

Computations or simulations may seem the ideal answer to a race car aerodynamicist's dream. After all, no real car is necessary. Unfortunately, at the present time such methods have only limited capabilities and require resources which may be expensive even for the race car industry. Long-term investment (over several years) in this direction and the gradual development of such capabilities may prove to be very useful.

The conclusion is that the field of fluid dynamics is quite complicated; no one tool is perfect for improving a vehicle, and sometimes more than one or even all options should be used. In this chapter we shall review each of the above tools and try to explain the delicate problems associated with its application.

Before turning to the main subject, let us clarify the types of aerodynamic information we expect from these tools. Typically, the collected data should include at least part or all of the following:

- Total aerodynamic coefficients, such as lift (on front/rear axle), drag, etc.
- Surface pressure distribution. This data can provide clues on how to improve vehicle shape
- Flow visualization data, such as streamlines (on or off the body), which can determine where the flow separates

There are many other types of useful aerodynamic data (e.g., boundary layer thickness, climatic impact on air conditioning, deposition of dirt due to reversed flow, etc.), but when designing race cars there is usually no time to generate more than the above listed data. So, armed with the knowledge about which data we are after, we can investigate how each of the aerodynamic tools can provide such information, and how reliable the corresponding results can be.

ROAD TESTING

The most significant advantage of road testing is that the actual vehicle is tested on an actual track. Also, the incremental effect of modifications can be quickly evaluated by measuring a vehicle's maximum speed or its cornering speed in a given turn.

But, when conducting a test there is usually an object to be tested (the race car), and there is the instrumentation that collects and analyzes the data. If the test object is moving, then only limited equipment can be carried on board. This problem is compounded when comparing two proposed vehicle configurations since they both must be drivable and the instrumentation has to be transferred from one vehicle to the other. Model changes, such as a different car nose, may interfere with instruments and make repeatability of road and test conditions more difficult. Therefore, the drawbacks of road testing are the limited ability to carry sensitive testing equipment, and the uncontrolled environment (winds). Also, while aerodynamic loads in a wind tunnel are measured by a stationary scale (or balance), during a road test an indirect method for similar measurements is utilized. Keeping this in mind, we will focus in this section on how to obtain information on aerodynamic lift, drag, surface pressure distribution, and flow visualization.

Measurement of Lift

Traditional lift measuring techniques in a road test are based on measuring suspension travel or strain due to aerodynamic load. Suspension travel for each of the wheels can be measured and the corresponding relative displacement of the suspension components can be translated into an equivalent lift or downforce. The immediate advantage of the method is that the load distribution between the wheels is readily available. The disadvantage is that the lift of the wheels themselves is not measured. This may pose a larger problem while testing open-wheel race cars than on cars with enclosed wheels, but for comparison studies (e.g., between two rear wings) it can yield good results.

Aerodynamic load on the suspension can also be measured by strain gauges mounted on the springs, as shown in Fig. 3.1, or by optical ride-height measuring gauges, as used on the vehicle in Fig. 3.2. The first method of measuring the strain on the suspension can also be used with active suspensions, where the ride height is kept unchanged.

In order to calculate the aerodynamic coefficients (e.g. lift and drag, as in Eqs. 2.13 and 2.15), vehicle speed (dynamic pressure) must be measured simultaneously. This is usually done with a pitot tube, as shown in Fig. 3.2, which directly measures the dynamic pressure ($\frac{1}{2}\rho V_\infty^2$). The actual probe will also measure side slip (side winds), angle of incidence, and air temperature. Since such measurements are aimed at the undisturbed flow condition, the probe is mounted high and forward where disturbances due to the vehicle itself should be negligible.

Fig. 3-1. Lift and drag measuring system used in a road test: 1) vehicle body, 2) leaf spring to measure rear lift, 3) nonrotating antenna for torque signals, 4) rotating transmitter of drive shaft strains, 5) receiver and preprocessor of torque signals, 6) strain gauges to measure front lift (one per side). Reprinted with permission from SAE Paper 850287 Copyright ©1985 SAE, Inc.

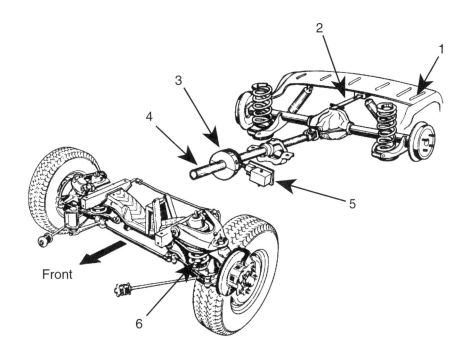

Fig. 3-2. The Nissan P-35, prototype car equipped for aerodynamic road testing (note the large velocity probe in front). Courtesy of NPTI.

Measurement of Drag

The measurement of drag in a road test is somewhat complicated by the fact that, in addition to the aerodynamic drag, a vehicle's resistance to motion includes driveline friction and tire rolling resistance. Tire resistance usually varies only slightly with speed (as shown in Fig. 2.20), except at very high speed. Measuring aerodynamic drag by means of road tests will require documentation of the tire's rolling resistance versus speed at a given normal load. Such data is usually available from race tire manufacturers. The combined rolling resistance (including tires and mechanical friction) can be measured in an experiment described schematically in Fig. 3.3 (as in Ref. 3.1). In this case the vehicle is towed inside a box that seals it from the outside air, and an internal load cell measures the tow force (which now has no air resistance component).

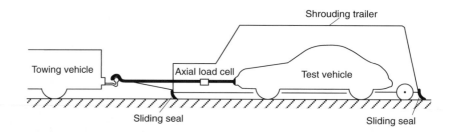

Fig. 3-3. *Method of towing a vehicle under a shrouded trailer for measuring tire's rolling resistance.*

Once the value of the tire resistance and the mechanical friction values are known, the aerodynamic drag can be evaluated through measuring the total longitudinal resistance. Several methods have been used in the past, and they can be based on measuring loads on the suspension, on the driveshafts, by measuring the vehicle's top speed (flat out), or by using the deceleration technique.

In some experiments (Ref. 2.3) the driving force was measured by measuring the torque on the driveshaft. Special strain gauges were glued on the shaft and the strain due to the driving torque was transmitted magnetically to a nonrotating receiver (see Fig. 3.1). This information was calibrated to measure total driving force. By subtracting the tire's rolling resistance from this force the aerodynamic drag was calculated.

A far simpler arrangement is when the vehicle is towed and the tension in the tow cable is recorded. This method was used in Ref. 2.3, as well, and its primary disadvantage is the disturbance in the flow created by the towing vehicle (even with a fairly long tow cable).

Maximum-speed experiments on a straightaway, which are frequently used when testing race cars, can provide good comparative information about the vehicle's drag (assuming that side wind effects are negligible when compared with the race car's speed). By simply recording the maximum engine RPM of each design under full throttle conditions, a fairly accurate comparison of the

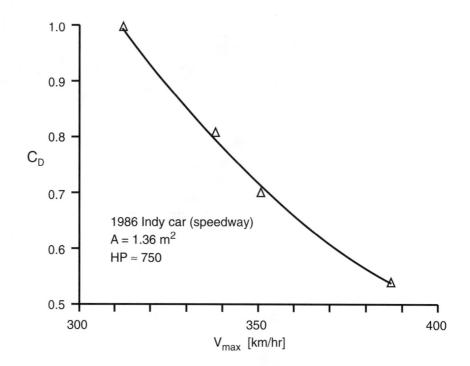

Fig. 3-4. *Effect of the drag coefficient on the maximum speed of an Indy car.*

1986 Indy car (speedway)
$A = 1.36 \ m^2$
$HP \approx 750$

aerodynamic drag can be obtained. Typical results of such an experiment with an Indy car initially set up at a speedway configuration are presented in Fig. 3.4. The solid line is the curve-fit over four separate runs (shown by the triangular symbols) to measure the car's maximum speed. During those runs, the downforce was increased, resulting in an increase in the drag, too. This increase in the resistance considerably reduced the vehicle's maximum speed even when the gear ratio was changed to match the new maximum speed.

The coast-down method has been used successfully in the past (Refs. 3.2 to 3.4), where the test vehicle is brought to a certain initial speed and then allowed to coast to a stop. The drag coefficient is determined from data of both the rate of deceleration and the distance travelled. Although the experiment in principle is simple to perform, it requires the evaluation of inertial effects. As a result, it is more sensitive to external (atmospheric) disturbances than would be expected from a constant-speed test, and a large number of repetitions for each data point are required.

As an example, Fig. 3.5 describes a typical speed-versus-time diagram during a coast-down test for a passenger-type vehicle. The rate at which the vehicle slows down (negative acceleration) is proportional to the force applied, according to Newton's second law. The external force is the resistance that slows down the vehicle and is a sum of the tires' rolling resistance and the aerodynamic drag. Based on this principle, which is explained with more details in the Equation sidebar, the vehicle drag can be estimated. In practice, the procedure is complicated by the fact that the inertia of rotating parts (wheels, gearbox, etc.) and driveline friction must be included in the analysis.

Fig. 3-5. *Typical variation of the vehicle's speed versus time during a coast-down test.*

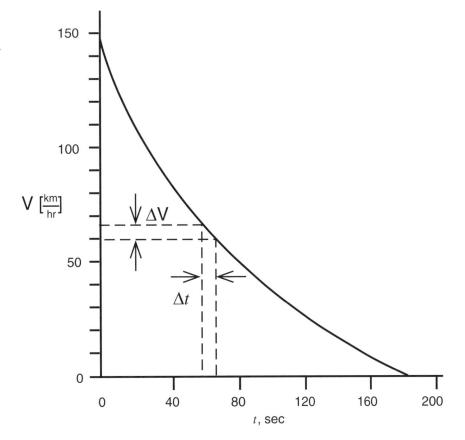

The Evaluation of Vehicle Drag from Coast-Down Tests

In order to demonstrate how aerodynamic drag is evaluated during a coast-down test, recall Newton's second law of motion, that the acceleration a into the direction of the acting force F is related by the formula:

Eq. 3.1

$$ma = F$$

where m is the mass (including inertia of rotating components) of the vehicle. For our purpose the force will be the drag (plus rolling resistance) and the acceleration will be negative since the vehicle's speed decreases during the coast-down test. Now, if we select a small time interval Δt on the curve of Fig. 3.5, during which the speed was reduced by ΔV, then we can estimate the vehicle's deceleration by $\Delta V / \Delta t$. Based on these quantities and Newton's equation we can estimate the total resistance D during this interval as

Eq. 3.2

$$D = -m\frac{\Delta V}{\Delta t}$$

and the minus sign is a result of the decreasing vehicle speed (since ΔV is negative). The next step is to subtract tire rolling resistance and account for inertial effects due to wheel rotation, and then by using Eq. 2.13 the drag coefficient is calculated.

Measurement of Surface Pressures

Measurement of the surface pressures in a road test or in a wind tunnel are basically the same, apart from the fact that in a road test the data reduction system must be more robust. Even this last disadvantage may disappear as telemetry improves and computer components become smaller and less sensitive to vibrations and temperature variations.

The surface pressure on a vehicle can be measured by drilling a small hole in the surface and connecting this point to a transducer, as shown in Fig. 3.6 (the hole should be flush and drilled normal to the outer surface). This method measures the local static pressure. For calculating the corresponding pressure coefficient (Eq. 2.11) the dynamic pressure is needed, too, which can be measured by a pitot tube (as shown in Fig. 3.2 or Fig. 2.12).

Fig. 3-6. Schematic description of mounting a static pressure port on the vehicle's surface.

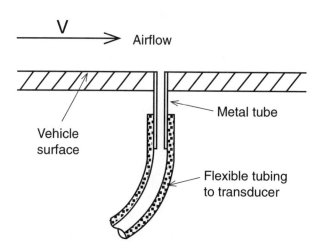

In order to obtain a comprehensive pressure distribution on the vehicle (such as in Fig. 2.15) a large number of pressure holes must be drilled and connected to a central measuring unit (transducer). Two such transducers are shown in Fig. 3.7. Each is capable of measuring a fairly large number of individual pressures (usually 32, 48, etc.). Note the array of small metal tubes to which flexible tubes are connected. The advantage of such transducers is that a large number of pressure-sensing tubes can be connected locally, inside the model, while only one cord carries the signal to the data acquisition system. In wind tunnel experiments, this is a great advantage, since no tubes will extend behind the model. (Not too long ago, all the pressure tubes were connected to a large manometer outside the wind tunnel test section. The cross section of these tubes was almost as large as the cross section of the model). The third transducer in Fig. 3.7 is a surface-mounted type, which is very sensitive to time-dependent variations in pressure. Because of its small size it can be glued onto the surface without the need to drill holes in the bodywork.

Fig. 3-7. Transducers used for surface pressure measurements. Clockwise from top: 48 port, made by Scanivalve; 48 port, made by PSI; surface mounted, made by Endevco.

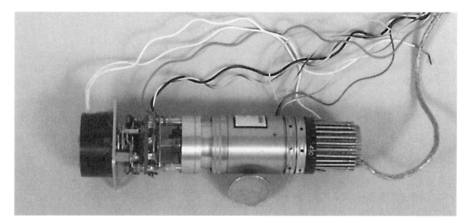

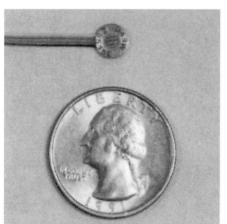

Performing surface pressure measurements in a road test is also complicated by the limited volume available on the vehicle for carrying test equipment. The complexity created by the large number of tubes and wires in such experiments can be seen in Fig. 3.8, where the side panel of the Nissan P-35 prototype car was removed to expose the internal instrumentation.

Lastly, when measuring surface pressures by the method described in Fig. 3.6, there is always the possibility that in a road test some holes will be plugged by dust or small flying insects.

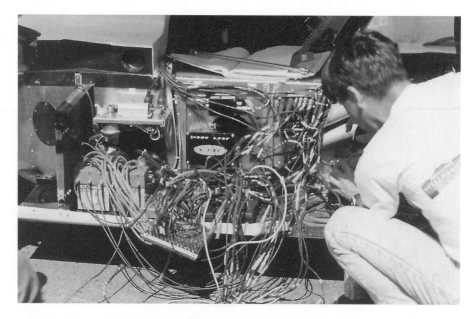

Fig. 3-8. *This deluge of tubes and wires used in the road test of the Nissan P-35 race car demonstrates the extent of the packaging problem in a road test. Courtesy of NPTI.*

Flow Visualization

Information such as the location of flow-separation lines or the direction of the flow into the cooling inlets on the sidepod of an F-1 car can provide valuable input on whether the surface shape needs to be modified. Because of the role of flow visualization methods in shedding light on why certain situations occur, they have been extensively developed, and several books are written on this topic (Ref. 3.5). However, for race car applications, visualizations primarily serve to show general flow directions and flow-recirculation areas. Therefore, I shall mention only the most frequently used methods, which are common to both road and wind tunnel testing.

In principle we can divide flow visualization methods into on- and off-the-surface. In the first group you frequently see the use of tufts (short strings of yarn glued at one end to the surface), which easily bend into the flow direction. Fig. 3.9 shows such a test on a highly streamlined solar race car. In such cases of attached flow the tufts are stable and point into the flow direction, while in case of a separated flow they fluctuate rapidly and often point away from the expected flow direction.

Fig. 3-9. *Visualization of the flow direction near the vehicle's surface by tufts. Photograph shows the SDSU-Suntrakker solar-race-car during the 1993 World Solar Challenge, held in Australia.*

Similar information can be obtained by observing traces of a viscous fluid (usually oil with some coloring dye) which is smeared by the flow near the surface. Fig. 3.10 shows the results of such a test, where the surface oil flow indicates that sufficient flow enters the cooling intake behind the front wheel of a prototype race car.

Fig. 3-10. Visualization of the flow direction near the vehicle's surface by tinted oil flow. Here traces of the oil flow indicate the direction of cooling air (from right to left) flowing into an inlet behind the front wheel of the Nissan P-35 prototype race car. Courtesy of NPTI.

The second type of flow visualization, the off-body method, is usually more difficult to execute during a road test since the most common tool in this category is the use of smoke traces in the flow. The smoke traces in the wind tunnel test shown in Fig. 3.11 were generated by a rake of tubes mounted ahead of the model. When using the same approach in a road test the rake usually has to be mounted on the test vehicle itself, which is probably why this method is unpopular on the road.

In road tests, results of the flow visualizations are generally recorded by a TV camera mounted on the vehicle or on a chase car. Using a chase car is considered exciting; however, interference between the two vehicles and camera stabilization are a major difficulty.

Fig. 3-11. Visualization of off-body streamlines by smoke injection. This figure shows the 1924 Rumpler's Tropfenwagen which was retested in 1979 to verify its low drag coefficient of $C_D = 0.28$. Courtesy of R. Buchheim, Volkswagen, AG.

Conclusions on Road Testing

Comprehensive road testing of a race car's aerodynamics is usually more expensive and more difficult than a similar wind tunnel test, and is possible only if a full-scale test vehicle exists. Therefore, comprehensive aerodynamic road tests are less popular, whereas partial aerodynamic testing is a very frequent part of most experimental programs. Such tests include "flat out" tests and suspension travel measurements for lift evaluation. In most road testing, obtaining absolute values for the aerodynamic loads is quite difficult, but measuring their incremental (relative) values is usually very accurate (and believed to be indisputable).

WIND TUNNEL METHODS

The basic idea behind building a wind tunnel is simple: Instead of chasing a flying airplane or a moving car with all the measuring instrumentations, the test model (and supporting instruments) stays stationary while the air moves relative to it. (Of course there is always somebody who will suggest testing a model on top of a speeding truck.) Wind tunnels allow test conditions to be well controlled and, in principle, are independent of external atmospheric conditions.

As simple as this idea looks, it turns out that there are many ways of constructing a wind tunnel and even more problems associated with each approach. In the following sections I will highlight the options and design features of various wind tunnels and present some of their advantages and disadvantages for generating the desirable aerodynamic data.

Types of Wind Tunnels

In an elementary wind tunnel the air is blown, usually by a fan (in certain wind tunnels high-pressure tanks or jets are used). We will limit our discussion to automotive-type wind tunnels, and one possible example is shown in Fig. 3.12.

Fig. 3-12. Schematic description of a basic open-return wind tunnel.

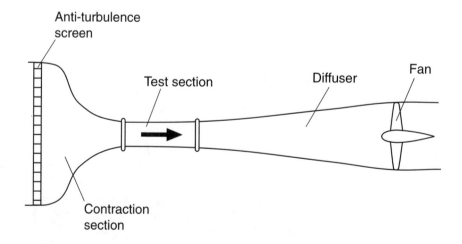

In this case a fan drives the air. Since the airflow density is near constant, the highest speed is reached at the smallest cross-section, which is used as the test section for vehicle or model placement. The test section may have a rectangular, circular, oval, or similar cross section. Ahead of the test section is an inlet contraction that directs the flow smoothly into the test section, with the objective to obtain a uniform velocity (free stream) in the test section. The ratio between the inlet area and the test section area is called *the inlet contraction ratio*. Larger contraction ratios usually result in more uniform free-stream conditions. Of course, larger contraction cones cost more and tie up more space. The large anti-turbulence screen at the inlet can be made of small honey-comb elements or from several simple screen meshes. Its primary purpose is to reduce the effect of outside wind currents and to straighten the inflow so that flow quality (including the turbulence level) behind the screen will be as uniform as possible. The diverging section behind the test section (the diffuser) reduces the speed ahead of the fan.

All wind tunnels will have these basic elements. The primary differences will be due to open- or closed-circuit air flows and to different test-section shapes. The wind tunnel shown in Fig. 3.12 is usually called an open-return type and many small-scale wind tunnels are built like that. However, it is logical not to waste the momentum of the air ejected behind the fan by building a return tube so that the air will circulate. Then the fan works only against the resistance created by the friction on the walls and model. Such a tunnel is a closed-return type, shown in Fig. 3.13.

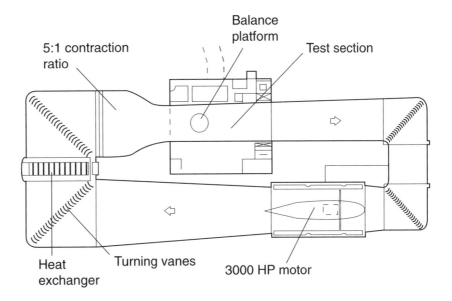

Fig. 3-13. *Plan view of General Motors' closed-return wind tunnel in Detroit, MI. Reprinted with permission from SAE Paper 820371 Copyright ©1982 SAE, Inc.*

Balance platform

5:1 contraction ratio

Test section

Heat exchanger

Turning vanes

3000 HP motor

The test section can be of a closed type, as in Figs. 3.12 and 3.13, or an open type as shown in Fig. 3.14. (The configuration in Fig. 3.14 is frequently called the Gottingen-type tunnel, after one of the first wind tunnels built in Gottingen, Germany). With an open test section the inlet contraction cone acts like a nozzle and the model is submerged in its jet. The simplest open jet tunnel has an open-return circuit, often called the Eiffel type.[1] A schematic description of such a type is shown in Fig. 3.15.

In general, open-return (or open-circuit) tunnels will have lower construction cost, and are attractive when materials such as smoke (for flow visualization), or exhaust gas products (from a running engine) should be purged. Also, if ambient conditions are constant, then test-section temperature will not change during a long test (as in the closed-return wind tunnel).

There are two important disadvantages to this design. The first is the effect of ambient conditions on the free-stream flow. If the tunnel is placed outside,

---

1. After Gustav Eiffel, 1832–1923, French engineer, builder of bridges and the Eiffel tower in Paris, France, and a pioneer in aerodynamic sciences.

Fig. 3-14. *A closed-return wind tunnel with an open test section, Gottingen type (Daimler Benz AG, Stuttgart, Germany, after Kuhn, A. "The Large Daimler-Benz Wind Tunnel," ATZ, Vol. 80, 1978, p. 27).*

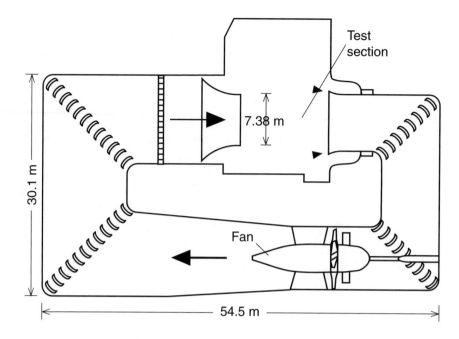

Fig. 3-15. *Open-return wind tunnel with an open test section (Eiffel type).*

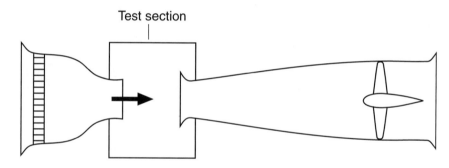

then winds may have a strong effect on the flow quality and velocity profile in the test section. Furthermore, noise from the test section, from the fan and its drive unit, and from the exit nozzle radiates directly outside, and in the case of larger wind tunnels this may present a real annoyance to the neighborhood. Also, by the virtue of using fresh ambient air, such a tunnel in a cold climate would freeze its operators. The second disadvantage is that more power is required to drive this type of wind tunnel than an equivalent closed circuit design. Consequently, a large number of small, open-circuit tunnels can be found in universities and other educational establishments, where by placing them inside larger rooms the disadvantages generally disappear.

Because less energy is required to drive closed-return tunnels, and since they are not sensitive to ambient winds, most larger wind tunnels are based on the closed-circuit design. The major disadvantages are its relatively higher cost and the accumulation of smoke (if present) or the buildup of temperature (due to friction) during long runs. To overcome this, many wind tunnels have air exchange vents as shown in Fig. 3.16. The air exchangers in this schematic are located on both sides of the tunnel, behind the fan, so that the plates direct a portion of the flow outside. These air exchange passages are permanently open and constantly exchange the internal flow with ambient air.

Another solution to this problem is used in the large GM wind tunnel shown in Fig. 3.13, where a huge heat exchanger serves for temperature control. If

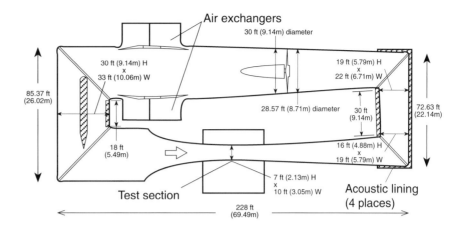

Fig. 3-16. *The NASA Ames 7-by-10-foot wind tunnel with air exchangers (open to the ambient air).*

the wind tunnel is intended for climatic and air-conditioning purposes as well, then only the closed-return-type wind tunnel can be used and in this case a heat exchanger must be included in the circuit.

A large number of automotive wind tunnels have open-jet test sections (Fig. 3.14 or 3.15) since larger models can be mounted and the effect of test-section walls is smaller. Accessibility is easier to the models and operators can hide outside the jet boundaries, using long probes to inject smoke near the model. Also the static pressure outside the jet varies far less than in the case of a closed test section (where a longitudinal pressure change may be present) and therefore drag measurements are considered to be more accurate. On the other hand, the open jet tends to dissipate through its mixing with the surrounding air, and therefore open test-section length is limited (shorter) and more power is required to drive the air compared to a closed test section.

A third alternative for test-section configuration is the slotted wall design. Fig. 3.17 shows this approach, where longitudinal slots are opened in the test-section walls and ceiling. Up to 30% of the wall area is left open so that larger

Fig. 3-17. *Schematic description of a slotted-wall test section.*

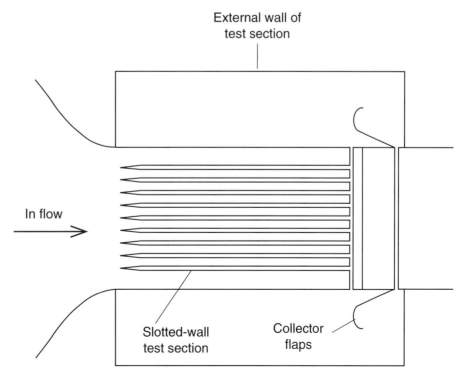

models can be tested. The presence of a model in the test section forces some part of the flow to move in and out through the slotted walls, and usually an outer wall will seal the inner circuit from external air.

Of course, the aerodynamicist's dream is a very large, closed test-section tunnel, but this is usually very expensive and not available for automotive testing. As mentioned, most automotive wind tunnels are the closed-return type with an open test section. For example, the phantom-view of the Volkswagen wind tunnel in Fig. 3.18 demonstrates the large size and complexity of a facility used for full-scale testing. Other large-scale wind tunnels, but with closed test section and slotted walls, include BMW in Munich, Volvo in Goteborg, Porsche in Weissach, and DNW in Emmeloord. The slotted-wall test section of the Porsche wind tunnel is shown in Fig. 3.19.

Today, nobody would consider developing an airplane without extensively testing it in a wind tunnel. Following the same thought, nobody would build an automobile—and particularly a race car—without testing it in a wind tunnel,

Fig. 3-18. Phantom view of the VW wind tunnel in Wolfsburg, Germany. Courtesy of Volkswagen AG.

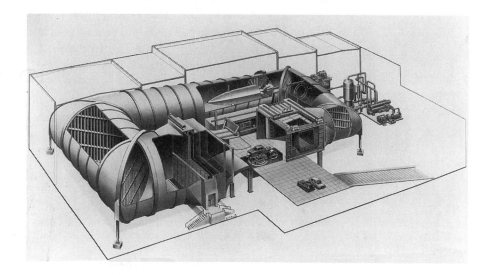

Fig. 3-19. Three-quarter view of the slotted-wall test section in the Porsche wind tunnel (Weissach, Germany). Reprinted with permission from SAE Paper 920346 Copyright ©1992 SAE, Inc.

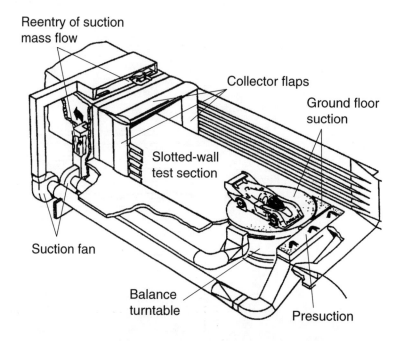

Reentry of suction mass flow

Collector flaps

Ground floor suction

Slotted-wall test section

Suction fan

Balance turntable

Presuction

even though they are not intended to fly. This probably explains the rapidly increasing number of wind tunnels built for general automotive and race car testing. A partial list of those facilities is provided in Appendix 2. The most interesting observation is that the number of wind tunnels serving the racing industry has grown tremendously during the recent years (most of those wind tunnels identified as serving the race car industry were built in the late 1980s or early 1990s).

Up to this point, the discussion has focused on the wind tunnel facility itself. Next we will address the installation of the model in the test section. The process of matching a particular vehicle model with a wind tunnel raises three important issues:

- Model size and the blockage it creates in the test section
- Simulation of the moving road
- Mounting of model and its rotating wheels in the test section

The next three sections first explain the problems related to these issues, and then describe some of the most common solutions.

Model Size and Test-Section Blockage

Let us start by demonstrating the dilemma faced when trying to match model and wind tunnel sizes by the simple example presented in Fig. 3.20. At the top of the figure a streamlined body moves through open air, causing the nearby

A

Fig. 3-20. Streamlines near a body in an open free stream (A), and when constrained by two rigid walls (B).

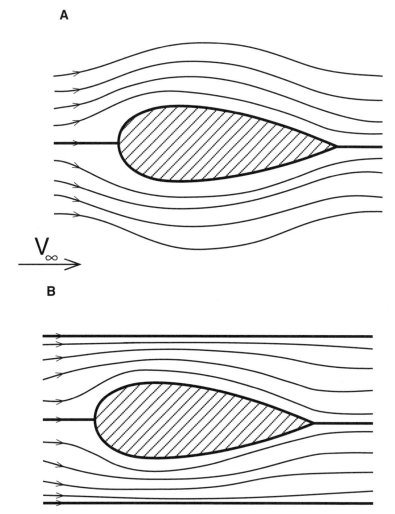

V_∞

B

streamlines to deform due to its presence. This disturbance in the flow is local; far from the body the streamlines will not be affected but stay parallel and straight. If this body is placed within two walls, as shown by the lower part of the figure, then the confinement forces the nearby streamlines to adjust to the wall shape. In practice, a too-close wall will cause the flow to move faster in the gap between the model and the walls, creating larger lift and drag readings. So the first part of the dilemma is that the largest possible test section is desirable to reduce the effects of the wall in an effort to obtain results closer to open-road conditions. However, the cost of wind tunnels and their operation increases with size, as does the power requirement. See Fig. 3.21.

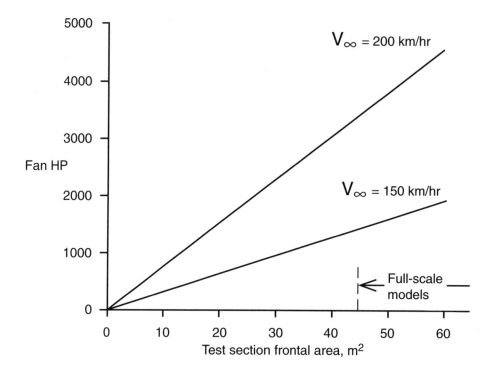

Fig. 3-21. Trends in wind tunnel power requirements versus test section cross-section area.

For example, in most commercial areas it will be difficult to continuously run a 500 HP fan motor because of power limitations. Based on this figure, with such power limitation, the test-section area will be less than 5 m^2 and model size will be probably less or near 1/4 scale. For comparison, the fan (rated over 17000 HP) of the German-Dutch wind tunnel is shown in Fig. 3.22. It is clear that only large organizations with huge budgets can afford a full-scale automotive wind tunnel (which is why very few exist worldwide).

The other part of the dilemma is model size, which according to the rationale of Fig. 3.20 should be the smallest possible. But model designers prefer larger models (even full-scale) so that more details can be incorporated into the model. If the actual car is used, then it has details such as radiators and cooling ducts, which cannot be reproduced exactly in smaller scale. Also, testing the actual car at the actual speed will result in the correct Reynolds number (see Chapter 2), and for race cars with wings this is very important. But if the car is

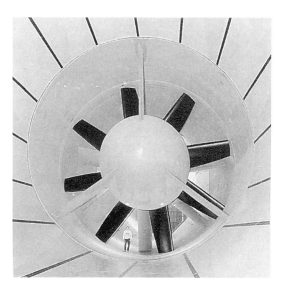

Fig. 3-22. The large fan that drives the air in the German-Dutch wind tunnel, rated over 17000 HP. Courtesy of DNW.

in its early design stages and does not exist, then a model must be prepared anyway. In any case, a quick glance at the Table in Appendix 2 shows that the number of full-scale automotive wind tunnels is very small, so we can conclude that most race car designers will be forced to prepare and test a small-scale model (in the 1/5th- to 1/2-scale range).

Still, the conflict remains: For minimum wall interference in a given wind tunnel facility, model size should be kept as small as possible, but from the model detail and accuracy point of view its size should be the largest possible. There is always a compromise between the requirements of the model designer and the available wind tunnel facility, and in most cases the effect of the test section walls is *not* negligible!

The most obvious interference between the model and the wind tunnel test-section walls is called *solid blockage* (Ref. 3.6 p. 364). Recall how flow speed will increase near the model as explained in Fig. 3.20. Since the local velocity at the test section is higher than it would be in a free flow outside the wind tunnel, the aerodynamic coefficients are overestimated.

In addition to this blockage effect there is a reflection effect that changes the lift of lifting surfaces near solid boundaries (as in the case of "ground effect"). Consequently, so-called "wind tunnel corrections" are used for the larger blockage ratios. A variety of wind tunnel correction methods are listed in Refs. 3.6 and 3.7. (Ref. 3.6, page 371, recommends that maximal model to test-section frontal-area ratio does not exceed 7.5%, while Hucho, Ref. 1.6, p. 403, suggests a limit of 5%.)

Most of the wind tunnel wall correction methods are based on the ratio between the model frontal area and the wind tunnel test section (or open jet) cross-section area. In its simplest form an equation is provided, similar to the one shown in the Equation sidebar, which allows an immediate correction of the test results. Some of the more elaborate correction methods require the measurement of the pressure along the test section, which is then used with a computational method to estimate the required corrections.

Example for Wind Tunnel Corrections   Wind tunnel wall corrections are used to modify the data so that it will be closer to the open air condition. Most of these wall correction methods are based on the ratio between the model frontal area A and the wind-tunnel test-section (or open jet) cross-section area C. For example, one of the simplest formulas for the blockage correction in a closed test section is (from Ref. 3.6, p. 371):

Eq. 3.3
$$\frac{(1/2\rho V_\infty^2)_c}{(1/2\rho V_\infty^2)_m} = \left(1 + \frac{1}{4}\cdot\frac{A}{C}\right)^2$$

Here the correction is applied to the dynamic pressure $1/2\rho V_\infty^2$ (defined in Eq. 2.7) and the subscript c stands for *corrected* and m for *measured*, respectively. This correction can be applied to any aerodynamic coefficient and, for example, when applied to the lift coefficient (Eq. 2.14) we can write that

Eq. 3.4
$$C_{L_c} = C_{L_m}\left[\frac{1}{\left(1 + \frac{1}{4}\cdot\frac{A}{C}\right)^2}\right]$$

To demonstrate the principle of this equation let us assume a large blockage ratio of A/C=0.075 (7.5%) and assume that we have measured a lift coefficient of C_{L_m} = 0.300 in the wind tunnel. The corrected lift coefficient value (estimated for the road), based on the correction of Eq. 3.4, is

$$C_{L_c} = 0.300 \cdot \frac{1}{\left(1 + \frac{1}{4}0.075\right)^2} = 0.289$$

The simple example in the Equation sidebar only demonstrates the principle of using wind tunnel corrections. In practice, other (and more complicated) corrections are used, and the particular method used depends on wind tunnel and model shape. In general, open-jet test sections are less sensitive to blockage corrections, and the magnitude of these corrections (Ref. 3.6, p. 433) can be as low as 1/4 of the equivalent closed test-section corrections.

Before concluding this section let us examine the approximate frontal areas for a variety of sports and race cars:

Table 3.1 Typical Frontal Area of Some Sports and Race Cars

Vehicle Type	Frontal Area A
Open Wheel (F-1, Indy)	1.5 m^2
Sports Cars (IMSA GTO)	1.7 m^2
Prototype (IMSA GTP)	1.8 m^2
Production (Porsche 928s)	1.9 m^2

Suppose we want to test the vehicles from Table 3.1, and we want to limit the blockage to less than 7.5%, then less than ten wind tunnels from the list in Appendix 2 can be used. So it is clear that the availability of a proper-size wind tunnel and the limit of maximum blockage ratio are the factors that determine model size.

Simulation of Moving Ground

The need to simulate a moving ground (or road) in the wind tunnel considerably complicates wind tunnel testing. Before listing the various solutions to the problem, let us prove first that there is a problem. This can be demonstrated by observing Fig. 3.23. As you can see, there is a difference in the shape of the boundary layers between the on-the-road and in-the-wind-tunnel conditions. Now recall the fact (presented in Chapter 2) that in the boundary layer the airspeed near the surface of a stationary object slows down to zero. A closer

Fig. 3-23. Generic shape of the boundary layer for a vehicle moving on the road (A), and for a vehicle mounted in a wind tunnel with fixed walls and floor (B).

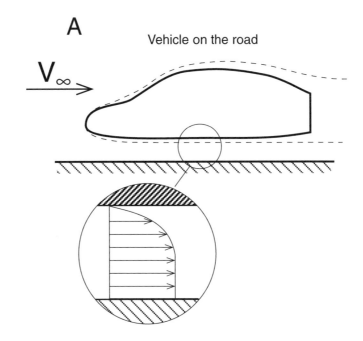

A   Vehicle on the road

V_∞

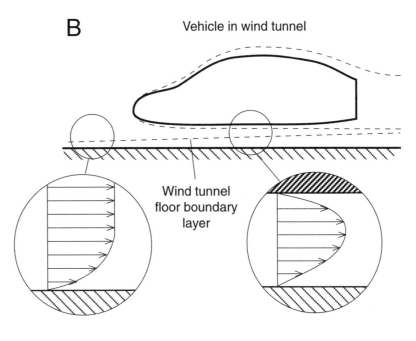

B   Vehicle in wind tunnel

Wind tunnel floor boundary layer

look at the velocity profile between the car and the road reveals a velocity deficiency near the vehicle's surface, as shown within the top circle.

In the wind tunnel, the tunnel floor is a stationary object relative to the air flow, and even without a car in the test section a boundary layer exists on the floor. This is shown by the second circular insert which samples the velocity profile ahead of the model in the wind tunnel. When a car is placed in the wind tunnel, the velocity profile under the vehicle (right-hand circle) is the result of the two boundary layers, one formed on the ground and one on the vehicle's lower surface.

The main questions are: How thick are those boundary layers, and how large an effect do they have on the aerodynamic results? Fig. 3.24 presents measured boundary layer thickness values in the full-scale GM tunnel. This data indicates that even when applying boundary layer suction ahead of the model, boundary layer thickness is close to 0.1 m. If we test a truck with a ground clearance of 0.6 m at a speed of 200 km/hr, then there is no need to worry about the effect of the floor boundary layer. But if a race car, with a ground clearance of 0.05 to 0.1 m, is tested, then it is likely that you will be unable to determine the effectiveness of the ground-effect aerodynamic wizardry. Consequently, in the following paragraphs we shall list some of the more common remedies to this problem.

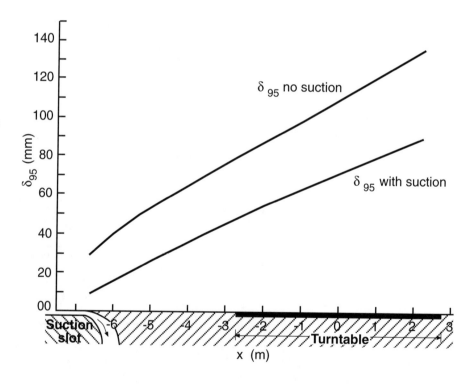

Fig. 3-24. *Test-section boundary layer thickness in the GM wind tunnel (after Ref. 3.8). δ_{95} is the boundary layer thickness at which 95% of the velocity outside this boundary was obtained. Reprinted with permission from SAE Paper 820371 Copyright ©1982 SAE, Inc.*

The first option is to elevate the model above the boundary layer. Since the boundary layer thickness increases toward the rear of the vehicle, it should also be tilted forward a bit. The problems with this idea are the (usually) large effects due to the change in the vehicle's pitch angle and due to the clearance left by the elevated wheels (which must be filled by some soft foam in order to avoid large suction forces resulting from the flow between the wheels and the ground). Therefore, this approach is seldom used.

A variation of this option is to introduce an elevated ground plane as shown in Fig. 3.25A. The basic idea here is that the region with the thicker boundary layer on the wind tunnel floor is avoided and the model is now placed in a much

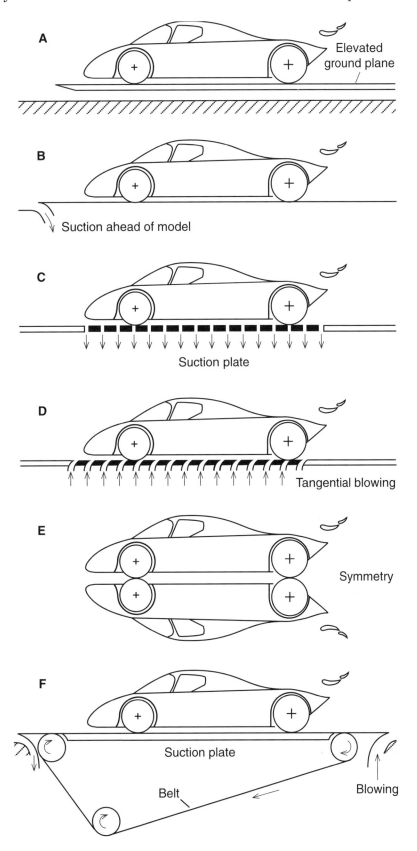

Fig. 3-25. *Various methods for simulating moving ground in a wind tunnel.*

A — Elevated ground plane

B — Suction ahead of model

C — Suction plate

D — Tangential blowing

E — Symmetry

F — Suction plate / Belt / Blowing

thinner boundary layer (formed only by the elevated plate). In this case, too, the model can be raised and the gaps underneath the wheels sealed with foam. This approach is probably the simplest and is used in small university-type wind tunnels.

The second simplest solution is to apply a spanwise suction slot ahead of the model (Fig. 3.25B). The suction in effect removes the boundary layer so that the new layer formed under the vehicle is much thinner. Because of its simplicity, this approach is used in many full-scale wind tunnels. To be effective, the thickness of the new boundary layer starting behind the suction slot should not exceed 10% of the vehicle's ground clearance.

An improvement over the suction method is to have slots under the vehicle as well, as shown in Fig. 3.25C. This suction plate is considered by many to be one of the better solutions, but its execution is somewhat complex and expensive. A closer observation of Fig. 3.19 reveals that in the Porsche wind tunnel such a suction plate is used, in addition to a presuction slot ahead of the model.

When mentioning suction techniques to an aerodynamicist, this will immediately trigger the question: Why not do the same, but with blowing? As a matter of fact, this seems more logical since tangential blowing adds the momentum which was lost in the lower boundary layer of the airstream (see Fig. 3.25D). Like the previous method, this is effective but expensive.

The only question about these two methods is: Should the suction or blowing vary under the model or should it be constant? Many aerodynamicists believe that due to the interaction between the vehicle and the floor, the suction (or blowing) should vary accordingly and not be constant.

As another solution, the principle of symmetry should not be ruled out as a legitimate approach. The basic idea here (Fig. 3.25E) is that the symmetry line dividing the two identical models is also a streamline. Therefore, the ground simulation is automatically obtained. Of course both models should be exactly the same (including the changes during the test) and this can increase the cost twofold. Also the wind tunnel test-section size needs to be increased to accommodate the two models and this makes this approach less attractive (this is probably why I have yet to see a test like this).

The last solution is the moving-belt ground simulation, shown in Fig. 3.25F. This approach is the most popular among race car designers but is not free of some major problems. First, the model is usually supported by a "sting," which is attached either to the back or to the roof of the model and interferes with the flow toward the rear wings. The second problem is how to measure the loads on the rotating wheels that are in contact with the belt (some tunnels use a narrow belt, running between the wheels only, so that this problem is avoided). The third problem is that the high suction under some race cars (prototypes, Indy, etc.) may suck up the belt. This is cured in the more expensive installations with an additional suction plate placed under the belt. The last problem is the limited speed of the belt ($\approx$ 150 km/hr) which is usually less than the wind tunnel full-speed capability (some recent moving belt systems are capable of running up to 250 km/hr). The moving belt system shown is one of the better designs since it has both a suction slot to remove the tunnel floor boundary layer ahead of the model, and blowing behind the belt to further push back the boundary layer that starts behind the belt system. A typical installation of a race car model above the moving belt in the test section of the Imperial College wind tunnel, in London, is shown in Fig. 3.26.

Fig. 3-26. *An open-wheel race car mounted in a test section with moving ground simulation. Courtesy of Mr. J. O'Leary, Dept. of Aeronautics, Imperial College.*

Methods of Mounting a Model in a Test Section

In this section the focus is on the model and its mounting in the test section. Some of the most frequently used engineering solutions are described in the following paragraphs.

The simplest method for testing an actual car in a full-scale wind tunnel is by placing its wheels on the tunnel floor (or ground plane, as shown in Fig. 3.27). Here, the wheels rest on small panels which are separated from the floor of the tunnel and are connected to a six-component scale. A typical setup of this kind (without the elevated ground plane) which is used by many full-scale facilities is shown in Fig. 3.28.

The four small circular panels (or plates) are mounted on top of four struts, which are directly connected to the load measuring device (called *balance*, or

Fig. 3-27. *One approach for mounting a wind tunnel model using an elevated ground plane technique. The aerodynamic loads are measured by the scale mounted under the tunnel.*

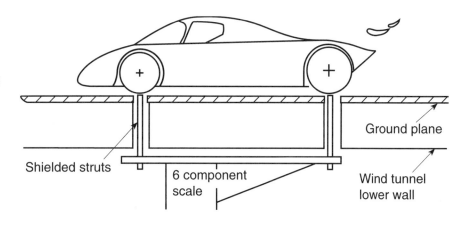

Shielded struts

6 component scale

Ground plane

Wind tunnel lower wall

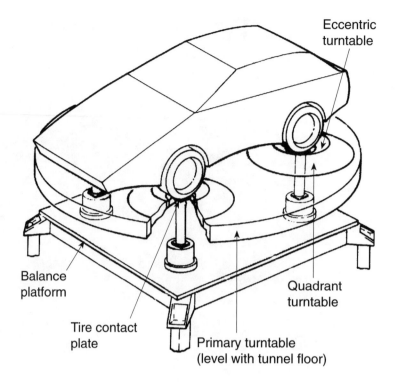

Eccentric
turntable

Balance
platform

Quadrant
turntable

Tire contact
plate

Primary turntable
(level with tunnel floor)

Fig. 3-28. Schematic view of the various turntables used to mount the vehicle on the balance (of a "drive-in" full-scale wind tunnel). Reprinted with permission from SAE Paper 820371 Copyright ©1982 SAE, Inc.

scales). The balance is isolated from the wind tunnel floor in order to record loads due only to air flow. This is accomplished by two additional sets of eccentric turntables placed flush with the tunnel floor and rotating relative to each other, as shown in Fig. 3.28. In addition, these turntables can be moved relative to the large turntable so that a small gap always exists between the plates holding the vehicle wheels and the rest of the wind tunnel floor. This adjustment must be made for each vehicle entering the wind tunnel. The large (primary) turntable serves for yawing the model, and at the same time the four struts on the balance turn in a synchronized manner to avoid contact between the load measuring system and the wind tunnel floor.

If we want the vehicle's wheels to rotate during the test, then we can use motors mounted on the scale. Their speed is synchronized with the airspeed in the test section. In this case the weight of the model is supported by struts (or plates) mounted inside the wheels, as shown in Fig. 3.29. The gap between the floor and the wheel is sealed by brushes or some other flexible seal to avoid air flow under the wheels. This technique can be used with most of the moving ground simulation methods shown in Fig. 3.25, and its only disadvantage is that it cannot be used with a moving belt system.

When a moving belt is used for ground simulation, then the model is usually supported by a sting which is mounted either behind (Fig. 3.30) or above the vehicle (Fig. 3.31). From the aerodynamic point of view, the rear-mounted sting creates less interference than the roof-mounted one. The forces and moments are measured by a six-component balance, which is mounted between the model's body and the sting. This is a highly sophisticated measuring element, shown in Fig. 3.32. By cutting holes and various shapes into the metal core of this balance, its structure becomes sensitive in particular spots to loads such as drag. Once these spots are identified, strain gauges are glued there,

Fig. 3-29. Typical method for mounting a model with rotating wheels on a fixed ground plane.

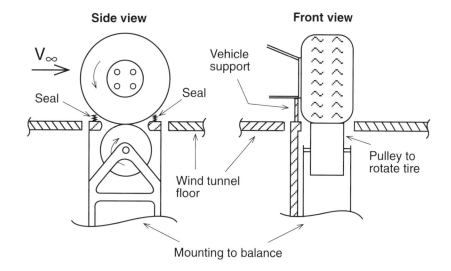

Side view

Front view

V_∞

Seal

Seal

Vehicle support

Pulley to rotate tire

Wind tunnel floor

Mounting to balance

Fig. 3-30. Typical rear sting mounting for suspending a model with rotating wheels above a moving belt system.

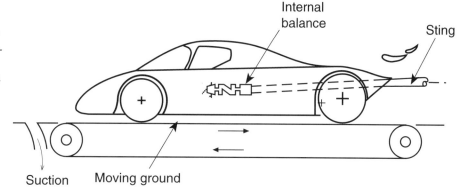

Internal balance

Sting

Suction

Moving ground

Fig. 3-31. Typical ceiling-mounted sting for suspending a model with rotating wheels above a moving belt system. Courtesy of Mr. J. O'Leary, Dept. of Aeronautics, Imperial College.

and by measuring their resistance, the balance can be calibrated to measure aerodynamic loads.

Wheel rotation is usually obtained by the contact between the wheel and the moving belt. In this case the forces between the belt and the model may introduce an error into the measured loads. In one solution the wheels are perma-

Fig. 3-32. *Schematic of an internal balance to measure forces and moments (six components).*

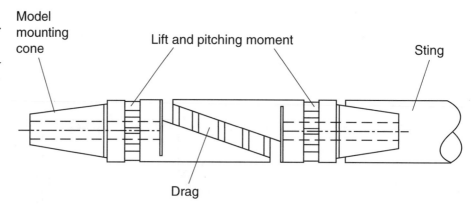

nently attached to the floor and are rotated by the moving belt. The rest of the model is attached to the balance, which measures only the loads on the vehicle body. This setup is used with many small-scale models, and the rotating wheels can help in holding down and stabilizing the moving belt.

The big disadvantage of such a setup is that the effect of the body on the wheels is not measured directly, and this can lead to some errors when testing open-wheel race cars (e.g., F-1, where the wheels dominate the vehicle's aerodynamics). An open-wheel race car model using this mounting method is shown in Fig. 3.33. The above mentioned shortcomings were corrected in this setup by measuring the aerodynamic loads on the wheels via strain gauges glued onto the struts holding the wheels. This method is quite accurate for drag but less dependable for measuring the lift of the rolling wheels.

Fig. 3-33. *Method of mounting rotating wheels separately from vehicle's body. Note that wheels are mounted on the floor and rotated by the belt, while the 35%-scale race car's body is suspended from above. Courtesy of Dr. Kevin P. Garry, Cranfield University.*

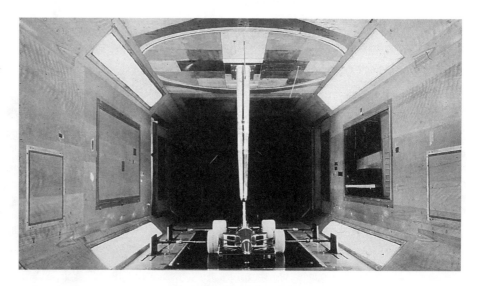

Another option is to soften the suspension so that the wheels are only lightly touching the belt. Then in a separate experiment the vertical and axial forces between the wheels and belt are measured with the belt running and the air flow off. This can be used later to correct measured lift and drag data. One of the disadvantages of using sting mounts in such moving-belt experiments is the flexibility of the balance, which may lead to model vibrations during the test. Therefore, this method is more attractive for small-scale testing with light models, though it has been used on full-scale vehicles as well (see, for example, the model in the DNW tunnel in Fig. 3.34). This problem is less severe when the model is supported from above (as in Fig. 1.14 and 3.31), but in this case the disturbance of the sting may affect the flow on the roof and toward the rear wing of a race car.

Finally, a sting balance can be mounted under the model, as in Fig. 3.35, where it is used with an elevated ground plane. This approach is similar to using the scales (Fig. 3.27) but the force-measuring unit is more compact.

Fig. 3-34. A full-size Opel Calibra held by a rear sting over a moving belt in the German-Dutch wind tunnel. Courtesy of DNW.

Fig. 3-35. Small-scale model mounted above a fixed ground plane. The load measuring balance is attached below the model. Reprinted with permission from SAE Paper 850283 Copyright ©1985 SAE, Inc.

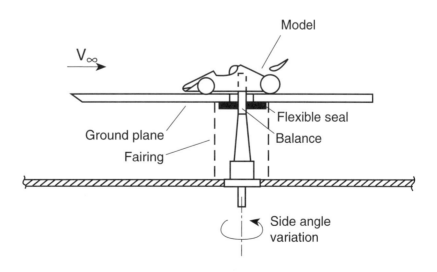

In the first part of this section I described various methods for placing the model in the wind tunnel test section The placing of the wheels on the wind tunnel floor (or the simulated road) was briefly discussed, and it is important to realize the sensitivity of the measured results to the geometry of the wheel/wind tunnel floor contact area.

For example, if the gap between the wheels and the floor is not sealed (as shown in Fig. 3.36), then the flow in this gap will reduce lift (e.g., increase downforce by up to $\Delta C_L \sim -0.45$), while the effect on drag is much smaller. The effect of wheel rotation is significant, too, and in open-wheel race cars (F-1, Indy, etc.) the incremental downforce can be about $\Delta C_L \sim -0.14$ more than without rotating wheels (that is, more downforce with the rotating wheels).

Fig. 3-36. Effect of gap between the stationary wheels and the ground on a prototype race car model lift coefficient (Reynolds number based on model length, $Re_L = 3.3 \times 10^6$). Reprinted with permission from Ref. 2.9.

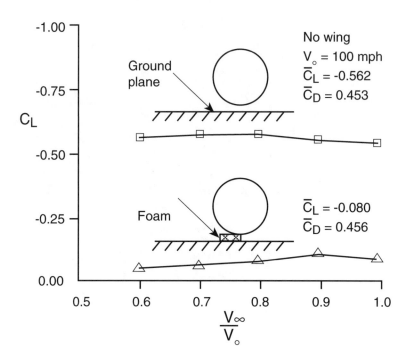

Fig. 3.37 (from Ref. 3.9) shows this effect versus varying ground clearance $e/2R$ for an isolated wheel (note that the coefficients are calculated based on the wheel's frontal area). The effect of wheel rotation on drag is usually an increase on the order of $\Delta C_D \sim -0.02$ for open-wheel race cars, but in sedans a similar decrease is measured, as shown in Fig. 3.38. This can be explained by the forward motion of the upper separation line on an open wheel (thus larger drag) and by the effect of pumping more air under the car for the sedan (hence less drag). Note that rotation effect will increase with increased tire surface roughness (tread height, etc.). (For additional information on the effect of rotation on the location of the separation point on race car wheels, see Chapter 6.)

Flow Quality and Reynolds Number Effects

Another topic that should be addressed is the difference in flow quality between the wind tunnel and the road. In principle, in still air on the road, turbulence is negligible; in closed-return wind tunnels turbulence is measurable (0.1%–1% is not unheard of). Also, because of the tunnel walls the velocity in the test section is not uniform (slower near the walls). Typical results are shown in Fig. 3.39 for the DNW wind tunnel (and here the numbers are very small).

Another effect that must be accounted for is the distortion of the flow field due to the presence of the model. This problem is associated with high blockage testing where wind tunnel speed is measured by a pitot tube(s) placed far ahead

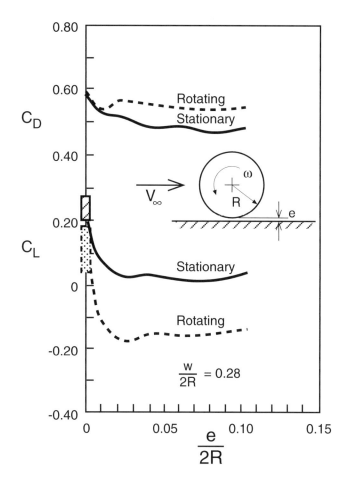

Fig. 3-37. *Drag and lift of isolated stationary and rotating wheels versus ground clearance. Coefficients based on wheel frontal area (after Ref. 3.9). The range of C_L shown for zero ground clearance indicates the range of results obtained with a variety of ground-to-wheel seals.*

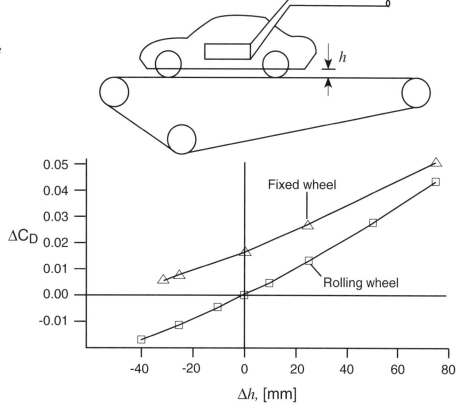

Fig. 3-38. *Influence of wheel rotation and ground clearance on the drag coefficient of an automobile (referenced to the production vehicle with ~180 mm ground clearance). Reprinted with permission from SAE Paper 910311 Copyright ©1991 SAE, Inc.*

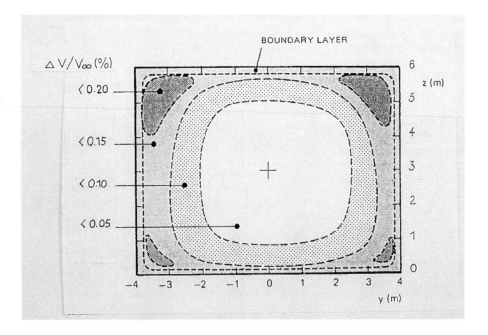

Fig. 3-39. *Variation in the test- section free-stream velocity in the center of the German-Dutch wind tunnel test section. Courtesy of DNW.*

of the model. But as shown in Fig. 3.40, the pitot tubes placed near the tunnel ceiling will record a speed which is higher than the average far-field velocity. This is a result of a rather large blockage (e.g., $A/C \sim 12\%$) in this experiment, which caused the shown distortion in the velocity profile ahead of the model.

A frequently blamed source for the differences between wind-tunnel and actual on-road aerodynamics is called the "Reynolds number effect." By observing the definition of the Reynolds number in Eq. 2.2, it can be concluded that in order to keep this number unchanged, the size of the vehicle multiplied by the speed should be kept constant. For example, testing a 1/5-th scale model at 5 times the expected speed will fulfil this condition. However, based on Fig. 3.21, an increase in wind tunnel test-section speed is very expensive (and a fivefold increase is not realistic; not to mention the possibility of supersonic speeds). Therefore, the Reynolds number is usually compromised.

The next question is: How will a lower Reynolds number test compare with actual full-scale performance? The answer is that if the flow is attached in the lower Reynolds number case, then it will also be in the higher Reynolds number case, and the effects on automobile aerodynamics will be fairly small (and limited to effects of Reynolds number on the friction in the boundary layer). However, if the flow is separated from curved surfaces (such as wheels, wings, etc.) in the lower Reynolds number case, then, due to reattachments, large differences are possible when comparing this to the larger Reynolds number case. This sensitivity to the Reynolds number is demonstrated by the following two examples.

For the first example, consider the lift coefficient of the symmetric airfoil in Fig. 3.41. The lift initially increases with increasing angle of attack, until a point called "stall," where the flow separates, resulting in a reduction in the lift of the airfoil. The interesting observation is that with and increase in the Reynolds number the flow separation (stall) is delayed, and considerably larger lift coefficients can be generated. (A more complete discussion on airfoils and wings is presented in the next chapter.)

Fig. 3-40. *Distortion of the velocity profile ahead and near the vehicle, when placed in a wind tunnel test section. Reprinted with permission from SAE Paper 890601 Copyright ©1989 SAE, Inc.*

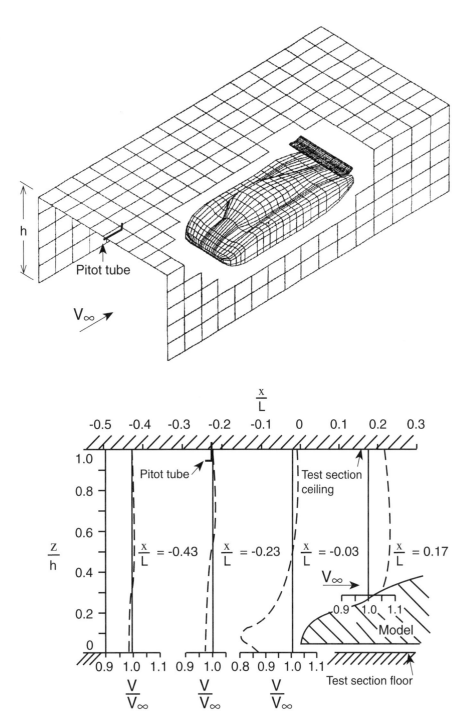

The significance of this data can be interpreted based on the following example: Suppose that a race car wing is developed at a Re number of 0.3 x 10[6] (using the wing chord for the length in the Reynolds number definition). The maximum lift coefficient is obtained just before the wing stalls, and the corresponding value in Fig. 3.41 is about 0.8. However, at a higher speed and scale (e.g., at Re = 3.0 x 10[6]) the maximum value of the lift coefficient can be as high as 1.5! This, of course, is not reflected by the low Reynolds number tests and

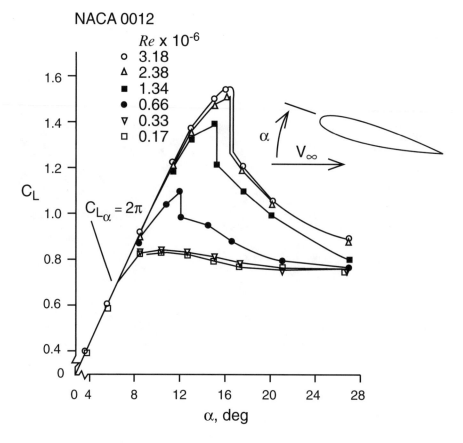

Fig. 3-41. *Effect of Reynolds number on the lift coefficient of a symmetric NACA 0012 airfoil. Note, that the length scale used for the Reynolds number in this case is the airfoil's chord length (from Ref. 2.2 p. 525, Copyright ©1977 AIAA - Reprinted with permission).*

the vehicle based on these experiments may end up generating only half of the potential downforce of its wing.

The second example, Fig. 3.42, shows an isolated stationary wheel placed on the wind tunnel floor. The aerodynamic lift and drag show a very rapid change, when the Re number is increased through the critical range of 0.1×10^6 to 0.3×10^6. This is possibly a result of a rapid change in the location of the separation lines on the wheel. When the Re number increases across this range, the separation point (or line) behind the wheel, shown in the inset in this figure, moves backward, and the size of the separated flow region is reduced (from the

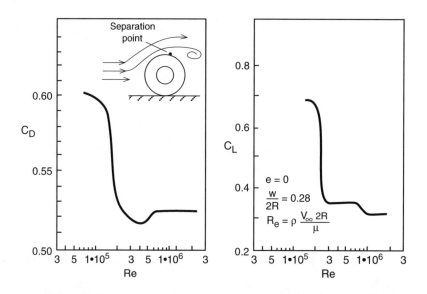

Fig. 3-42. *Trends in the variation of drag and lift for a stationary wheel (in contact with the floor), versus Reynolds number. Coefficients are based on wheel frontal area (after Ref. 3.9).*

top and the two side views). It is quite remarkable that such a small Reynolds-number increment has this strong effect on the lift and drag of the wheel—the lift by more than 50%.

Large portions of the Reynolds number effects occur at the range of Re$=10^5$ to 10^6. So when testing a 1/4-scale model, say, at 150 km/hr, and making decisions about a race car traveling at 300 km/hr, then those two points (based on the wing's chord) are exactly at the opposite edges of this troublesome range. If you are pleased with your 1/4-scale, low-speed results, then the actual vehicle will perform well, but your aerodynamic design will in all likelihood be *too* conservative.

Expected Results of Wind Tunnel Tests

Independent of the testing method, similar results are *expected* from both road and wind tunnel tests. For completeness, however, a brief summary is provided of the type of engineering data that can be obtained by wind-tunnel testing.

First and most obvious is load data. This includes downforce, drag, side force, and the pitching, rolling, and yawing moments. The primary parameters that will affect vehicle performance are downforce, drag, their ratio (L/D), and the front/rear axle distribution of the downforce (a 40%/60% ratio can be considered as satisfactory). Load measurements are usually done by balances (or scales). For improving the vehicle, sometimes more data is required, and surface pressure distribution can be measured and the flow features can be visualized. These techniques are basically the same as described for road testing, but

Fig. 3-43. *Pressure distribution along the centerline of a sedan-based race car. α_w is the rear wing angle of attack.*

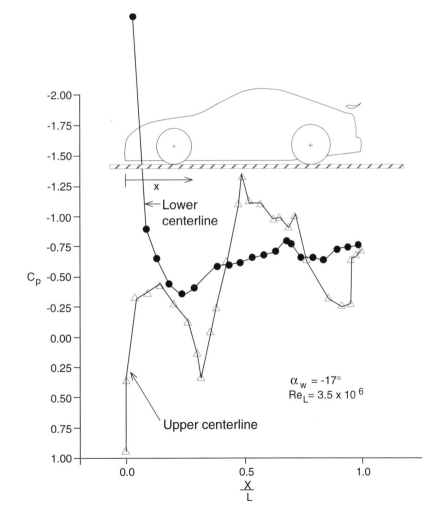

it is much easier to implement those methods in the wind tunnel. Typical pressure distribution, measured along the centerline of a 1/4-scale model of the race car (discussed later in Chapter 7) is presented in Fig. 3.43. Based on the shape of the pressure distribution, flow separation and other flow features can be investigated. In this particular case the stagnation pressure near the nose has a value close to $C_p = +1.0$. Because of flow separation behind the rear deck, the pressure does not recover to this high value, creating considerable levels of form-drag. Also, by identifying low- and high-pressure areas on the vehicle, cooling and ventilation intakes and exits can be located.

Qualitative information on the flow can be obtained by visualization techniques. Implementation in the wind tunnel, again, is much easier than in a road test, and typical examples for using surface tufts and smoke traces are shown in Fig. 3.44 and 3.45.

As was mentioned earlier, flow visualizations are primarily used as a diagnostic tool to improve a vehicle's design. This data can be obtained on the

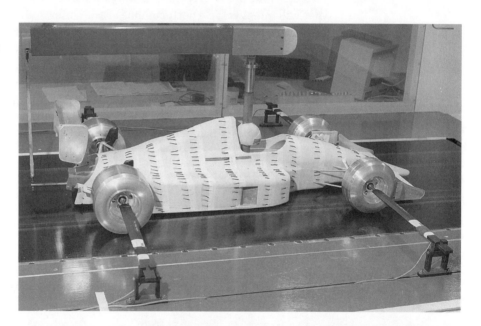

Fig. 3-44. Surface tufts for surface-flow visualization. Courtesy of MIRA.

Fig. 3-45. Use of smoke trace for off-body flow visualization in the wind tunnel test section. Courtesy of MIRA.

body's surface or off the surface and can help explain some of the results obtained from the load tests. For example, the tufts on the body of the F-1 car in Fig. 3.44 indicate attached flow, even at the cooling flow exit on the side pod. Note the attached flow region ahead of the rear wing, which is an indication of a good design, since flow separation there may hamper wing performance. The smoke trace in Fig. 3.45 is a good example for using off-body flow visualization in the wind tunnel. In this case the probe releasing the smoke can be moved to any area of interest to investigate the flow direction. This particular photo shows that the flow is attached on the upper surface of the body and the rear wing receives mostly undisturbed flow (an indication of a good design).

Conclusions on Wind Tunnel Methods

While it may seem as if wind tunnels can never exactly simulate actual road conditions (due to ground effect, wheel rotation, Reynolds number, etc.), the wind tunnel is, in fact, the primary tool used to study automotive and race car aerodynamics.

In regard to the accuracy of the data, many wind tunnel operators proudly advertize the microscopic accuracy of their balance system, but in reality some of the problems mentioned earlier refute this claim of high fidelity. And measuring lift coefficients with more than 2 digits behind the decimal point may not be necessary. The bottom line is:

- Understanding the aerodynamic problem is more important than having too sensitive equipment. Since vehicle improvement requires only incremental data (to judge if an idea is good), productive vehicle improvements can be achieved with minimum resources (good results have been achieved with 14% blockage in a wind tunnel with no moving ground belt)
- Whatever works satisfactorily in the wind tunnel, will usually work on the track (or on the road)
- A design optimized in a small-scale wind tunnel will be too conservative on the actual road, and the vehicle can be further improved

COMPUTATIONAL METHODS

Analytical tools should be simple to use and should rapidly predict trends in the particular problem being investigated. The difficulty in applying this logic to automotive aerodynamics rests in the complexity of fluid dynamic equations. In spite of the large advent in computational solutions, a detailed simulation of the partially separated flow field over a race car is difficult and still very time consuming and expensive. Therefore, the use of this tool is so far limited, and only the simplest (and least costly) forms of computations have been used to study localized problems (e.g., wing shape development for race cars).

The primary benefits from using a computational tool (once the method has been matured and validated) would be the quick response and the ability to improve and modify a vehicle's shape before it was built. Computational methods can also serve as a diagnostic tool for improving existing vehicles. When compared to other forms of experiment, computations have the advantage that the generated results can be used over and over to study new parts of the problem. In experiments, once the model is taken out of the wind tunnel, new questions cannot be answered. As an example, when placing the engine induction air inlet on the car, the warm flow from the radiators must be avoided. The inlet location can only be guessed at if this aspect was not studied during a wind-tunnel test. However, results of most computations will include the velocity field information, on and off the vehicle, and a simple tracing of the streamlines can quickly answer this question (without a rerun of the code).

Because of the importance and potential of computational methods, I will present a brief discussion of the fluid dynamic equations. Then I will discuss the current capability and maturity of some methods, as well as some examples of applications.

Fluid Dynamic Equations

The airflow over a vehicle should obey certain basic rules of physics, among them the conservation of mass and momentum. Solution of the flow over a car without temperature variations should be possible, based on those two equations.

The first equation states that the fluid mass is conserved. This equation is often called the continuity equation. To demonstrate this principle let us examine a stream tube, as shown in Fig. 3.46. The tube can be the result of a flow in an internal channel or an imaginary tube confined between streamlines (so the flow enters only through the left side and exits at the right side). The conservation of mass principle tells us that the mass flow rate entering the stream tube is equal to the exiting mass flow rate (or, for a fluid with a constant density the product of velocity and area are constant). For example, if the area at the inlet is 5 times larger than at the exit, then exit speed will be 5 times higher than the speed at the inlet. The algebraic formulation of this equation, along with some numerical examples, are presented in the Fluid Dynamic Equations a bit later in this chapter.

Fig. 3-46. *Generic stream tube and nomenclature used to describe the basic fluid dynamic equations.*

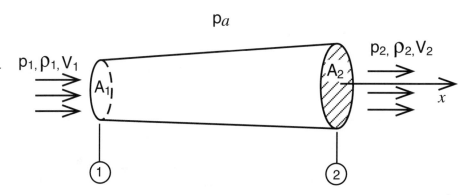

The second equation, the conservation of momentum, dates back to Sir Isaac Newton (1642–1727) who, among other things, postulated that the change of linear momentum on a particle is proportional to the force acting upon it. Catching a speeding baseball will exert a force in the catcher's hand. Similarly, when one of the periscopic devices shown in Fig. 3.47B catches the moving air, it will exert a force, because the horizontal movement of the air is halted. Another simple example that I can think of is the water hose I use to water the plants in the garden. The water exiting from the hose will push back my hands, similar to the exiting air in Fig. 3.47C. This is one example when the change in the momentum of a flowing fluid (water in this case) results in a force (other

A

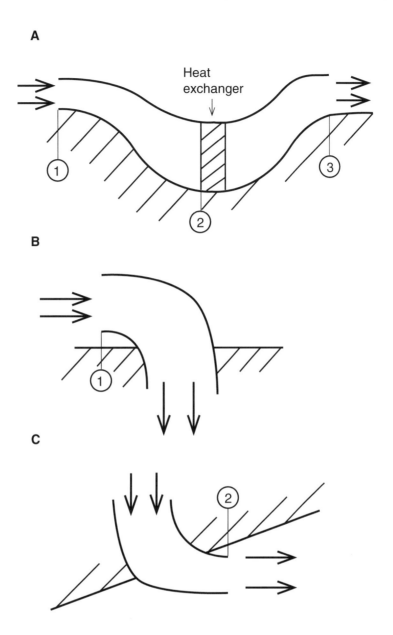

Fig. 3-47. Typical air ducts found on race cars, and the effect of their internal momentum.

examples are airplane jet engines or the space-shuttle rockets). More details about this principle are presented in the Equation sidebar.

The above simple examples demonstrate the physical meaning of the fluid dynamic equations. The continuity equation usually provides information on velocity due to changes in the geometry, while the momentum equation determines aerodynamic loads. For the practical solution of the flow field over a car, a three-dimensional method is required, which complicates the procedure considerably. In spite of this complexity, this science is rapidly developing and its progress is discussed in the next section.

continued on 3rd page following

Fluid Dynamic Equations   When referring to "Fluid Dynamic Equations," most people think of the conservation of mass and momentum (Newton's second principle). The complete form of these two equations is quite complicated, and in order to demonstrate their nature, only the so-called "one dimensional" form will be discussed here.

The first equation states that the fluid mass is conserved. This is often called the continuity equation. To demonstrate this principle let us return to the stream tube in Fig. 3.46. For our purposes the tube is an imaginary one confined between streamlines, so the flow enters only through A_1 and leaves only at A_2. If the density of the fluid at station 1 is ρ_1, the cross-section area is A_1 and the flow speed is V_1, then the mass-flow rate $\dot{m}$ entering at section 1 is

Eq. 3.5
$$\dot{m}_1 = \rho_1 V_1 A_1$$

and the units are mass/time (e.g., kg/sec). The dot on top of the $\dot{m}$ signifies the mass flow per unit of time. The continuity equation states that in a steady-state condition the mass-flow rate entering the tube equals the mass-flow rate leaving the tube

$$\dot{m}_1 = \dot{m}_2 = \dot{m}$$

Therefore, the subscripts 1 or 2 can be omitted. In terms of the local velocity and density (using Eq. 3.5) the above continuity equation can be rewritten as:

Eq. 3.6
$$\rho_1 V_1 A_1 = \rho_2 V_2 A_2$$

To demonstrate the continuity principle let us return to the Venturi tube of Fig. 2.13. Assume that the water is flowing into this tube at a speed of 0.2 m/sec at the inlet where $A_1 = 0.001 m^2$. The mass flow rate is then calculated by using Eq. 3.5, and the water density is taken from Table 2.1:

$$\dot{m} = \rho_1 V_1 A_1 = 1000\left(\frac{kg}{m^3}\right)0.2\left(\frac{m}{sec}\right)0.001 m^2 = 0.2\frac{kg}{sec}$$

If the throat area $A_2 = (1/5) A_1$, and water density is unchanged, then we can calculate the velocity there by using Eq. 3.6:

$$V_2 = V_1 \cdot \frac{\rho_1 A_1}{\rho_2 A_2} = 0.2 \cdot \frac{m}{sec} \cdot \frac{5}{1} = 1\frac{m}{sec}$$

The second equation, the conservation of momentum, dates back to Sir Isaac Newton (1642–1727) who, among other things, postulated that the change of linear momentum on a particle is proportional to the force acting upon it. My teacher at the high school wrote this down as:

$$\sum F = \frac{d}{dt}(mV)$$

and here $\sum$ represents a summation of all forces F acting, and $\frac{d}{dt}$ is a derivation (change) with time. Note that Eq. 3.1 is the same, but there it applied to the acceleration of a solid body. With fluid (air) flow, this equation must hold for any fluid particle, and when applied to the steady-state flow in the stream tube in Fig. 3.46 this yields:

Eq. 3.7
$$\sum F = \dot{m}_2 V_2 - \dot{m}_1 V_1 = \dot{m}(V_2 - V_1)$$

since $\dot{m}_1 = \dot{m}_2$.

The forces in a fluid can be a result of pressure, viscosity (friction), gravity or other external forces. If we limit ourselves to forces due to pressure and all other external forces acting on the tube boundary are called F, then we can write for the force into the x direction

$$\sum F = F + (p_1 - p_a) A_1 - (p_2 - p_a) A_2$$

Here the p_1 and p_2 are the static pressures at sections 1 and 2, respectively, and p_a is the reference ambient pressure. Substituting this into Eq. 3.7 results in

$$F + (p_1 - p_a) A_1 - (p_2 - p_a) A_2 = \dot{m}(V_2 - V_1)$$

In conclusion, by rearranging the terms in this last expression the momentum conservation equation can determine the force acting on the above stream tube:

Eq. 3.8
$$F = (p_2 - p_a) A_2 - (p_1 - p_a) A_1 + \dot{m}(V_2 - V_1)$$

or if we use Eq. 3.5 then

Eq. 3.9
$$F = (p_2 - p_a) A_2 - (p_1 - p_a) A_1 + \rho_2 V_2^2 A_2 - \rho_1 V_1^2 A_1$$

To demonstrate the usefulness of this equation, consider the three cases in Fig. 3.47. In Fig. 3.47A a cooling duct is shown. For example, we can use the continuity equation (Eq. 3.6) to calculate the velocity ahead of the cooler, at section 2 (assuming that we know the speed at section 1, which could be close to the vehicle's speed):

$$V_2 = V_1 \frac{\rho_1 A_1}{\rho_2 A_2}$$

If the density does not change in the diffuser (no temperature change) then $\rho_1 = \rho_2$ and both symbols can be omitted. Then the speed between the two sections 1 and 2 changes as the inverse of the area ratio ($V_2/V_1 = A_1/A_2$). The momentum drag D of the installation can be calculated by using Eq. 3.9:

Eq. 3.10
$$D = -F = -(p_3 - p_a) A_3 + (p_1 - p_a) A_1 - (\rho_3 V_3^2 A_3 + \rho_1 V_1^2 A_1)$$

and the minus sign indicates that the drag is a result of the fluid acting on the duct (reaction to the force acting on the fluid). Incidentally, if the exit velocity V_3 is large enough, the drag becomes negative (the duct will generate thrust).

Eq. 3.8 can be used to calculate the momentum drag caused by a cooling intake, as in Fig. 3-47B (or by retaining only the section 1 terms, in Eq. 3.10):

Eq. 3.11
$$D = (p_1 - p_a) A_1 + \rho_1 V_1^2 A_1$$

while the thrust T (acting in a direction opposite to D) due to the exhaust flow in Fig. 3.47C is

continued on next page

Eq. 3.12

$$T = (p_2 - p_a) A_2 + \rho_2 V_2^2 A_2$$

As a numerical example let us find the ram-drag of an air intake with an area of $A_1 = 0.01 m^2$, such as the one shown in Fig. 3.47B. If our vehicle travels at 250 km/hr (69.44 m/sec) and air density is again taken from Table 2.1, we can estimate the drag by using Eq. 3.11 (and neglecting the pressure term $(p_1 - p_a) A_1$):

$$D = 1.22 \left(\frac{kg}{m^3} \right) \left(69.44 \frac{m}{\sec} \right)^2 0.01 m^2 = 58.8 N$$

Type of Codes and Current Capabilities

Most computational methods for the solution of the airflow over vehicle shapes are based on solving the equations of continuity and momentum. Their simplified form is presented in Eqs. 3.5 to 3.9. Current codes differ primarily in the way they model the forces acting on a fluid particle (pressure and viscous forces), and in the numerical representation of the governing partial-differential equations. Fig. 3.48 shows the rapid development in computational capabilities of various methods. The ordinate indicates the complexity of the body about which the calculation is done. The abscissa indicates the complexity of the numerical model.

The simplest models will not have the effect of viscosity. Therefore, drag due to friction and flow separation cannot be predicted. These codes, sometimes called potential flow solvers, are now well developed and can compute the flow over a complex body usually in a few minutes. Consequently, from the avail-

Fig. 3-48. *Variation of fluid-dynamics computational capability over the years, versus complexity of model geometry.*

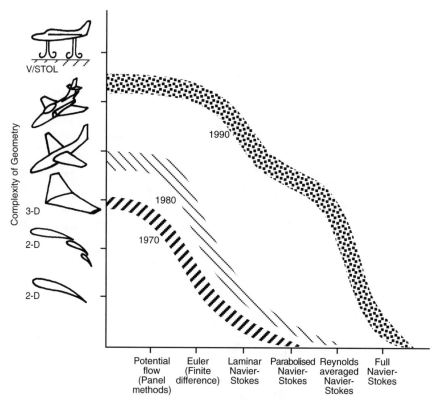

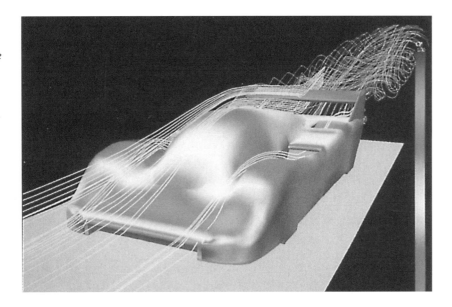

Fig. 3-49. *Results of panel code, showing the pressure distribution and off-body stream-lines on a Porsche 965 race car. Courtesy of M. Summa, AMI.*

ability point of view, they are suitable for race car application. As an example for this approach, the computed results over a prototype race car are shown in Fig. 3.49, depicting streamlines and surface pressure contours (shown by different colors). In cases of attached flows over highly streamlined vehicles or wings, this method is very useful. However, viscous flow-dominated areas near the rotating wheels and behind the vehicle cannot be modeled in a satisfactory manner.

The most complex computer codes include the effect of viscosity, and in principle should be capable of predicting surface friction and flow separation. These codes are based on solving the complete momentum equations, which are called the Navier-Stokes equations. In case of laminar flows the computer codes are more developed, as indicated by Fig. 3.48, than for various levels of modeling turbulent flow. However, the flow over most of the rear section of an automobile is turbulent and contains areas of massive flow separations. Thus, the appropriate solution requires modeling of the turbulence in the flow, and using a time-accurate approach to model the unsteady separated flows near the surface and in the wake. Such a solution requires considerable computational effort, perhaps days on the most modern computers, and therefore is very expensive.

As an example, the results of the viscous flow solution for the flow over a generic Mazda RX-7 automobile are shown in Fig. 3.50. This type of computa-

Fig. 3-50. *Viscous-flow (Navier-Stokes) simulation of the separated flow over a two-dimensional model of the Mazda RX-7 car. Copyright ©1987 AIAA, Reprinted with permission from AIAA Paper 87-1386.*

tion, in principle, contains the proper information on the viscous drag (friction), and on the flow separation (that causes form drag). Extending this computation to three dimensions, including details such as wheel rotation, would be expensive even for a large automobile manufacturer. This fact, and the current long computational turnaround times, limit the use of these methods for racing applications.

Returning to Fig. 3.48, the ultimate solution of the fluid dynamic equation (at the far right of the abscissa) will be the so-called "full," or "direct," simulation using a very fine grid, without modeling turbulent eddies. At this time the method is applicable only to very simple geometries because of the large computational effort involved.

Conclusions on Computational Methods

The most important conclusion is that from a user's standpoint none of the computer codes is mature enough for immediate use by a novice designer. This means that only after developing research-oriented and well-trained operators can this tool be productive (for a survey of computational tools by the automotive industry in 1993, see Ref. 3.10). However, once sufficient experience is gained, and after several validations against road and wind tunnel tests, computational capability can be very useful, especially for race car wing designs.

The primary advantage is the ability to generate detailed information after the code has been run. For example, aerodynamic loads on various body panels and wing components can be separated for a structural analysis. Load distribution and changes with angle of attack and side slip can be generated quickly to interact with vehicle dynamic codes to investigate effect of geometry changes on lap times. Various parametric studies, such as wing positioning, can be done before an actual model is built. This makes low-order computational methods (e.g., panel methods) attractive for tasks such as the preliminary or conceptual development of various vehicles. Also, the results of computations are more comprehensive than any single test. Such results include aerodynamic loads, surface pressure distribution, and flow visualization information, and all are the product of the same computation.

CLOSING REMARKS ON TOOLS

As was mentioned at the end of the introduction to this chapter, no one method for estimating the aerodynamic loads is perfect; a combination is required for a productive vehicle development program. However, by being aware of the pitfalls associated with the various methods, valuable data can be generated even with limited resources. This is especially evident when incremental data is sought on the value of some local modifications. When carefully used, most methods can generate good quantitative data.

It is also clear from this chapter that the field of fluid dynamics (and, again, air is a fluid, too) is still very complicated and sometimes unpredictable (nonlinear, in engineering terms). Therefore, many of the aerodynamic gimmicks may work in a small-scale model in the wind tunnel but won't work on the actual race car. Or they may not work in either case but the crew will put it on anyway because they think it does work, and so on. . . .

REFERENCES

3.1 Beauvais, F. N., Tignor, S. C., and Turner, T. R., "Problems of Ground Simulation in Automotive Aerodynamics," SAE Paper No. 68-0121, Detroit 1968.

3.2 Walston, W. H., Buckley, F. T., and Marks, C. H., "Test Procedures of the Evaluation of Aerodynamic Drag on Full-Scale Vehicles in Windy Environments," SAE Paper No. 76-0106, Detroit 1976.

3.3 Korst, H. H. and White, R. A., "Evaluation of Vehicle Drag Parameters From Coast-Down Experiments Conducted Under Non-ideal Environmental Conditions," *J. of Fluids Engineering*, Vol. 103, pp. 133-140, March 1981.

3.4 Roussillon, G., "Contribution to Accurate Measurement of Aerodynamic Drag on a Moving Vehicle from Coast-Down Tests and Determination of Actual Rolling Resistance," *J. of Wind Engineering and Industrial Aerodynamics*, Vol. 9, pp. 33-48, 1981.

3.5 The Japan Society of Mechanical Engineers, Editor: Nakayama Y., *Visualized Flow: Fluid Motion in Basic Engineering Situations Revealed by Flow Visualization*, Pergamon Press, NY, 1988.

3.6 Rae, W. H., and Pope, A., *Low-Speed Wind Tunnel Testing*, Second Edition, John Wiley and Sons, Inc., 1984.

3.7 Garner, H. C., Rogers, E. W. E., Acum, W. E. A., and Maskell, E.C., *Subsonic Wind Tunnel Wall Corrections*, AGARDograph 109, Oct. 1966.

3.8 Kelly, K. B., Provencher, L. G., and Shenkel, F. K., "The General Motors Engineering Staff Aerodynamic Laboratory—A Full-Scale Automotive Wind Tunnel," SAE Paper No. 82-0371, 1982.

3.9 Cogotti, A., "Aerodynamic Characteristics of Car Wheels," *Int. J. of Vehicle Design*, Technological Advances in Vehicle Design Series, SP3, Impact of Aerodynamics on Vehicle Design, pp. 173–196, 1983.

3.10 Hucko, W. H., and Sovran, G., "Aerodynamics of Road Vehicles," *Annual Review of Fluid Mechanics*, 1993, No. 25, pp. 485–537, 1993.

4

AIRFOILS AND WINGS

INTRODUCTION

A discussion on wings traditionally starts with a discussion on the wing section shape, the airfoil. We shall follow this approach and first demonstrate the aerodynamic significance of the airfoil geometry and its effect on lift and drag.

A three-dimensional wing consists of airfoil sections, but the shape of the wing planform in terms of sweep, taper, twist, and other geometrical parameters affects the overall performance as well. The second part of this chapter will focus on such planform shape effects of the finite, three-dimensional wing.

The definitions in this chapter follow standard aerodynamic practice: that is, the lift is the force acting in the upward direction. In order to clarify any confusion due to this definition, note that for race car applications the downforce can be obtained by using inverted wings, which create negative lift. So, wings sketched in this chapter will be airplane-type, compared to the inverted wings shown through the rest of the book.

Following the same spirit, in this chapter *only*, the reference area A used for defining the aerodynamic coefficients (as in Eqs. 2.13–2.15) is based on the wing surface area, and not on the frontal area of the complete vehicle.

AIRFOILS: BASIC DEFINITIONS

An airfoil is the two-dimensional cross section of a three-dimensional wing. The relevant terminology is explained in Figs. 4.1 and 4.2. A generic airfoil shape is shown by the shaded cross section in Fig. 4.1. It is called "two-dimensional" since this shape does not extend spanwise. Therefore, a two-dimensional airfoil can be viewed as the cross section of a rectangular wing with an infinite span b (and for this case, $b \rightarrow \infty$, in Fig. 4.1A). The sideview of this infinitely wide wing is shown in Fig. 4.1B, as is the angle of attack α (relative to the moving air). The letter c is usually used to denote the chord length of the airfoil (Fig. 4.2), while t stands for its maximum thickness. The leading edge is usually rounded and the trailing edge is pointed. Fig. 4.2 shows that an airfoil can be symmetrical or it can have a camber.

The streamlines over a generic airfoil moving through a fluid (such as air) are presented in Fig. 4.3. The streamline that stops under the leading edge is called the stagnation streamline since the flow stagnates (stops) at this point. The point itself is called a stagnation point. The overall effect of the airfoil on the surrounding fluid results in a faster flow above it and a slower flow under it. According to Bernoulli's equation (Eq. 2.5), because of this velocity difference the pressure above the airfoil will be lower than under it. The resultant force will act upward and is called *lift*.

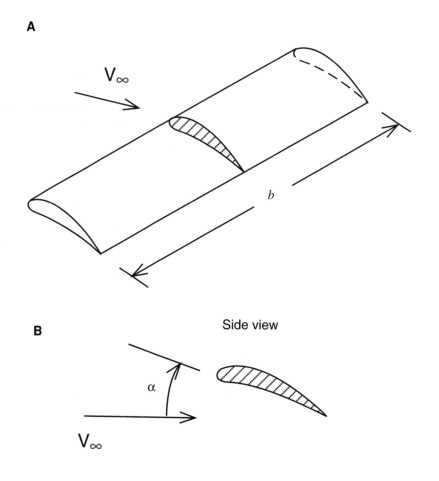

A

*Fig. 4-1. The airfoil is the shaded shape shown on the wing **A**. In the case of a rectangular wing, **B** shows the two-dimensional airfoil.*

B

Side view

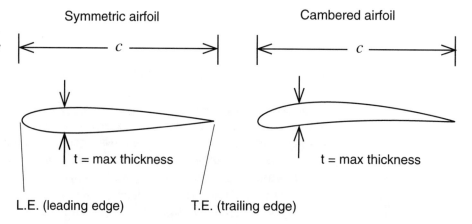

Fig. 4-2. Basic nomenclature used to describe an airfoil.

Symmetric airfoil

Cambered airfoil

t = max thickness

t = max thickness

L.E. (leading edge)   T.E. (trailing edge)

The shape of the pressure distribution is a direct outcome of the velocity distribution near the airfoil (see Eq. 2.4). For example, a fluid particle traveling along a streamline placed slightly above the stagnation streamline (in Fig. 4.3) will turn sharply to the left near the stagnation point. Since this turn is against the solid surface of the airfoil, the particle will slow down, resulting in a larger pressure near this point on the lower surface. But as it reaches the leading edge, it is forced to turn around it (but now the particle wants to move away from the surface), and therefore, its acceleration increases, resulting in a very low pressure near the leading edge.

*Fig. 4-3. Streamlines near an airfoil (**A**), and the resulting pressure distribution (**B**).*

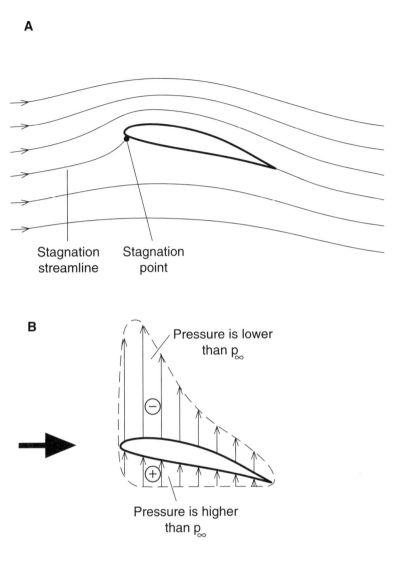

A similar particle moving under the stagnation streamline experiences no major direction changes, and will generally slow down near the airfoil and increase the pressure on the airfoil's lower surface. Thus, the (+) sign in Fig. 4.3B represents the area where the pressure is higher than the free-stream static pressure, while the (–) sign represents the area with lower pressure. Also, in most cases the contribution of the suction side (–) to the lift is considerably larger than that of the pressure side (+).

The next question is: How does an airfoil's geometry affect the shape of the pressure distribution? This can be partially answered by the example in Fig. 4.4. First, a typical pressure distribution on a symmetric airfoil at an angle of attack α is shown in the left-hand side. The vertical arrows depict the direction of the pressure force acting on its surface. The shape of the pressure distribution on an airfoil with a cylindrical arc-shaped camber, at zero angle of attack ($\alpha = 0$), is shown at the center of the figure. These two generic pressure distribution shapes can be combined to generate a desirable pressure distribution, as shown at the right-hand side of the figure. Because of this observation, airfoils are frequently identified by their thickness distribution (which is a symmetric airfoil) and by an additional centerline camber shape

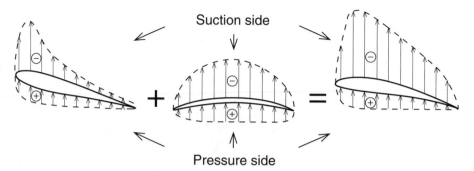

Suction side

Pressure side

Fig. 4-4. *The shape of the pressure distribution on a thin airfoil depends primarily on angle of attack and camber (thickness is important but has a smaller effect).*

(called camber line). The conclusion is that the shape of an airfoil's pressure distribution can be altered by varying the angle of attack and the camberline shape (the shape of the thickness distribution is important too).

After this short introduction, let us investigate the aerodynamic performance of airfoils and its dependence on an airfoil's geometry.

Airfoil Lift   A detailed description of the flow field over airfoils can be found in engineering text books such as Refs. 2.1 and 2.2. Our objectives here, though, do not include an elaborate mathematical discussion of the problem, so we can proceed to list four important conclusions derived from the above references (e.g., Ref. 2.2, pp. 138–139). These conclusions are:

1. The lift versus angle of attack, α, for a thin airfoil in an *attached* flow field is linear, as depicted in Fig. 4.5, where the lift slope is 2π ($\pi = 3.141592654$). In

Fig. 4-5. *Effect of camber on an airfoil's lift coefficient (stall region is not shown).*

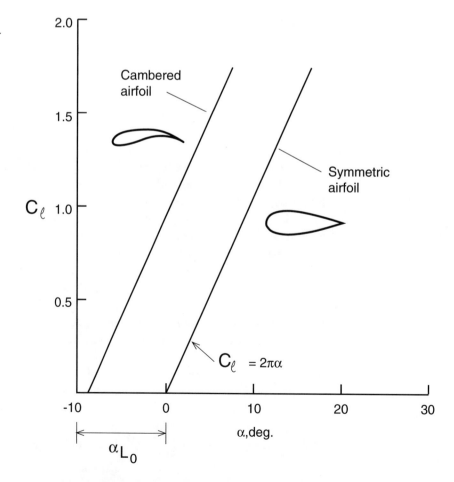

other words, the lift is directly proportional to the angle of incidence, and the multiplier is 2π. This is depicted graphically for a symmetric, thin airfoil by the right-hand line in Fig. 4.5, whose shape (inclination) is given by Eq. 4.1.

An airfoil's camber does not change the lift slope and can be viewed as an additional angle-of-attack effect α_{Lo} (as shown by the left-hand curve in Fig. 4.5). The symmetric airfoil will have zero lift at $\alpha = 0$ while the cambered airfoil with an effective angle of attack will have larger lift. Calculation of α_{Lo} for a given shape of camberline is somewhat more complicated (see Ref. 2.2, p. 128), and for wings with moderate camber its magnitude is on the order of a few degrees.

Lift Coefficient of an Airfoil

An airfoil is the two-dimensional side-view of a wing with infinite span, as shown in Fig. 4.1. The lift coefficient C_l of such an airfoil is defined and calculated per unit width of the airfoil. So, when using Eq. 2.14, the reference area becomes the chord c multiplied by a unit width:

$$C_l = \frac{l}{\left(\frac{1}{2}\rho V_\infty^2\, c\right)}$$

where l is the lift per unit width. The increase in the lift of a symmetric airfoil, as the angle of attack α increases, is given by the formula

Eq. 4.1
$$C_l = 2\pi\alpha$$

Note that C_l is a nondimensional number and α is measured by radians, so the value in degrees must be multiplied by $\pi/180$. For a cambered airfoil the coefficient 2π does not change, but there is an increment in the effective angle of attack by α_{L0}. Thus, the symmetric airfoil will have zero lift at $\alpha = 0$ while the cambered airfoil will have a lift of $C_l = 2\pi\alpha_{L0}$, even at zero angle of attack. Consequently, for a cambered airfoil, Eq. 4.1 can be rewritten as:

Eq. 4.2
$$C_l = 2\pi\,(\alpha + \alpha_{L0})$$

As an example, consider a symmetric airfoil at an angle $\alpha = 8$ deg. With the aid of Eq. 4.1, the lift coefficient is:

$$C_l = 2\pi 8\left(\frac{\pi}{180}\right) = 0.877$$

and the actual lift force can be calculated by using Eq. 2.14. The effect of thickness t/c is to slightly increase lift. For a symmetric Joukowski airfoil (details on this airfoil shape and the above formula appear in Ref. 2.2) the lift slope correction due to thickness is $0.77\,t/c$. Consequently, the modified form of Eq. 4.1, for a thick airfoil is:

Eq. 4.3
$$C_l = 2\pi\left(1 + 0.77\frac{t}{c}\right)\sin\alpha$$

and note that here $\sin\alpha$ is used instead of α.

Fig. 4-6. *Effect of thickness on the aerodynamic coefficients of symmetric NACA airfoils (based on data from Ref. 4.1). Note that the thickness of the 0006 airfoil is 6%, of the 0009 is 9%, and for the 0012 is 12%.*

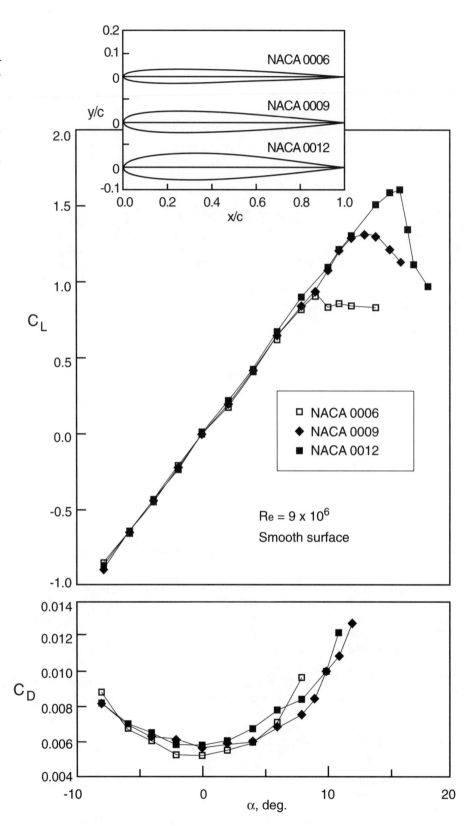

2. The trailing edge of the camberline has the largest effect on the airfoil's lift (compared to the rest of the camberline). Therefore, the lift can be changed, without changing the airfoil angle of attack, by changing the camberline geometry (e.g., by flaps, or slats). The largest increment will be observed if the change is near the trailing edge region. This is why most airplane wings have trailing edge flaps.

3. The above formulation is valid for attached flows only! To explain the meaning of this conclusion let us back up a bit: In the early 1930s, NACA, the forerunner of the NASA organization, developed a systematic set of airfoil shapes, many of them listed in Ref. 4.1. As an example, the measured performance of three symmetric NACA airfoils, with increasing thickness, is presented in Fig. 4.6. The lift curve seems to follow the trend suggested by Eq. 4.1 (or Fig. 4.5) but at a certain point the wing stalls and no additional lift is gained by increasing the angle of attack. This is caused by flow separation, which is shown in Fig. 4.7. At the left-hand side, the attached flow case is described, which is applicable to the linear (straight-line shaped) region of the lift curve in Fig. 4.5 and Fig. 4.6. However, at the larger angles of attack, the streamlines do not follow the airfoil surface shape and separate (right-hand side), causing the lift curve to bend. It is the flow separation that alters the pressure distribution, as shown in Fig. 4.8, primarily reducing the magnitude of the suction on the upper surface, resulting in a loss in lift and a large increase in drag.

Fig. 4-7. Schematic description of the streamlines near an airfoil with attached flow and with separated flow.

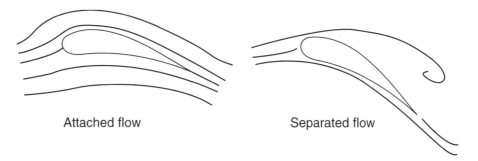

Attached flow   Separated flow

Fig. 4-8. Pressure distribution on a GA(W)-1 airfoil in separated flow with the computed pressure distribution for the attached flow case. From Maskew et al., "Prediction of Aerodynamic Characteristics for Wings with Extensive Separations," paper No. 31 in AGARD/NATO CP-291, "Computation of Viscous-Inviscid Interactions," 1980.

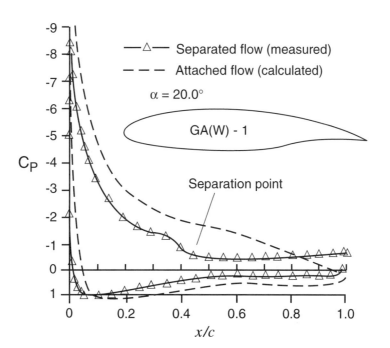

So, for a predictable and reliable airfoil performance, the stalled condition must be avoided.

When the airfoil is very thin and/or its leading edge is fairly sharp, the stall is abrupt. This is called "leading edge separation." For thicker airfoils, especially with large camber, the separation gradually develops at the trailing edge, and hence is called "trailing edge separation." For the latter type airfoils, the stall is less abrupt, as shown in Fig. 4.9.

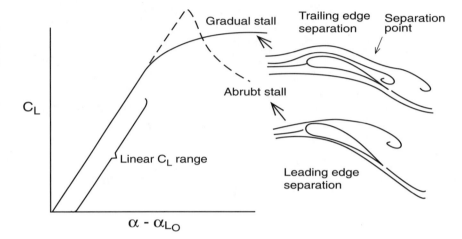

Fig. 4-9. Effect of stall on the lift versus angle of attack curve, for two airfoil types.

4. Now we can return to discuss the effect of airfoil thickness on lift. Mathematical models (e.g., Ref. 2.2, p. 159) show that increasing thickness t/c slightly increases an airfoil's lift slope. The formulation for a particular set of airfoils is given by Eq. 4.3. However, the small change (suggested by Eq. 4.3) in the lift slope is only marginally detectable in the experimental data presented in Fig. 4.6. On the other hand, for the larger angles of attack, the data in Fig. 4.6 suggests that thicker airfoils can have a larger maximum lift coefficient $C_{L_{max}}$ (and a delayed stall). This trend is shown again in Fig. 4.10, but it stops when the airfoil becomes too bulky (near a thickness ratio of about 12%).

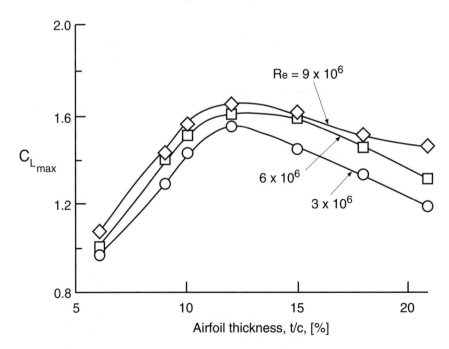

Fig. 4-10. Effect of airfoil thickness on its maximum lift coefficient for the NACA 63 series airfoils (data from Ref. 4.1).

Airfoil Drag   The drag of an airfoil, for the attached flow case, is a result of the friction caused by the viscous boundary layer. This is shown schematically in Fig. 4.11. The thicker the boundary layer, the more the fluid is slowed down and the larger the drag.

Fig. 4-11. Schematic description of the boundary layer development on both sides of an airfoil, in an attached flow.

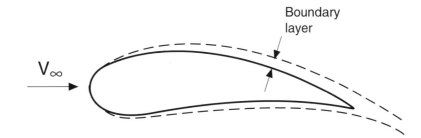

Now, referencing Fig. 2.9, we can clearly state that with a laminar boundary layer, less drag is expected than with a turbulent boundary layer. This can help to establish a simple model for the effect of the Reynolds number on attached boundary layer drag: The undisturbed flow in Fig. 4.11 will initiate a laminar boundary layer at the airfoil's leading edge, but with increasing distance on the surface or due to higher speeds V_∞ (= higher Re number) a transition to turbulent boundary layer will take place. We can conclude that an earlier transition from laminar to turbulent boundary layer (which is usually a result of higher Reynolds numbers) causes larger turbulent friction regions, resulting in more viscous drag. Along the same lines, surface roughness will increase the friction coefficient and promote boundary layer transition. Thus, on a smoother surface, friction drag is smaller and transition is delayed.

Based on the connection between boundary layer thickness and drag, we can speculate on the effect of thickness and camber on airfoil performance. Both of these geometrical properties tend to increase the boundary layer thickness on the upper surface (suction side) and therefore an increase in drag is expected. The drag data, near zero angle of attack, in Fig. 4.6 demonstrates this trend for varying airfoil thicknesses. At the larger angles of attack, though, the sharp turn of the streamlines near the leading edge cause a thicker boundary layer on the upper surface of the thinner airfoils, so the trend is reversed (but the logic of thicker boundary layer resulting in more drag remains).

If the flow over the airfoil is partially separated, due to large camber or high angles of attack, then following the terminology in Chapter 2, a form drag will result. This separated-flow drag is usually much larger than the friction drag and is accompanied by a loss of lift. A quick glance at Fig. 4.8 reveals that for a partially separated air flow the large suction at the leading edge is reduced (and in full stall completely eliminated). This suction pulls the airfoil forward and balances the form drag (near zero for the attached-flow case), and when reduced by flow separation will immediately increase the form drag.

The drag coefficient variation of an airfoil versus angle of attack α is now easily summarized. For example, consider the drag data presented in Fig. 4.6. At the lower angles of attack the boundary layer is the thinnest and the drag is the lowest (e.g., the zero lift drag coefficient of a NACA 0009 is close to $C_d = 0.0055$). With increased angle of attack the boundary layer becomes thicker, and the drag increases. Near the maximum lift, usually some trailing edge separation exists, and this form drag sharply increases the section drag.

Airfoil Moment   The aerodynamic lift and drag are the result of integrating the surface pressure distribution (Fig. 4.3 and 4.4). It is possible to represent the resultant force due to this pressure distribution by a single force F as shown in Figure 4.12. One of the more interesting conclusions from basic airfoil theory (Ref. 2.2, Chapter 5) is that this force acts at the quarter chord of a symmetric airfoil and points in the lift direction. Consequently, this point, called the *center of pressure*, is located near the quarter-chord location ($x_{cp} = c/4$) for a symmetric airfoil. If we measure the moments relative to this point, $C_{m_{c/4}} = F \cdot \frac{c}{4} / \left(\frac{1}{2} \rho V_\infty^2 A \right)$, then the result will be zero, since the aerodynamic force F acts at this point. Experimental data for a symmetrical airfoil, as in Fig. 4.13, verifies this within the attached flow region. Only at high angles of attack, near stall, does the center of pressure move backward.

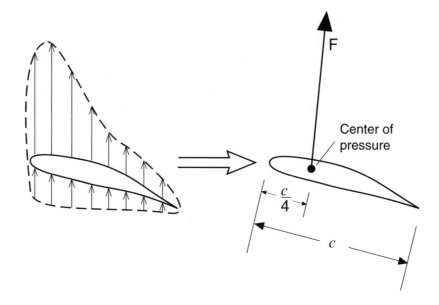

Fig. 4-12. *The contribution of the pressure distribution from the airfoil's upper and lower surfaces can be represented by a single force F, placed at the center of pressure.*

Fig. 4.13 indicates, too, that the moments do not vary with angle of attack (except near stall). The point about which the pitching moment is independent of angle of attack is called the "aerodynamic center"; for most airfoils it is near $c/4$.

For cambered wings the center of pressure can be in a different location and may vary with angle of attack, whereas the aerodynamic center will be near the quarter chord. For example, the center of pressure for the circular arc-shaped airfoil, at zero angle of attack (Fig. 4.4), is at the center because of fore-aft symmetry. It will move forward with increased angle of attack, while the aerodynamic center remains near $c/4$.

For race car applications the location of the aerodynamic center is less significant, while the location of the center of pressure is more important; a small backward shift of the center of pressure on the rear wing of a Formula One car can visibly influence performance.

Effect of Reynolds Number   The effect of an airfoil's Reynolds number on race car aerodynamics may be noticed as a vehicle's speed varies, but it becomes extremely important when extrapolating small-scale wind tunnel data to full-scale conditions. Most of those effects were mentioned in previous sections, and they usually indicate that with higher Reynolds numbers airfoil performance improves. For the

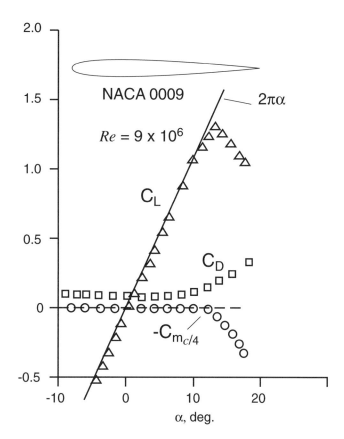

Fig. 4-13. *Typical set of aerodynamic data (lift, drag, and pitching moment) for a NACA 0009 Airfoil (data from Ref. 4.1).*

completeness of the discussion, let us recap some of the effects of the Reynolds number on airfoil performance:

Boundary layer thickness and the friction coefficient (Fig. 2.9) usually decrease with increasing Reynolds number (for both laminar and turbulent boundary layers). Consequently, within the full-scale vehicle range ($Re = 3\times10^6 \to 9\times10^6$) the drag coefficient of an airfoil (in attached flow) will decrease with increased Reynolds number (see Ref. 4.1 for such data on a variety of NACA airfoils).

For flows with higher Re number the boundary layer is thinner and the flow outside the boundary layer has higher momentum, a combination that delays flow separation (and airfoil stall). This is shown clearly in Fig. 3.41. For an Re number of 0.17×10^6 the airfoil stalls at $\alpha \approx 8°$, while for an Re number of 3.18×10^6 the stall is delayed to $\alpha \approx 14°$. This results in a considerable increase in the maximum lift coefficient $C_{l_{max}}$, which is documented in Fig. 4.10. The stall pattern in Fig. 4.9 is affected too by the change in the Reynolds number. At the lower values of Reynolds number (Fig. 3.41), a gradual trailing edge stall moves forward as the airfoil's angle of attack increases, while at the higher range (e.g., at $Re = 3.18\times10^6$) the stall is an abrupt leading edge separation.

Another interesting phenomenon which may affect race car aerodynamics is a laminar bubble in the boundary layer. This effect was mentioned briefly in Chapter 2, and is illustrated for the case of an airfoil in Fig. 4.14. The boundary layer that starts at the airfoil's leading edge is laminar initially but, typically, for $Re > 0.2\times10^6$ a transition to turbulent boundary layers occurs along the upper surface (suction side). For airfoils with highly cambered upper surface (or less cambered but at high angles of attack) the laminar boundary layer starts to separate. But the increased thickness of the boundary layer results in a transition to a turbulent boundary layer, which is less sensitive to stall. Consequently, the flow reattaches, creating a bubble with an enclosed area of recirculating flow.

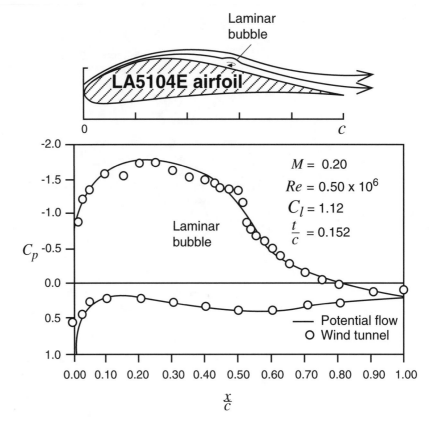

Fig. 4-14. *Signature of the laminar bubble on the pressure distribution of an airfoil (Courtesy of Douglas Aircraft Co. and Dr. Robert Liebeck).*

Fig. 4.14 shows the effect of this bubble on an airfoil's pressure distribution, where the solid line stands for the expected curve without such a bubble, while the symbols depict the sharp local drop in the pressure distribution due to this bubble. The effect of this laminar bubble on race car development is significant in the case of small-scale testing where the Reynolds number of the wings is near 0.2×10^6 to 0.5×10^6. The resulting wings will be far less loaded (to avoid stall and high drag) than they would have been in full scale, resulting in a conservative design. Furthermore, an airfoil designed for this flow range that performs well on the scaled-down model may be less attractive in full scale.

Desirable Pressure Distribution

Up to this point in this book, some of the most important observations in the field of low-speed aerodynamics have been presented. In this section I will combine some of those previous conclusions and use them to evaluate effective designs, with the pressure distribution being the preferred diagnostic tool. Therefore, let us start with a brief summary of some of the more important previous conclusions:

- Surface friction and resulting drag is lower in a laminar (vs. turbulent) boundary layer
- With a favorable pressure gradient (see Chapter 2) the boundary layer in an undisturbed free stream will stay laminar for longer distances along the body surface (transition is delayed)

- Flow separation in a turbulent boundary layer is delayed (vs. laminar boundary layer)
- Favorable pressure gradient delays separation (which may occur later in the unfavorable pressure distribution region)

The above conclusions suggest that for low drag, large laminar boundary layer regions must be maintained on the airfoil. However, the opposite is true when high lift coefficients are sought. In this case an early "tripping" (causing transition by surface roughness, vortex generators, etc.) of the boundary layer can help to increase the maximum lift coefficient. Consequently, for race car application two basic types of airfoil designs are likely: the first is a low drag design (possibly with moderate lift) for high-speed tracks, while the second one is designed for maximum lift (downforce) for road races with fast un-banked turns.

The principle of obtaining large laminar boundary layer regions for low drag applications is demonstrated in Fig. 4.15. The upper surface and the corresponding pressure distribution shape for a hypothetical baseline airfoil are shown by the broken lines. For this case there is a sharp suction peak and the pressure gradient is adverse over the whole upper surface. (Recall that we have called a gradually increasing pressure *unfavorable*, or adverse. In terms of the pressure coefficient C_p this curve will have a downward slope, and such an area is indicated by the lowest arrow on Fig. 4.15.) At the higher Reynolds numbers (e.g., Re > 10^6) the transition will take place behind the suction peak (see left peak in broken lines) and the boundary layer on the upper surface will be turbulent from this point to the trailing edge.

Fig. 4-15. *Effect of small modifications of an airfoil's upper surface on the resulting pressure distribution.*

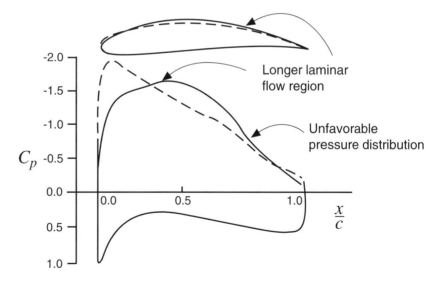

This pressure distribution can be modified (at the same angle of attack and without changing the lift) by drooping the leading edge and adding more front camber. This is shown by the solid line in Fig. 4.15, which results in a favorable pressure distribution on the front half of the airfoil's upper surface. The second airfoil will have less drag (for the same lift) due to a longer laminar boundary layer on the upper surface. Also, the modified airfoil will have its maximum thickness and its center of pressure farther back (aft loaded).

Based on the above rationale, NACA developed a low-drag airfoil series. The advantage of the low-drag design over the earlier airfoil design is shown in Fig. 4.16. The shape of the early NACA 2415 airfoil is shown in the inset. The maximum thickness of the low-drag airfoil (NACA 64_2-415) is moved to the 40% chord area, which is farther back than the location of the maximum thickness on the NACA 2415 airfoil. The effect of this modified design on the drag coefficient is indicated by the comparison between the drag-versus-lift-coefficient plots of the two airfoils. In the case of the low-drag airfoil, a bucket-shaped low-drag area is shown, which is a result of the large laminar flow regions. However, when the angle of attack is increased (resulting in C_l larger than 0.7) the boundary layer becomes turbulent and this advantage disappears.

Fig. 4-16. Variation of drag coefficient versus lift coefficient for an early and later low-drag NACA 15% thick airfoils (data from Ref. 4.1).

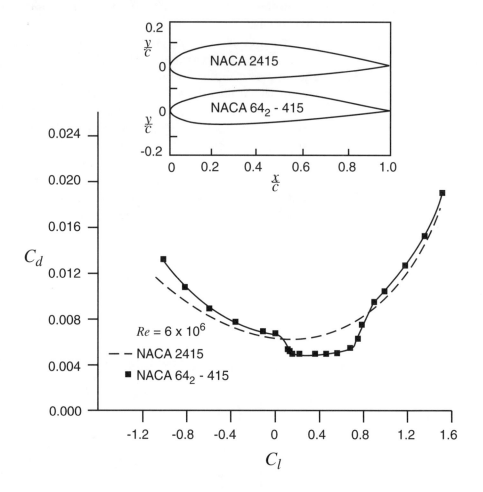

In order to obtain large lift coefficients, the boundary layer on the upper surface should become turbulent as close as possible to the leading edge. Furthermore, since flow separation develops in an adverse pressure environment, the primary question is how much variation of the suction on the airfoil's upper surface can be achieved without flow separation (or in graphic form: How steep can the downward C_p slope be?).

Having an early idea about the shape of a desirable pressure distribution for maximum lift applications can help to design the airfoil's shape to fit such an ideal pressure distribution shape. Indeed, Liebeck (Ref. 4.2) has developed a family of airfoil upper surface pressure distributions that will result in the most delayed flow separation, as shown in Fig. 4.17. In principle, these generic curves depend on the Reynolds number (in the case of Fig. 4.17, the Re number is 5 x 10^6), and airfoils having any of the described upper pressure distributions will have an attached flow on that surface.

The maximum lift coefficient will increase toward the center of the group. The bold curve represents the pressure distribution yielding the highest lift due to the upper surface pressure distribution (within this group). In practice, the sharp corners on these "target pressure distributions" should be avoided. A more realistic pressure distribution is shown by the broken lines. An airfoil shape based on using one of these pressure distributions is shown in Fig. 4.18, along with the experimental and computed pressure distribution (maximum lift is $C_l \approx 1.8$, at $\alpha = 14°$, and at Re number of 3 x 10^6). Note that at the lower angles of attack there is a favorable pressure gradient near the front of the airfoil where a laminar boundary layer can be maintained for low drag (transition is near the maximum thickness section).

Even though the shape of the pressure distribution was used in this section to diagnose airfoil performance, the shape of the streamlines and the location of the stagnation point near the leading edge are important as well. This is

Fig. 4-17. *Family of possible airfoil upper surface pressure distributions resulting in an attached flow on the upper surface (for Re number 5 x 10^6). (From Liebeck, Ref. 4.2. Copyright ©1978 AIAA, Reprinted with permission).*

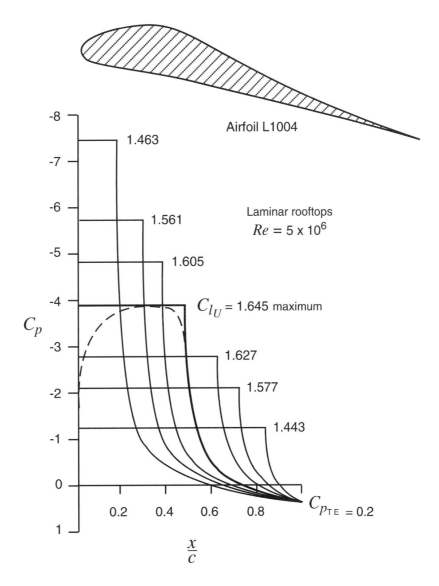

Fig. 4-18. Shape of the L1004 airfoil and theoretical and experimental pressure distribution on it at various angles of attack (From Liebeck, Ref. 4.2. Copyright ©1978 AIAA, Reprinted with permission).

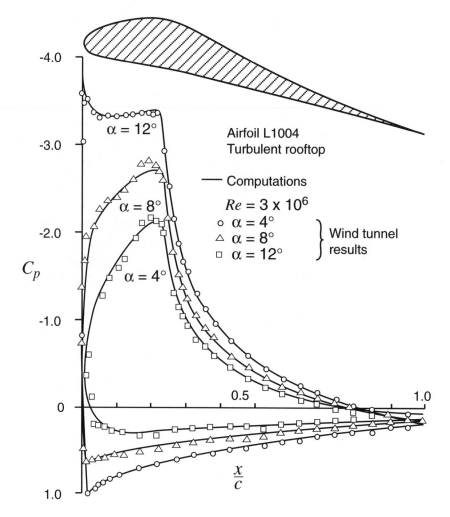

shown in Fig. 4.19, where at the left a traditional leading edge is shown with the fluid rapidly accelerating around it. This may create a thick boundary layer and an early transition on the upper surface. This can be avoided by drooping the leading edge, as shown at the right side (see also Fig. 4.15). When the stagnation point is near the leading edge, a sharper leading edge can be used (for a fixed angle of attack design—which is the case for most race cars), resulting in a better lift/drag ratio. But, when wing angles of attack vary over a wider range (as in the case of airplane wings) then the stagnation point location is not fixed, and a larger leading edge radius is required (to avoid separation of the flow turning around the sharp leading edge). The location of the stagnation point can be easily identified on the lower surface pressure distribution (e.g., in Fig. 4.14 or Fig. 4.18). At this point $C_p \approx 1$.

The effect of the previous considerations on airfoil shape can be summarized in a simplistic form: For a high lift application, highly cambered airfoils will be used; for a low drag application, less cambered and possibly thinner airfoils will be selected.

The task of developing airfoil shapes for a particular operation range has led to the development of numerous special "airfoil design" computer codes. Most of these computer programs are capable of predicting the location of boundary layer transition and flow separation point (if present). Some of these codes

Fig. 4-19. *Effect of leading edge shape on the nearby flow for a typical airfoil (**A**), and on one with drooped leading edge (**B**).*

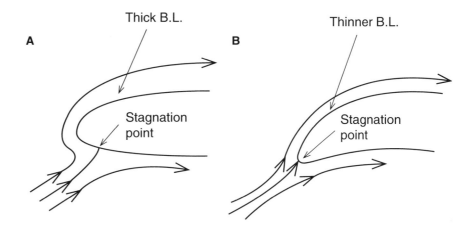

have inverse capability, where the pressure distribution is modified and the corresponding (or closest possible) airfoil shape is computed by the program. For example, one of the earliest such codes is the Eppler code (Ref. 4.3) and one of the more recent (and advanced) is the ISES code (Ref. 4.4).

Developing an excellent airfoil shape, however, cannot ensure a good wing design, or even a satisfactory performance, when mounted on a race car (due to the large interference and finite-span effects, as will be explained later).

FINITE WINGS

A complete wing shape is usually identified by the two-dimensional airfoil section (or sections), and by the planform shape. The influence of airfoil shape on the aerodynamic properties was discussed in the previous section. Here we shall focus on the effects of a wing's planform shape. Prior to investigating the influence of those geometrical details on wings' aerodynamics, let us describe briefly those geometrical properties.

> ***Wing Aspect Ratio and Taper Ratio***   The aspect ratio R of a wing is a measure of how wide it is compared to its chord. The actual definition is:
>
> **Eq. 4.4**
> $$ R = \frac{b^2}{S} $$
>
> where S is the wing area, b is the span, and for the rectangular wing $R = b/c$.
>
> The taper ratio compares the chord length between the wing tip and its root. For a wing with a tip chord c_t and a root chord c_0 , the taper ratio λ is defined as:
>
> **Eq. 4.5**
> $$ \lambda = \frac{c_t}{c_0} $$

The most common planform shapes (or top view) of planar wings are shown in Fig. 4.20. The simplest shape is the rectangular wing with a span b, and a constant chord c (Fig. 4.20A). The aspect ratio AR is then defined as the ratio between the square of the wing span divided by its area (see Eq. 4.4). This, in fact, is a measure of the width of the wing span compared to its chord. The wing can be swept, and in Fig. 4.20B the wing leading edge is swept backward by an angle Λ. In this case the wing has a taper, as well, and the tip chord c_t is smaller than the root chord c_o. The taper ratio λ is defined by Eq. 4.5, and it simply describes the ratio between the tip and root chord lengths. The wing planform can have an elliptic shape, as shown in Fig. 4.20C, and in this case the wing chord varies along the span, in a manner similar to an ellipse. The triangular shape of Fig. 4.20D is seen on many high-speed aircraft, and can be viewed as a swept-aft rectangular wing with a taper ratio of zero. Any wing can be twisted so that the tip has a different angle of attack from its root chord, and it can be tilted upward at its tips (called *dihedral*) or downward at the tip, compared to the wing root (called *anhedral*).

Fig. 4-20. *Several basic wing planform shapes (all with the same span b).*

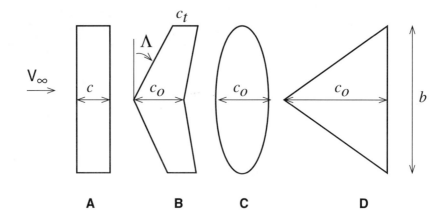

Effect of Planform Shape

Our survey of airfoil aerodynamics indicated that lift is a result of the difference between positive pressure distribution on one side and negative pressure (suction) distribution on the other side. In a finite wing the pressure difference cannot be maintained near the wing side edge (tip), so the magnitude of this pressure difference between the upper and lower surfaces (and resulting lift) near the tip is drastically reduced. Furthermore, the air will flow around the wing tip from the high- to the low-pressure side, creating two strong vortices, shed near the wing tips, as shown in Fig. 4.21.

The strength of the vortex is directly related to wing lift, and the mathematical aspects of this problem are presented in many text books (e.g., Ref. 2.2, Chapter 8). The two vortices cause the flow to circulate around the vortex axis (or core) in the direction indicated in the figure. The combined effect of the two vortices is to induce a downwash in the area between the vortices, including the wing area from which they originate. Thus, the lift of the wing is reduced by this effect, which is large for low aspect-ratio wings (since the vortices are closer to the wing) and small for high aspect-ratio wings. Incidentally, an airfoil can be viewed as a wing with infinite aspect ratio, where due to the infinite spanwise distance this effect is zero.

Fig. 4-21. Trailing tip vortices behind a finite wing.

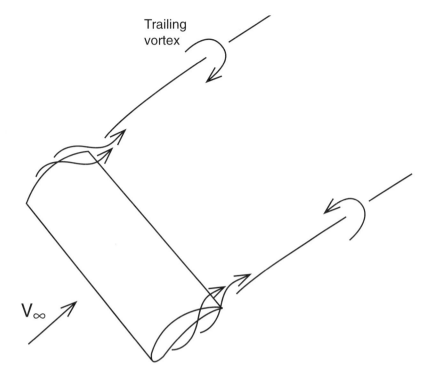

Because of the strong effect of the tip vortices shown in Fig. 4.21, wing lift depends on its aspect ratio. This effect of wing planform shape can be accounted for simply by replacing the lift coefficient slope, 2π, with the $C_{L\alpha}$ term in Eq. 4.2, which was used for the two-dimensional thin airfoil. (Note that C_l, with lower case l, was used for the two-dimensional airfoil lift per unit span, where the reference area was $A = c \cdot 1$.) Consequently, with this minor modification, the airfoil formula can be used for calculating the lift coefficient of a three-dimensional wing, as well, as shown in Eq. 4.6. The lift coefficient slope, $C_{L\alpha}$, for a variety of rectangular wing configurations is given in Fig. 4.22. For an unswept rectangular wing (for which, $\lambda = 0$) the slope $C_{L\alpha}$ is considerably less than 2π, especially when wing aspect ratio is less than 7. This particular curve can be approximated by using theoretical results derived for an elliptic wing (Ref. 2.2, p. 203) and the corresponding formula is given by Eq. 4.7. The immediate conclusion, implied by Eqs. 4.6 and 4.7, is that wings with a larger aspect ratio (larger span) will have a larger lift coefficient slope.

The effect of wing sweep (e.g., $\lambda = 30°$ on Fig. 4.22) is to further reduce $C_{L\alpha}$, and the effect is similar for both fore- and aft-swept wings. In addition to reducing the lift, wing sweep changes the spanwise loading (or the local section lift coefficient C_l). This is depicted by Fig. 4.23 where the spanwise loading of three wings with the same area, angle of attack, and aspect ratio is presented. The unswept wing's lift is considerably higher than the lift of the two swept wings. Its maximum loading is at the center, whereas the lift near the tips drops to zero. The forward-swept wing will have larger loading near its root and less near its tip, while aft-swept wings will have more lift toward their tips. From the wing structural point of view, when generating the same lift, the root bending moments will be smaller for a forward-swept wing than for a wing with the same aft sweep. The primary reason that forward-swept wings were not used often on airplanes in the past is the aeroelastic divergence problem that causes the forward cantilevered wing to be aeroelastically unstable.

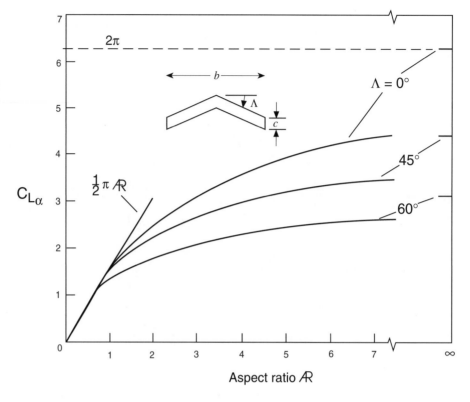

Fig. 4-22. *General trends showing the effect of wing aspect ratio on the lift coefficient slope of planar, rectangular wings.*

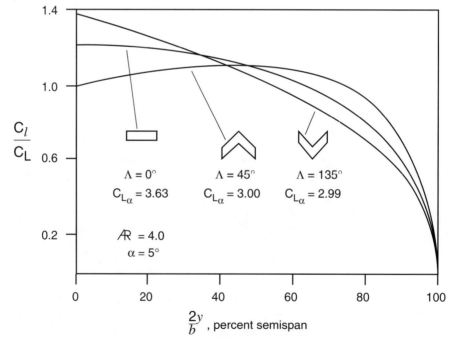

Fig. 4-23. *Effect of wing sweep on the spanwise loading of untapered planar wings. Reprinted with Permission of ASME, from J. Fluids Eng., Vol. 107, Dec. 1985, p.441.*

Figure 4.23 also demonstrates the loss of lift near the wing tips (edge effect) of finite wings mentioned in the first paragraph of this section. In comparison, the lift slope of an airfoil is near $C_{L\alpha} = 2\pi = 6.28$, while lift slope of a finite wing is zero at the tip and less than 2π at the center, due to the downwash of the trailing vortices. This lift deficiency near the tips affects the rest of the wing. Based on Fig. 4.23, the lift slope for the three rectangular wings with an $AR = 4.0$ is in the range of 2.99–3.63. Indeed, this value is far less than the two-dimensional value of 6.28, which clearly indicates the strong influence of wing aspect ratio on wing performance.

Lift Coefficient of a Finite Wing The lift coefficient of a three-dimensional wing is defined by Eq. 2.14:

$$C_L = \frac{lift}{\left(\frac{1}{2}\right)\rho V_\infty^2 A}$$

The lift coefficient C_L can be calculated by a formula similar to Eq. 4.2:

Eq. 4.6

$$C_L = C_{L_\alpha}(\alpha + \alpha_{L_0})$$

and the only difference is that the lift slope of 2π was replaced by $C_{L\alpha}$. Typical values for this coefficient are given in Fig. 4.22. Theoretical estimation of this coefficient for an elliptic wing (Ref. 2.2, p. 203) provides the following relation for the lift slope versus aspect ratio

Eq. 4.7

$$C_{L_\alpha} = \frac{2\pi}{1 + 2/(AR)}$$

As an example let us calculate the lift coefficient of two rectangular wings with symmetric airfoils of 0.5 m chord, at an angle of attack of 8 deg. The first will have a span of 2 m, and the span of the second wing is 4m. The aspect ratios of the two wings, based on Eq. 4.4, are 4, and 8, respectively. Next, we can calculate the lift slopes for the two wings, using Eq. 4.7:

$$C_{L_{\alpha1}} = \frac{2\pi}{1 + 2/4} = 4.19$$

$$C_{L_{\alpha2}} = \frac{2\pi}{1 + 2/8} = 5.02$$

and both are less than the two-dimensional value of 2π. The lift coefficient is now calculated by Eq. 4.6

$$C_{L1} = 4.19\frac{8\pi}{180} = 0.585$$

$$C_{L2} = 5.02\frac{8\pi}{180} = 0.599$$

and clearly the wider wing has more lift, per unit area.

The taper ratio, as defined in Eq. 4.5, also affects the spanwise loading of untwisted wings, as shown in Fig. 4.24. Here the local lift coefficient increases toward the tip with decreasing taper ratio λ. For very small taper ratios the tip will have a tendency to stall first, an unfavorable behavior that can be corrected by twist (to reduce the angle of attack toward the tip).

Fig. 4-24. Effect of taper ratio on the spanwise variation of the lift coefficient for untwisted wings. Reprinted by permission of Prentice-Hall, Englewood Cliffs, N.J. from Bertin, J. J., and Smith, M. L., "Aerodynamics for Engineers," Second Edition 1989, p. 258.

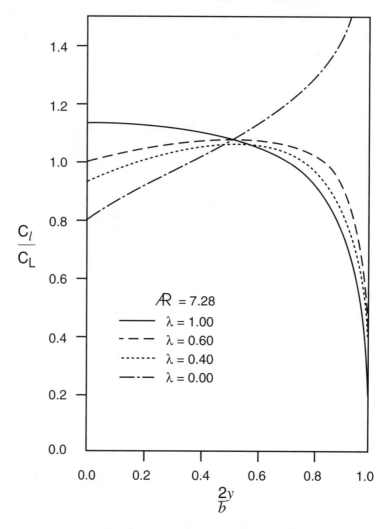

One of the most important effects, relevant to race car aerodynamics, is the influence of ground proximity on the performance of wings. This is presented in Fig. 4.25. In general, wing lift increases due to ground effect, independent of its shape and angle of attack. The magnitude of this effect can be large, where for ground clearance of less than $h/c = 0.5$, the lift can easily increase by 50%.

The effect of wing dihedral (see definition of Υ in Fig. 4.26) far from the ground is similar to sweep: It reduces the lift slope (as shown by the lower curve). This trend continues near the ground for positive dihedral angles. However, for negative values of the dihedral (anhedral) angle, the increase in lift of the wing portion near the ground is largely due to ground effect, as shown on the upper two curves.

The first important effect of the wing trailing vortices (Fig. 4.21) was to reduce lift. However, as a result of their downwash the free stream is now reaching the wing at a slightly reduced angle of attack, tilting the lift vector, and

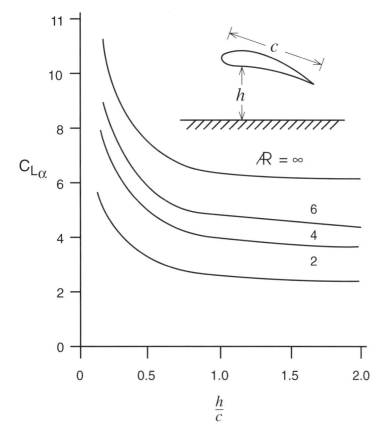

Fig. 4-25. *Effect of ground proximity on the lift coefficient slope of rectangular wings. Reprinted with Permission of ASME, from J. Fluids Eng., Vol. 107, Dec. 1985, p.441.*

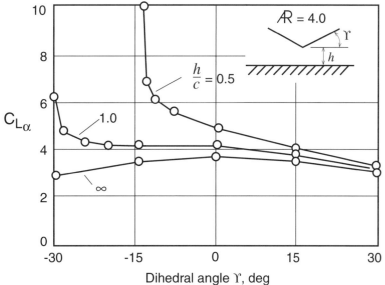

Fig. 4-26. *Effect of dihedral on the lift coefficient slope of rectangular wings in ground effect. (After Kalman et al., J. Aircraft, Vol. 8., No. 6, p. 412. Copyright ©1971 AIAA, Reprinted with permission.)*

resulting in an "induced drag." This portion of the drag is a direct result of the lift, and the effect is large for small-aspect-ratio wings, whereas it becomes negligible for very large aspect ratios.

An approximate formula for the induced drag was developed for elliptic wings (with an elliptic planform) and is given in Eq. 4.8. This equation indicates that the induced drag, C_{D_i}, will increase with the square of the lift, but will decrease with increased wing aspect ratio. Therefore, the overall effect of increasing wing aspect ratio is to increase the lift and reduce the induced drag (and improve lift/drag ratio). Most wings used on race cars operate near their highest lift range and have low aspect ratios. Consequently the induced drag is usally very large and certainly requires careful attention to minimize it.

Induced Drag The induced drag is a by-product of the lift of a finite wing. An approximate formula for the induced drag of elliptic wings (usually with elliptic planform; for other shapes, see Ref. 2.2, p. 209) shows the following trend:

Eq. 4.8
$$C_{D_i} = \left(\frac{1}{\pi\,\mathcal{R}}\right)C_L^2$$

This equation indicates that the induced drag, C_{D_i}, will increase with the square of the lift, but will decrease with increased wing aspect ratio.

To demonstrate the application of this equation we can continue the example that we've started in the discussion on Eq. 4.7. Thus the aspect ratio of the two wings is 4 and 8, respectively, and their induced drag, based on Eq. 4.8, is then:

$$C_{D_{i1}} = \frac{1}{\pi 4}0.585^2 = 0.027$$

$$C_{D_{i2}} = \frac{1}{\pi 8}0.599^2 = 0.014$$

and, clearly, the lift/drag ratio of the wider wing is better.

The total drag of a finite wing, therefore, consists of the induced drag C_{D_i} and of the viscous drag C_{D_0} (e.g., as described in Fig. 4.6 for a two-dimensional airfoil section):

Eq. 4.9
$$C_D = C_{D_i} + C_{D_0}$$

The viscous drag C_{D_0} can be further divided into the surface skin friction contribution, and, if present, to drag due to flow separation (form-drag).

The total drag of a finite wing, therefore, consists of the induced drag C_{D_i} and of the viscous drag C_{D_i} (e.g., as described in Fig. 4.6 for a two-dimensional airfoil section). Those two components must be added, as indicated by Eq. 4.9. For more detailed study, the viscous drag C_{D_0} then can be further divided into the surface skin friction contribution, and, if present, to drag due to flow separation (form-drag). Such information for some of the standard airfoil shapes is provided in Ref. 4.1, in a form that resembles the data presented in Fig. 4.16.

An interesting anecdote tells about Jean Le Round d'Alembert, 1717–1783, a French engineer who studied the performance of airfoils. His analytical study indicated that an airfoil must have zero induced drag, as we have seen for the wing with infinite span. Of course he did not know about the viscous and form-drag components. This observation, that an airfoil in attached flow has no induced drag, is called *d'Alembert's paradox*. The important point here is that even today people have difficulties realizing that by using a very high-aspect-ratio wing, the drag can be reduced to almost negligible levels.

The most important and often overlooked conclusions from this short section are

- The lift (slope) of a wing *decreases* with decreasing aspect ratio (span)
- The (induced) drag of a wing *increases* with decreasing aspect ratio

Slender Wings and Vortex Lift

The previous sections emphasized the importance of maintaining attached flow while generating lift. However, there are many lifting surfaces that utilize separated flow fields in order to generate lift. The most interesting case, relevant to race car aerodynamics, are slender delta wings that utilize the "vortex lift" principle, shown in Fig. 4.27.

Fig. 4-27. Leading edge vortices developing on highly swept delta wings at large angles of attack.

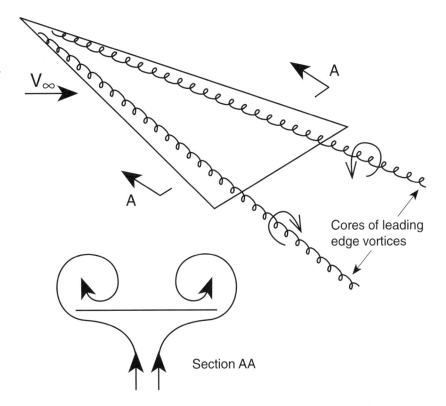

Here the flow turns around the highly swept back leading edge and separates on the upper surface, along the leading edge. This phenomenon occurs primarily at larger angles of attack ($\alpha \approx 20°$ and more) and with very thin or even sharp leading edges. The cross-section view of the flow field (section AA in Fig. 4.27) indicates that two concentrated vortices form above the wing, and the flow around the two cores rotates in opposite directions. Such a vortex flow can also be generated by the side edge of a slender rectangular wing, and the similarity between those two flows is depicted by Fig. 4.28.

In the case of a slender, thin, rectangular wing, a separated leading edge bubble is present as well. Contrary to the round leading edge of airfoils, in these cases a sharp leading or side edge is desirable since this will increase the strength of the separated vortex. The effect of the separated vortices on the upper surface pressure distribution is shown in Fig. 4.29. The strong vortices,

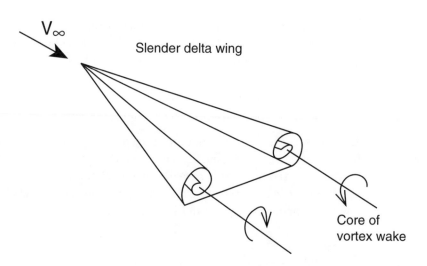

Fig. 4-28. *Similarity between the leading edge vortices on a delta wing and the side edge vortices on a low-aspect-ratio rectangular wing (at higher angles of attack).*

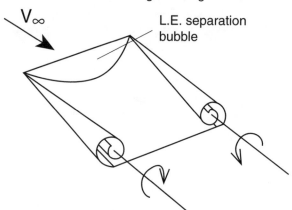

Fig. 4-29. *Schematic description of upper surface pressure distribution on an AR=1 delta wing at α= 20˚. Reprinted with permission from Ref. 2.2, Copyright ©1991 McGraw Hill, Inc.*

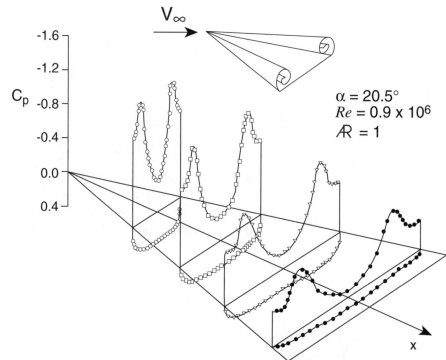

placed above the wing induce high speed and low pressure (see Bernoulli's equation, Eq. 2.5) under the vortex core, and their pressure signature is clearly visible on this figure. The effect of the side vortices, in the case of a slender rectangular wing, is similar to the effect described for the delta wing.

The aerodynamic lift of such slender lifting surfaces can be estimated by using the previous logic of a lift-slope multiplied by the angle of attack, as shown by Eqs. 4.10 and 4.11. These formulas are usually valid for wings with very small aspect ratios. The second formula (Eq. 4.11) is based on a curve-fit to experimental data, and is also valid for higher angles of attack. The drag of such wings is, in general, larger than the lift of attached-flow wings (with well-defined airfoil shapes) and it can be estimated by Eq. 4.12.

Near the nose section of many race cars, small inclined plates (dive plates) are used which utilize the above described principle to generate aerodynamic force (as will be shown later in Chapter 6). An additional importance of utilizing such vortex-generated force is that the vortices created by these sharp plates can interact with other surfaces and create additional aerodynamic force. This fact was realized by aircraft designers, and modern high-speed airplanes have such highly swept lifting surfaces, called *strakes* (see Fig. 4.30). For example, if such a strake is added in front of a less swept-back wing then the vortex originating from the strake will induce low pressures, similar to those shown in Fig. 4.29, on the upper surface of the main wing. Therefore the total gain in lift will surpass the lift of the strake alone, as shown in Fig. 4.30.

Vortex Lift of Slender Wings The aerodynamic lift of such slender lifting surfaces is estimated by classical slender-wing theory (Ref. 2.2, p. 221), which is applicable primarily to very slender delta wings $AR < 1$) at low angles of attack,

Eq. 4.10
$$C_L = \left(\frac{\pi}{2}\right) AR \cdot \sin\alpha$$

This formula does not account for the vortex lift and therefore its use is limited to angles of attack of $\overset{\cdot}{\alpha} < 10°$. For larger angles of attack (in the range of $10° < \alpha < 30°$), and for wings with aspect ratios of less than 1.3, the lift coefficient can be approximated by the formula

Eq. 4.11
$$C_L = (a_1 + a_2 AR) \sin\alpha$$

and here $a_1 = 0.963$, and $a_2 = 1.512$ for delta wings, while $a_1 = 1.395$, and $a_2 = 1.705$ for rectangular wings, respectively. The resultant aerodynamic force in the case of the vortex lift is acting perpendicular to the wing surface and, therefore, the drag can be estimated by:

Eq. 4.12
$$C_D = C_L \tan\alpha$$

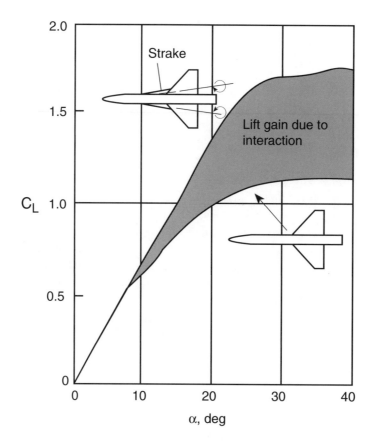

When comparing the lift-versus-angle-of-attack diagrams for the case of vortex lift (Fig. 4.30), with that of an airfoil (Fig. 4.13), a stall condition can be detected on both figures. In the airfoil, the lift loss at the larger angles of attack
was attributed to flow separation, whereas in the vortex lift the loss is caused
by "vortex burst." This condition occurs when the well-organized structure of
the leading-edge vortex breaks down, as shown in Fig. 4.31 (notice the smear-
ing of the dye lines towards the trailing edge). Since the vortex core has burst,

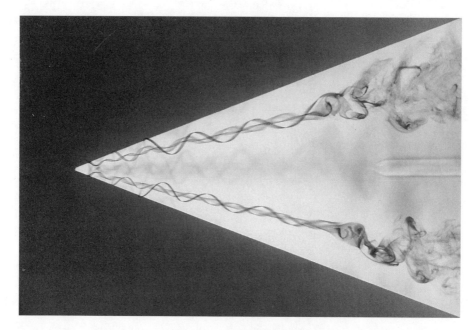

*Fig. 4-31. Flow visual-
ization of the break-
down of leading edge
vortices on an AR=1
wing at $\alpha = 35°$. (Courtesy of G. Malcolm, Ei-
detics Int.)*

and the vortex is dispersed, its suction effect on the wing is reduced, causing a loss of lift, similar to wing stall.

It is important to observe that the drag of wings utilizing vortex lift (Eq. 4.12) is larger than the drag of attached-flow-based wings (Eq. 4.8) and this limits their application. Also, vortex lift can be generated only with highly swept leading edges (e.g. $\Lambda > 70°$) and its useful angle-of-attack range for race cars (where vortex burst is not present over the wing) is $15° < \alpha < 40°$.

High Lift Wings   In numerous situations, the wing design should produce the maximum possible aerodynamic lift (or downforce, in the case of a race car). Typical options to obtain higher lift include: an increase of wing area, increase in camber, and delaying flow separation by slotted flap design or by blowing. If the wing planform area is fixed (e.g., by regulations) then the most popular option is to use multi-element airfoil shapes. A three-element shape is shown in Fig. 4.32.

Fig. 4-32. *Methods of increasing effective airfoil camber to achieve high lift: by using multi-element airfoil design and by trailing edge blowing, or circulation control.*

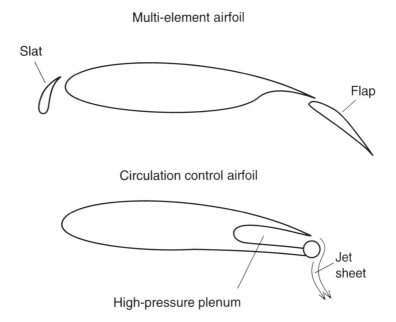

The option of blowing a high-speed jet near the airfoil's trailing edge, or the "circulation control airfoil," was used successfully in high-lift airplanes and is capable of generating very high lift coefficients. In a race car, the only available high-speed jet is the exhaust, and its use for this purpose may pose a few problems (such as sudden braking in the midst of a high-speed turn, followed by a sudden drop in exhaust pressure and resultant loss of downforce). Therefore, our discussion is focused on the more traditional high-lift design, namely the use of multi-element airfoils.

The basic principle behind the multi-element design is that the airfoil camber can be increased far more than with a single element airfoil. Additional benefits include energizing the boundary layer, and a favorable interaction between the wing elements, resulting in a gain in the combined lift (for more details, see Ref. 4.5).

The high-lift capability of the multi-element design was realized in the beginning of this century. Handley Page was among the first to show experimentally that with more elements, larger maximum lift coefficient can be obtained.

His results are shown in Fig. 4.33 where an RAF 19 airfoil (boundaries shown by the dashed line) was broken up into different numbers of elements. The numbers in the figure indicate the number of slots, that is, a two-element airfoil will have only one slot, a three-element airfoil two slots, and so on. This Figure clearly indicates that with more elements, higher angles of attack can be reached, and in this case the maximum lift is close to $C_{L_{max}} = 4.0$.

Fig. 4-33. *Lift coefficient versus angle of attack for the RAF 19 airfoil broken up to different numbers of elements (note that a two-element airfoil has 1 slot, a three element airfoil has 2 slots, etc.) (From Smith, Ref. 4.5, Copyright ©1975 AIAA, Reprinted with permission).*

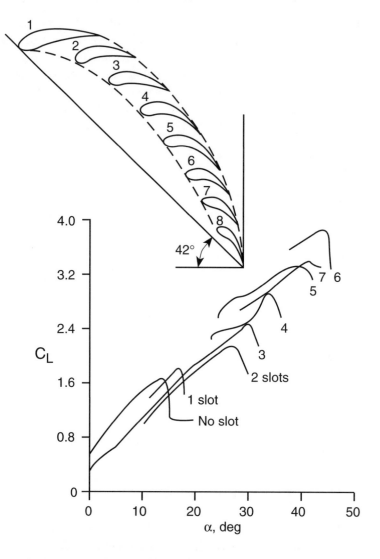

Instead of investigating the extremes of the number of airfoil elements, let's address the role of the first element (called the *slat*) and the last element (called the *flap*) in a basic three-element high-lift wing. The shape of such an airfoil is shown in Fig. 4.34, along with the pressure distribution, at $C_L = 3.1$. As was mentioned earlier, the trailing edge portion of the camberline has the largest effect on airfoil lift. This is demonstrated in Fig. 4.35, where the effect of 50° flap deflection shows the large increase in the lift at a given angle of attack. However, the increased lift in this case causes faster flow around the leading edge. To avoid flow separation, the leading edge must be drooped (Fig. 4.19). In the particular example in Fig. 4.35, drooping the leading edge slat (at angles of attack larger than 5°) will clearly delay flow separation (stall) but will not increase lift.

Fig. 4-34. *Pressure distribution close to the maximum lift coefficient on a three-element wing. Slat angle is –42°, trailing edge flap angle is 10°, and section lift coefficient is 3.1 at Re number = 3.8 x 10⁶.*

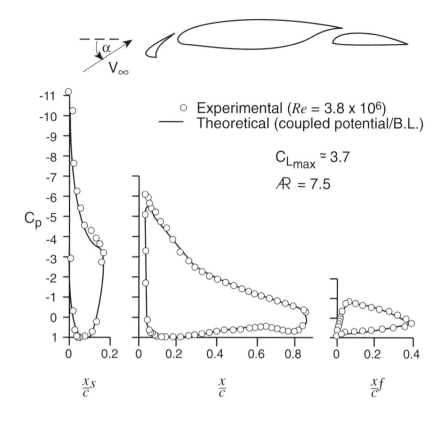

Fig. 4-35. *Generic trends showing the effect of leading edge slats (used above α = 5°) and trailing edge flaps on the lift curve of a high-aspect-ratio, airplane-type wing.*

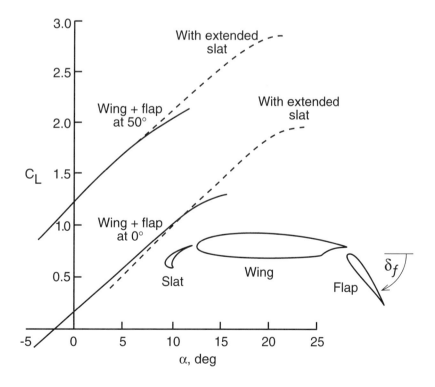

In conclusion, extending the slats will extend the range of angle of attack for maximum lift but will not increase the lift curve slope (which depends on planform shape). Also, a typical high-lift airfoil may have several trailing edge flaps for increased camber, but usually only one small leading edge slat.

Most of the high-lift airfoil shapes were developed for high-aspect-ratio wings (e.g., airplanes). On the other hand, most race car regulations limit the width of wings, resulting in a small aspect ratio. Consequently, most of the airplane-type multi-element airfoils need to be modified before they can be used for racing cars. To demonstrate this effect, computed results for the two-dimensional (high AR case) pressure distribution on a four-element airfoil are shown on the upper part of Fig. 4.36. Similar data at the centerline of an Indy car rear wing (AR=1.5), with the same airfoil section and the same angle of attack, are presented in the lower part of the figure. Clearly, the C_p range of the

Fig. 4-36. Pressure distribution on a two-dimensional four-element airfoil (top) and at the centerline of an AR=1.5 rectangular wing, having the same airfoil section and angle of attack (bottom) (used on a 1987 March Indy car). (From Ref. 4.6, Copyright ©1989 AIAA, Reprinted with permission.)

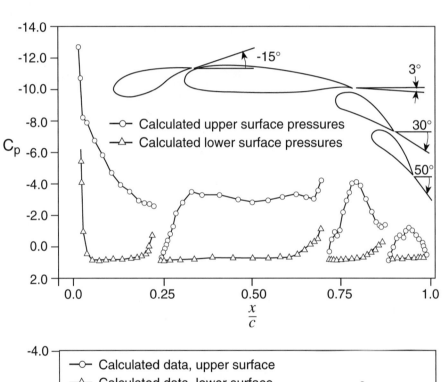
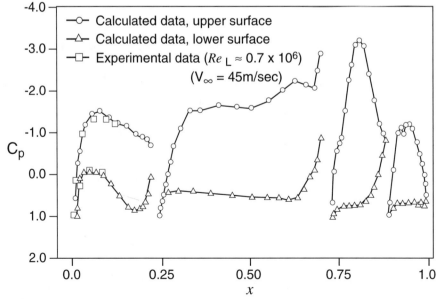

three-dimensional data is much smaller than the two-dimensional (high AR) data, and the shape of the two pressure distributions is entirely different. The pressure gradients in the lower figure are strongest near the second trailing edge flap. Flow separation at a larger angle of attack may be initiated here. In the two-dimensional data, flow separation is more likely behind the sharp suction peak on the slat.

Before concluding this section, let's briefly address the question of maximum possible lift. The technical literature (e.g., Ref. 4.5) lists fairly high limits. Two-dimensional lift coefficients of 4, and even 5, are considered to be possible with multi-element designs (and unpublished airplane company reports have indicated values near $C_L = 5$). For smaller aspect-ratio wings a maximum lift coefficient of $C_{L_{max}} = 1.2AR$ is frequently quoted, in association with wings of AR smaller than 6.

Wing Performance Enhancement

In this section we will survey some of the add-on tricks used to improve wing performance. In terms of the fluid-dynamic jargon those devices can be active (e.g., jets, polymer injection, acoustic excitations, etc.) or can be passive (as a permanent fixture), but only the latter are described here since racing regulations rule out the first type.

One of the best known add-on devices is the vortex generator, shown in Fig. 4.37. These can resemble small wing shapes or have more complex geometries as shown by the four typical shapes. A typical vortex generator is a bit taller than the local boundary layer thickness, and the swirl of the vortices it creates helps to add fresh momentum (from the free stream) into the boundary layer. If such vortex generators are placed near the expected separation line, the added momentum can delay flow separation.

The overall effect is usually a gain in maximum lift and a reduction in drag at the higher lift coefficient (as a result of the smaller separated flow regions). At lower lift coefficients, though, the vortex generators may increase the drag as indicated in Ref. 4.7. Most vortex generators can be constructed from simple sheet metal and some are commercially available as a glue-on strips.

Similar improvements in the high lift coefficient range are claimed for the wavy trailing edge device, which mixes the higher pressure flow from the wing

Fig. 4-37. *Typical shapes of vortex generators used on wings.*

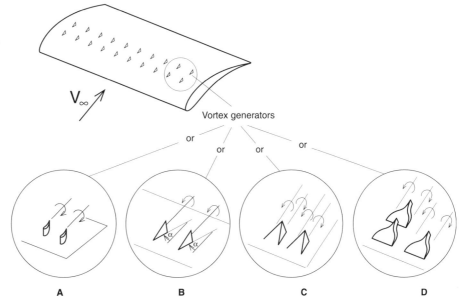

V_∞

Vortex generators

or   or   or   or

A   B   C   D

lower surface with the flow on the upper surface (Fig. 4.38). This mixing reduces wing trailing edge separation, and larger maximum lift values were reported with such a trailing edge in Ref. 4.8.

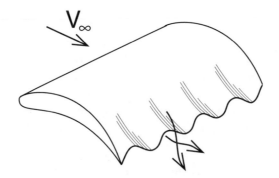

Fig. 4-38. *Wavy trailing edge which may increase maximum lift by increased mixing near the trailing edge.*

The previous methods were aimed at delaying flow separation, but drag reduction can also be achieved by reducing the viscous-flow skin friction near the surface. One such technique uses streamwise microgrooves, or riblets, shown in Fig. 4.39. The grooves are usually very small and hardly visible. Thin films with adhesive back with various sizes of grooves are commercially available. The riblets are glued onto the surface with the triangular grooves oriented parallel to the streamlines. Drag reduction of up to 8% is reported in the literature (Ref. 4.9). The tiny surface grooves seem to reduce the skin friction created within the boundary layer.

Recall that in the boundary layer the velocity slows down to zero near the wall, as depicted by the velocity profile in Fig. 4.39c. In the lower layers of a typical boundary layer, without riblets, spanwise vortices are formed (because of the viscous shear flow due to the wall). This vortex filament develops a wavy instability, which results in partial lifting off of the vortex. As the vortex lifts into the moving fluid, it breaks up into longitudinal streamwise vortex filaments, which eventually entangle and lead to a fully chaotic turbulent flow. The riblets seem to interact at the stage where the longitudinal vortex filaments exist, as shown in Fig. 4.39b. At this stage these vortices are stabilized by the grooves, and the creation of momentum-loosing, turbulent flow is delayed. Furthermore, the lower viscous layer is more "orderly" and as a result the local skin friction is reduced. Therefore, it is possible to gain drag reduction from delaying the transition to turbulent boundary layer and also from the reduction of the turbulent stress near the wall, as well.

In order for the riblets to produce measurable results, they must be placed parallel to the stream, and their size should fit the prevailing Reynolds number of the flow. Apart from the difficulty that the riblet film cannot be painted, this device can be used on race cars, especially where the flow direction is known (e.g., on wings).

An interesting trailing edge device is the so called Gurney flap which is frequently used on race cars but only recently was applied to airplane wings. Such a flap is a small plate, mounted at large angles (close to 90°) onto a wing's trailing edge. Its height is on the order of a few percent of the wing's chord (usually less than 5%). The effect of the flap on the flow is described in the inset to Fig. 4.40, and flow visualizations indicate that the trailing edge boundary layer

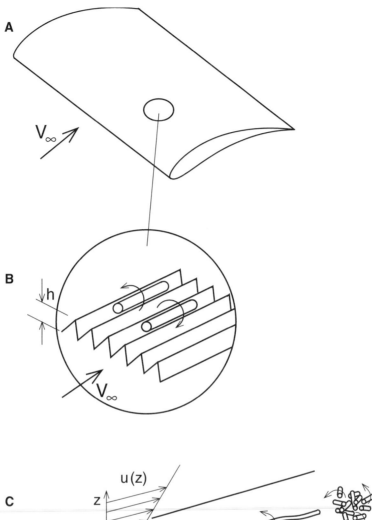

Fig. 4-39. *Schematic description of the effect of riblets on the structure of the turbulent flow near a solid surface. The evolution of vorticity in the boundary layer is sketched after Kline et al., J. Fluid Mech. Vol. 30, Pt. 4, 1967, p. 770.*

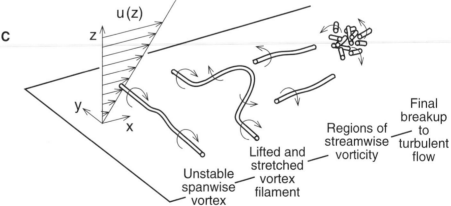

thickness on the suction side is reduced as a result of the sharp turn at the trailing edge. Again, for wings that operate near high lift coefficients, this reduces trailing edge separation and increases lift. The advantage of this flap is in its simplicity, which can help to trim the aerodynamic loads on a car by just changing the flap size (or by removing it). At lower lift coefficient values, when the wing trailing edge boundary layer is thin, the drag will increase and wing lift/drag ratio will be reduced with the addition of this trailing edge flap.

The more surprising application of such trailing edge flaps is on the two side fins (or end plates) on a race car's rear wing (as shown in Fig. 4.40). The experimental data clearly indicate that the lift is increased when using this device.

Fig. 4-40. *Effect of small 90° flaps on the aerodynamics of a small-aspect-ratio rectangular wing (rear wing of an 1987 Indy car). Reprinted with permission from SAE Paper 890600 Copyright ©1989 SAE, Inc.*

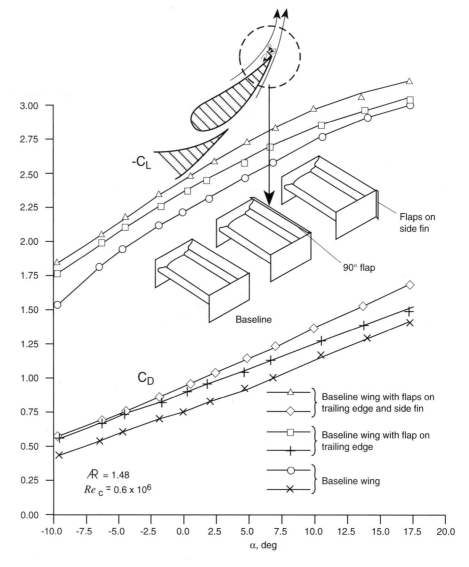

Its effect is to create an effective camber for the end plate, and the suction side of the plate under the main wing reduces the pressure there (increasing downforce, in the case of an inverted wing).

The above discussion leads us directly into a discussion about the importance of side fins (or end plates). To comprehend their aerodynamic effect we must return to Fig. 4.23, which describes the loss of wing lift near its tips. This loss can be reduced by maintaining a pressure difference between the upper and lower wing surfaces near the tip, which can be accomplished by adding wing tip devices such as the end plates shown in Fig. 4.41. Furthermore, any improvement in lift near the tip will have an effect across the whole wing. The potential of wing tip devices was discovered a long time ago and many airplanes have various tip treatments to improve their wing's lift/drag ratio. Usually, the rule of the-larger-the-better applies to end plates, and their generic effect can be estimated by the simple formula of Eq. 4.13. Basically, a larger end plate will increase a wing's effective aspect ratio, thus increasing lift (Eq. 4.7), and reducing induced drag (Eq. 4.8).

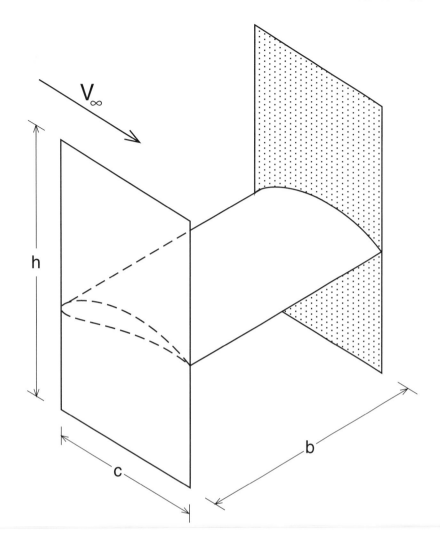

Fig. 4-41. *End plate parameters affecting the performance of a rectangular wing.*

Effect of End Plates   End plates, or side fins, mounted at the tips of wings can increase their lift. Their effect can be estimated by the simple formula suggested by Hoerner (Ref. 2.21, p. 3.9). According to this model, the side fin increases the effective wing aspect ratio *AR* by the ratio

Eq. 4.13
$$AR = AR_{actual}\left(1 + 1.9\frac{h}{b}\right)$$

The wing span *b* and side fin height *h* are depicted in Fig. 4.41, and the actual aspect ratio of a rectangular wing is $AR_{actual} = b/c$. So if we want to calculate the effect of end plates on a wing's lift, we have to increase the aspect ratio by using Eq. 4.13. The lift then is calculated, as before, by using Eq. 4.6 and 4.7, and the induced drag by using Eq. 4.8.

BASIC LIFTING SURFACE INTERACTIONS

Up to this point we have covered the aerodynamic performance of an isolated airfoil or wing. Contrary to airplane wings, in road vehicles the lifting surfaces may be closely placed and can interact with the vehicle and with each other. In this section I will present some of the most basic lifting surface interactions.

For the data presented in Figs. 4.42–45 a large-aspect-ratio wing is assumed, and these interactions can be viewed, essentially, as airfoil interactions (a NACA 65_2-415 section, at an angle of attack of $\alpha = 5°$, was used for the computations). Also, these interactions are far-field type, where the distance between the wings is larger than, say, half the chord, and not near-field type as in the case of multi-element airfoils.

As a first example, consider the tandem airfoil configuration shown in Fig. 4.42. The effect of the interaction can be visualized by representing a wing (or airfoil) by a single vortex (see Ref. 2.1 or 2.2), and then the two airfoils can be represented by two vortices, as shown at the lower part of Fig. 4.42. This simple model indicates that when the horizontal separation Δx is decreased, the aft vortex induces an upwash on the front vortex, resulting in an increase of the front wing's lift. For the same reason, the aft wing experiences a downwash and its lift will be reduced. The computed results show that this interaction increases with reduced distance, Δx, and the effect becomes very strong when the distance is less than 3 chords. The combined lift of the two airfoils does not change, as indicated by the $C_{L_F} + C_{L_R}$ curve in this figure.

Another interesting interaction is when two airfoils approach each other along a vertical line (as in the case of the biplane). Then the interaction reduces the lift of both airfoils (Fig. 4.43). Since both elements lose lift, the combined lift is reduced as well. This is an interesting conclusion, since biplanes are used

Fig. 4-42. *Effect of horizontal separation on the lift of tandem airfoils.*

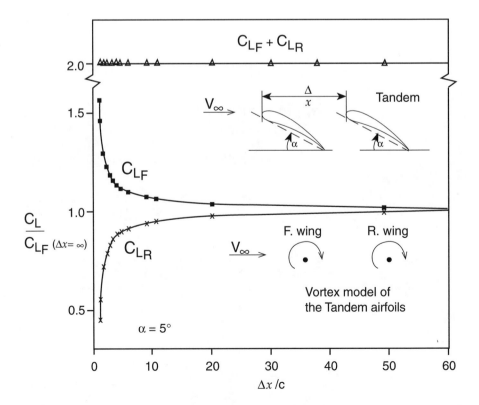

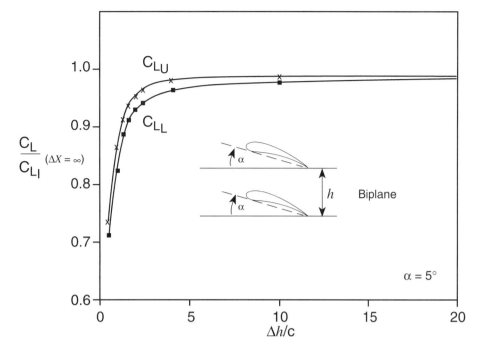

Fig. 4-43. *Effect of vertical separation on the lift of a biplane (airfoils).*

on many race cars, which indicates that there must be other benefits from using this approach. (Those benefits are usually a result of the interaction of the lower wing with the vehicle's body, while the upper wing operates in a less disturbed airstream. For more details see Chapter 6.)

The third interaction is the stagger, shown in Fig. 4.44. In this case the vertical separation h/c is fixed and the horizontal separation Δx is varied. The two-vortex model (of Fig. 4.42) can be used here, too, to explain the lift variation.

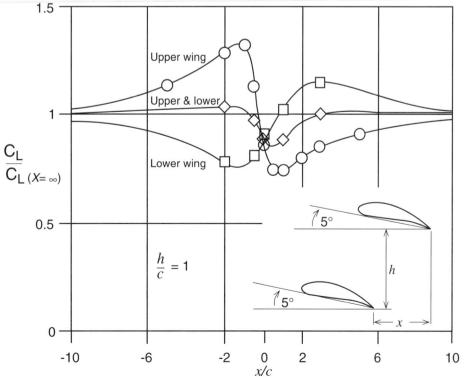

Fig. 4-44. *Effect of horizontal separation on the lift of two staggered airfoils.*

When the upper airfoil is placed ahead of the lower one, its lift will be increased by the upwash from the lower airfoil, and the trend is reversed when it is placed behind the lower airfoil. The lower airfoil experiences an opposite effect and for positive x/c its lift will be increased. The combined lift is not affected much by the horizontal shift, apart from a small dip when the airfoils are placed exactly one above the other.

The last interaction is when an airfoil and its mirror image approach each other (Fig. 4.45). However, the symmetry line can be viewed as a ground plane, and therefore this interaction describes the ground effect, discussed both in Chapter 1 and earlier in this chapter. This case is the opposite of the biplane, and here the lift of both wings increases (or the lift of the single airfoil near the ground). The effect becomes noticeable for ground clearances of less than a half chord, as indicated by Fig. 4.45 (see Fig. 4.25 for the finite wing case).

Fig. 4-45. *Effect of ground proximity on the lift of an airfoil.*

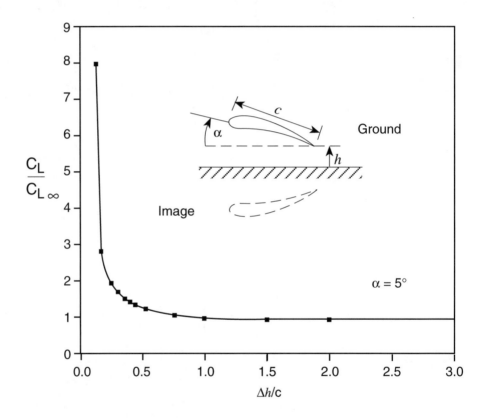

The above simple examples introduce the concept of aerodynamic interaction, which influences the complete vehicle aerodynamics, and when properly used can considerably increase the effectiveness of the design. However, on an actual car many regions of separated flow exist and, occasionally, the aerodynamic interaction is completely opposite to what is expected.

EXAMPLES OF VARIOUS AIRFOIL SHAPES

In this section a variety of airfoil shapes are presented along with their pressure distributions (two-dimensional pressures, except for the last three). In airplane applications, two-dimensional pressure distribution can help select the airfoil shape and estimate wing performance. Most race cars, though, have very small aspect-ratio wings (as low as $b/c = 1.5$), and the wings operate in close proximity to other body parts, such as wheels. Therefore, the following examples serve only to demonstrate the diversity of the various airfoil shapes. Their actual application to race cars requires three-dimensional pressure distribution data (which can be obtained either from experiments or computations).

When searching for a single-element airfoil shape, the simplest option is to examine the large variety of shapes developed by NACA, many of which are listed in Ref. 4.1. Most of these airfoils can be very efficient when used in the lower lift coefficient range (e.g., $C_L < 0.8$).

As a representative example, the NACA 64_2-415 airfoil is presented in Fig. 4.46. This airfoil will have a very low drag (as shown in Fig. 4.16) due to almost 40% laminar boundary layer in the lower range of angle of attack (up to $\alpha = 4°$). At higher angles of attack, a suction peak develops near the leading edge (see pressure data for $\alpha = 5°$), causing early transition in the boundary layer and a sudden jump in skin-friction drag. The pressure distribution, shown in the figure for $C_l \approx 0.90$, corresponds to this condition with the higher drag. This can be verified by observing the $C_l \approx 0.90$ point in Fig. 4.16, which is located at the higher drag range at the right-hand side of the low-drag bucket. At the lower lift coefficients, such as at $\alpha = 1°$ ($C_l \approx 0.46$), the pressure distribution is favorable on both sides of the airfoil. This low-drag condition corresponds to the middle of the low-drag bucket in Fig. 4.16.

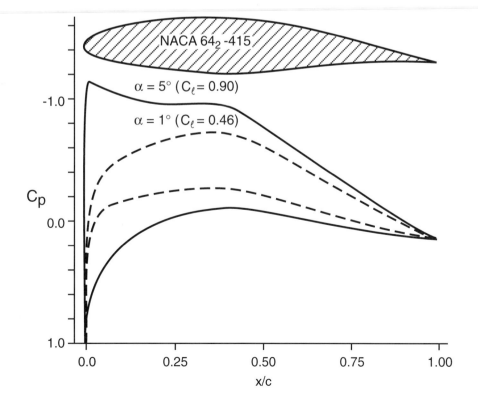

Fig. 4-46. *Two-dimensional pressure distribution on a NACA 64_2-415 airfoil at $\alpha = 1°$ and $5°$ (effective Re number is over 2×10^6).*

A more recent airfoil shape, shown in Fig. 4.47, is the NLF(1)-0414F airfoil developed by NASA (Ref. 4.10). This airfoil has very large laminar flow regions, as can be expected from the favorable pressure distribution shown. The coordinates of the section and the lift and drag for a variety of Reynolds numbers and angles of attack are provided in Ref. 4.10. Because of the low-drag capability, such an airfoil is suitable for the front wing of open-wheel race cars in a speedway setup (e.g., for Indy 500).

For higher lift applications, more camber is required, and to reduce the risk of flow separations multi-element airfoils are often used. However, racing regulations often dictate a certain geometry, against any common logic. Such is the case in the highly cambered airfoil shown in Fig. 4.48 where regulations specify the use of single-element airfoils. The two-dimensional (very high aspect-ratio) ideal pressure distribution shown in this figure is completely out of the "desirable" range shown in Fig. 4.17. Therefore, the flow will separate and the calculated lift coefficient of near $C_L = 4$ cannot be obtained. However, this airfoil, with an aspect ratio of 5.7, was used on an actual vehicle (Ref. 4.11) and there the flow was attached. This is a result of the smaller aspect ratio and the interaction with the vehicle body. Details of the performance of this airfoil when mounted to the vehicle will be presented in Chapter 6.

One way to increase airfoil camber without risking flow separations is to increase the number of airfoil elements. Fig. 4.49 shows the GA(W)-1 airfoil, which was developed for general aviation applications. Coordinates of the geometry and experimental lift and drag data on this airfoil section appear in Ref. 4.12. In the two dimensional case, flow separation on the flap begins at about $\delta_f = 40°$. The corresponding pressure distribution is also shown. For

Fig. 4-47. *Two-dimensional pressure distribution on a NLF(1)-0414F airfoil (effective Re number is 10^7).*

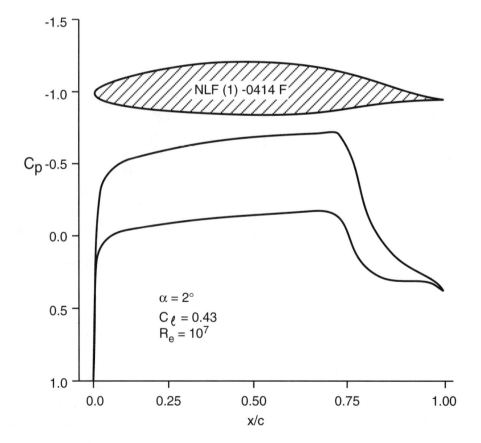

Fig. 4-48. Two-dimensional pressure distribution on a highly cambered rear wing of a sedan-based race car (effective Re number is over 2×10^6). Of course, this two-dimensional value of the lift coefficient is too high, and this airfoil can be used only on lower aspect-ratio wings (see later Fig. 6.68).

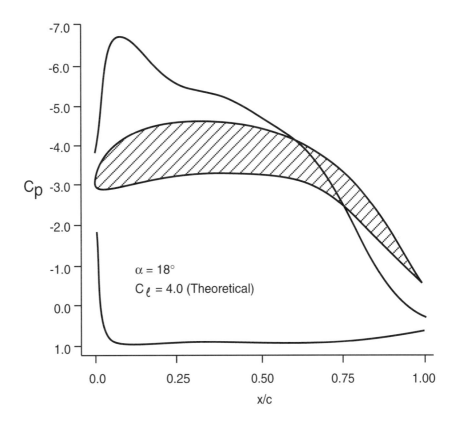

Fig. 4-49. Two-dimensional pressure distribution on a GA(W)-1 airfoil (effective Re number is 2.2×10^6).

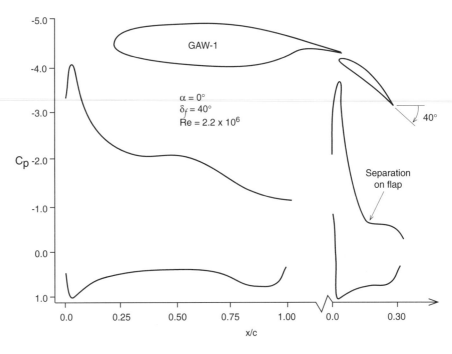

race cars, the main element should be placed near zero angle of attack, and flap angle should not exceed 40°.

The next two-element airfoil shape (Fig. 4.50) is the first example of a purpose-built race car airfoil used on a rear wing, not a modified airplane airfoil. This design represents the trend of increased camber, which is required for race car applications where an improved lift/drag ratio—and not the maxi-

Fig. 4-50. Two-dimensional and three-dimensional (along the centerline) pressure distribution on a two-element race car wing, designed for low drag (effective Re number is 2.2×10^6).

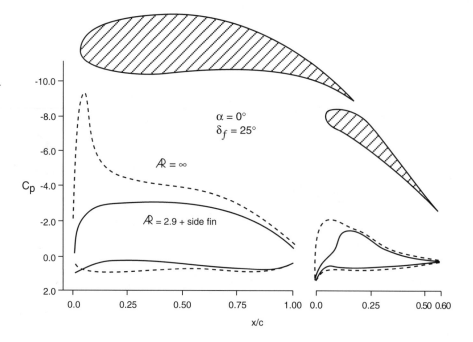

mum possible lift—is sought (remember, too, that an airplane wing must also have low drag at cruise, while such a race car wing is optimized only for the high lift condition).

The two-dimensional pressure distribution ($\mathcal{R} = \infty$) of this airfoil indicates that a suction peak exists near the leading edge. However, in actual applications ($\mathcal{R} = 2.9$) this suction peak is not present and a fairly large favorable pressure distribution exists near the leading edge. This difference in the shape of the pressure distribution increases as the wing aspect ratio is reduced, as it was demonstrated earlier by Fig. 4.36. Also, note that the flap of this airfoil has an adverse camber near the trailing edge. Although this design seems to reduce the camber and the lift, in practice this flap shape improves the overall wing lift/drag ratio near its maximum lift condition.

When the lift coefficient must be increased (to levels of over $C_L = 3.00$), then several elements are required, as shown in the last two examples. However, racing regulations can create some interesting airfoil shapes, as shown in Fig. 4.51. This Indy car rear wing (of a 1987 Lola) is a result of the requirements limiting wing dimensions within a square fixed by maximum horizontal and vertical dimensions (10' high and 28' long). The outcome of those limitations is an airfoil with high aft camber, where a large portion of the lift is generated by the flaps. Since such Indy car wings had a very small aspect ratio, only the three-dimensional pressure distribution is presented (in Figs. 4.51 and 4.52). The huge difference in the shape of the pressure distribution between the two- and the three-dimensional cases is shown in Fig. 4.36 (this wing was designed to replace the one in Fig. 4.51).

The extreme airfoil design shown in Fig. 4.52 is a result of the maximum length allowed by the same 1987 Indy car regulations. To obtain the largest angle of attack within the above specified dimensions, the leading edge was lowered considerably, whereas the trailing edge camber was increased as much as it was possible. The interesting feature of this 1987/8 Indy car wing is that the last flap is actually turned backward (towards the nose of the car), to further

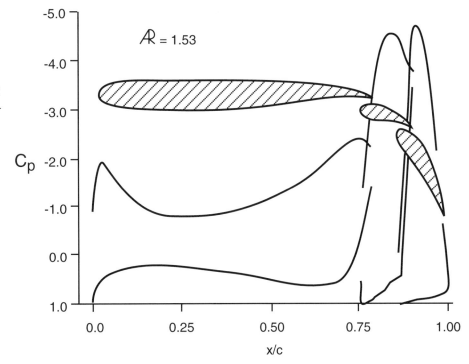

Fig. 4-51. *Three-dimensional centerline pressure distribution on a three-element race car rear wing, designed for maximum lift (effective Re number 2.2×10^6).*

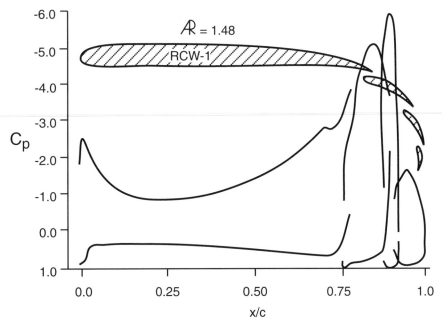

Fig. 4-52. *Three-dimensional centerline pressure distribution on a four-element race car rear wing, designed for maximum lift (effective Re number 2.2×10^6).*

increase rear camber. The three-dimensional pressure data suggest that the highest suction peak exists on the second flap, where flow separation is the most likely. However, on the actual wing (with $b/c \approx 1.5$ and with large end plates), the flow was attached on all the elements. Incidentally, experimental results with these wings indicated an increase of 13% in lift when using the section in Fig. 4.52 compared to the one in Fig. 4.36 (which was better than the baseline in Fig. 4.51).

Another interesting observation is that the last two multi-element airfoils shown here had no leading edge slats, similar to the slat shown in Fig. 4.35. This is because the leading edge suction peak (and the unfavorable pressure behind it) were small in these low aspect-ratio wings, and flow separation there was less likely. The addition of a slat at the leading edge of such a race car wing can be justified only on the ground of reshaping the pressure distribution to one with a favorable gradient, as shown in Fig. 4.36 (with the hope of less skin-friction drag).

The above examples show that for most cases, special airfoil shapes must be developed to meet certain regulation requirements. Knowledge of the target pressure distribution shape (from experiments or computations), along with some of the information presented in this chapter in regard to desirable pressure distributions, can help to form an opinion about the applicability of a certain airfoil. When this information is available, the suitable airfoil shape can be easily selected or even developed by changing the airfoil shape until the desirable pressure distribution is obtained. This iterative development is possible using either computations or wind tunnel measurements. In any case, such a systematic approach is far better than the time-consuming trial-and-error process used by some teams to select a correct airfoil shape from the huge selection available in the open literature.

As an appropriate epilogue to this section we must mention that a race car wing is a part of the car bodywork, and non-aerodynamic parts such as braces, small oil coolers, or TV cameras may be attached to it. At this point we already know that the suction side of the wing is more sensitive to flow separation. If attachments or modifications are needed on the wing, then the pressure side must be used. Typical examples demonstrating this principle are presented in Fig. 4.53. Clearly if some box must be mounted, then the proper way is shown in Fig. 4.53a. If a groove must be incorporated, then don't do it on the suction side (as on my Fiero GT). Attaching a strut to a wing is much better on the pressure side (but not practical when mounting a rear wing onto the gearbox). Lastly, along the same lines, the linkage holding the elements of a flapped airfoil should be placed on the pressure side.

Fig. 4-53. *The low-pressure side of an airfoil is far more sensitive to surface irregularities than the higher pressure side. These examples demonstrate common add-on mistakes.*

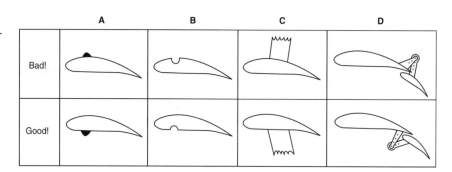

CONCLUDING REMARKS

This chapter described some of the basics of airfoil and wing aerodynamics. Since the pressure distribution on wings and bodies can be measured by well-established methods, this information was used to evaluate and suggest improvements in airfoil shape and wing design. The large effects of aspect ratio on improving wing performance were demonstrated, as was the basic effects of the interaction between two wings. The importance of such interaction between multiple wings and especially with the other components of a race car's body will be discussed in Chapter 6. Finally it must be noted again that throughout this chapter the reference area for calculating the lift and drag coefficients is based on the wing's planview area, and *not* on the vehicle's frontal cross-section area, as is customary in automobile aerodynamics (and used in all the other chapters). Also, all wings in this chapter assumed an airplane orientation with lift pointing upward, but are shown in their correct race car orientation (inverted) in the other chapters.

REFERENCES

4.1   Abbott, I. H., and von Doenhoff, A. E., *Theory of Wing Sections*, Dover, New York, 1959.

4.2   Liebeck, R. H., "Design of Subsonic Airfoils for High Lift," *J. Aircraft*, Vol. 15, No. 9, 1978, pp. 547-561.

4.3   Eppler, R, and Sommers, D. M., *A Computer Program for the Design and Analysis of Low-Speed Airfoils*, NASA TM 80210, Aug. 1980.

4.4   Drela, M., and Giles, M. B., "ISES: A Two-Dimensional Viscous Aerodynamic Design Analysis Code," AIAA Paper No. 87-0424, Jan. 1987.

4.5   Smith, A. M. O., "High Lift Aerodynamics," *J. Aircraft*, Vol. 12, No. 6, 1975, pp. 501-530.

4.6   Katz, J., "Aerodynamics of High-Lift, Low Aspect-Ratio Unswept Wings," *AIAA J.*, Vol. 27, No. 8, 1989, pp.1123–1124.

4.7   Bragg, M. B., and Gregorek, G. M., "Experimental Study of Airfoil Performance with Vortex Generators," *J. of Aircraft*, Vol. 24, No. 5, 1987, pp. 305–309.

4.8   Werle, M. J., Paterson, R. W., and Presz, W. M., "Trailing-Edge Separation/Stall Alleviation," *AIAA Journal*, Vol. 25, No. 4, 1987, pp. 624-626.

4.9   Walsh, M. J., "Riblets," Viscous Drag Reduction, *Progress in Astronautics and Aeronautics*, Vol. 123, 1990, pp. 203–261.

4.10   McGhee, R. J., Viken, J. K., Pfenninger, W., Beasley, W. D., and Harvey, W. D., "Experimental Results for a Flapped Natural-Laminar-Flow Airfoil with High Lift/Drag Ratio," NASA TM 85788, May 1984.

4.11   Katz, J., and Dykstra, L., "Effect of Wing/Body Interaction on the Aerodynamics of Two Generic Racing Cars," SAE Paper No. 920349, 1992.

4.12   Wentz, W. H., "New Airfoil Sections for General Aviation Aircraft," SAE Paper No. 730876, 1973.

5 AERODYNAMICS AND VEHICLE PERFORMANCE

INTRODUCTION

Aerodynamic loads may affect a vehicle's performance directly, as in the case of the drag force, or indirectly, as a result of lift or downforce changing the tires' friction coefficient. In order to understand how and why aerodynamic loads affect performance, the parameters influencing tire performance are presented first, and then some of the very basic concepts of vehicle dynamics are surveyed. We will finish by reviewing several examples of how aerodynamics improves high-speed handling, braking, and cornering of race cars.

TIRE PERFORMANCE

Even though the main topic dealt within this book is aerodynamics, we cannot forget that most vehicles ride on their tires. In fact, all forces such as driving, cornering, and braking are eventually created by the tires. To understand the effect of aerodynamics, we must begin with the basics of tire characteristics.

First, let us observe the simple experiment in Fig. 5.1, where a flexible material, such as a rubber eraser, is pushed sideways against a surface. Suppose the normal force F_z is fixed, then as we increase the side force, $F_x(action)$, a deformation of length Δx near the contact area results. Note that at the same time the "road" will act on the eraser with an equal reaction force, $F_x(reaction)$, but in the opposite direction.

This force at the contact area between the rubber and the surface is the one of interest to us. Typical results of measuring the magnitude of this side force versus the deformation Δx is presented at the right hand side of Fig. 5.1. The interesting observation is that at first, similar to a spring, the deformation and resulting force increase linearly (marked as "linear range"), but for larger Δx a

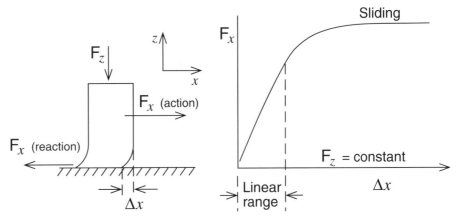

Fig. 5-1. *The relation between force and deformation for a flexible tire material. Δx measures the distance between the vertical line along the wall of the deformed material relative to its initial contact point.*

sliding will develop. The ratio between the normal force and the maximum sliding force is the classical friction coefficient μ_{max}. Coefficients for a variety of materials are given in Table 5.1

Table 5.1 Approximate Values For Sliding Friction Coefficients (Dry)

Materials	Sliding friction coefficient, μ_{max}
Steel on steel	0.1–0.2
Rubber on metal	0.4–0.5
Tire on road	0.5–0.9
Racing tire on road	1.2–1.5
Qualifying tire on road	1.4–1.7

Tire Adhesion The driving, braking, and cornering forces that act on a moving vehicle are created in the contact patch between the road and the tire. Because of the importance of the ratio between the force parallel to the ground and the normal forces (as shown in Fig. 5.1), let us define an adhesion coefficient, μ such that:

Eq. 5.1

$$\mu = \frac{F_x}{F_z}$$

This ratio resembles the friction coefficient, μ_{max}, which can be considered as the maximum value of the adhesion coefficient, μ. If the x direction is aligned with the vehicle's longitudinal axis, then μ can describe a braking coefficient, whereas when F_x is replaced by F_y then this can be called *cornering force coefficient*.

Based on the simple example presented in Fig. 5.1 we can conclude that in order for the tires to generate forces, the tire must deform, and some level of slip must exist between the road and the tire. *Slip* is another new term, and it describes (usually in percent) the difference between the velocity of the tire and the road. To demonstrate this principle, let us examine two important cases, the longitudinal and lateral slip of tires.

The longitudinal case is relevant to both acceleration and braking. Fig. 5.2 is the equivalent of Fig. 5.1, but for a braking tire. The tire's axle moves forward at a momentary velocity V, and the normal load is F_z. The braking force is created by slowing the wheel rotation relative to the road speed and creating wheel slip. Wheel slip is therefore a measure of the tire rotation speed versus road speed. For example, if the wheel rotates without any friction, then the slip is 0% ($V = R\Omega$, where R is the tire radius and Ω is the rotation rate). When it slides without any rotation (i.e., is locked), then the slip is 100%. A 15% slip, therefore, represents a case when tire rotation $R\Omega$ is 15% less than forward speed V.

Figure 5.2 indicates that for small wheel slip values, the increase in braking force is linear. Beyond approximately 15% slip, the axial force F_x (note that F_x is the road force on the tire) decreases with increased slip. The traction forces during vehicle acceleration are created in a similar manner, but then the tire

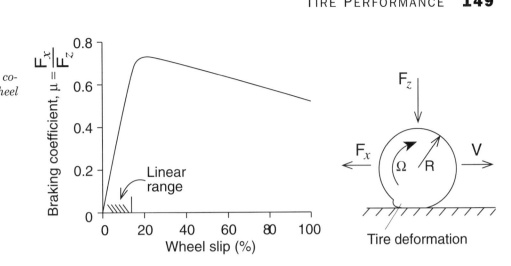

Fig. 5-2. *A tire's braking adhesion co-efficient versus wheel slip.*

rotates faster than the road speed; thus 100% slip is when the tire rotates but the forward speed is far less ($V<<R\Omega$); zero slip is again when tire speed is equal to road speed (note that there are other definitions for tire slip).

When cornering, the side force is created by a sidewise slip of the tire (as in Fig. 5.1). As a result of this slip, the actual direction of travel (vector V) is at an angle β to the direction of heading, as shown in Fig. 5.3. So the curve in this diagram describes the gradual increase of the side force F_y, when the normal force F_z is held constant. The lateral adhesion coefficient is now the ratio between the side and the normal force. Again, similar to the previous figures, for small angles of β (less than 4°) the slope of the curve is linear, whereas for large side-slip angles, tire slip is large (vehicle may slide) and certain tires will actually create less side force at those larger slip angles β. In practice, the tire should operate in the linear range because vehicle response to control inputs is then predictable. In layman's terms, the vehicle is not in an uncontrollable slide and, for example, will turn as expected when the steering wheel is turned.

This concept leads to a conclusion that a vehicle in steady-state cornering must maintain a slip angle relative to its heading (Fig. 5.4). For the vehicle body to assume a true tangential orientation relative to the circular path, all four wheels should maintain a side-slip angle, and this can be obtained only via four-wheel steering (as shown in the lower part of Fig. 5.4).

Fig. 5-3. *A tire's lateral adhesion coefficient versus side slip.*

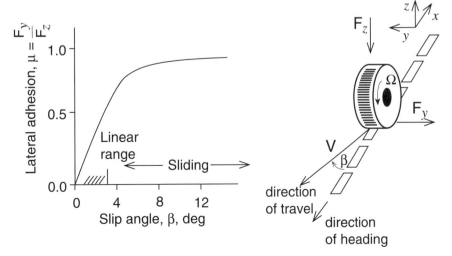

Fig. 5-4. *Orientation of wheels for a turning vehicle with front-wheel steering, and with all-wheel steering. Note that all wheels must have a side-slip angle in order to generate the cornering forces.*

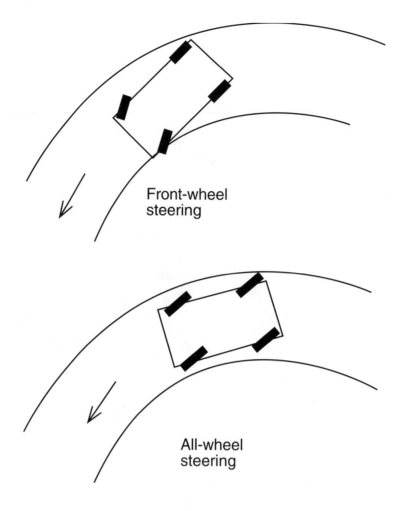

Front-wheel
steering

All-wheel
steering

The general performance of the vehicle and its tires depends, among other things, on suspension geometry, inflation pressure, normal load, tire construction, road surface conditions, etc. (For further details on vehicle dynamics see references such as Refs. 5.1–5.5.) Figs. 5.2 and 5.3 represent a force (or adhesion coefficient μ) created by tire slip, and usually a constant normal force F_z is assumed. But due to aerodynamic downforce the normal load may change, and for this purpose let us replot Fig. 5.3 in a dimensional form, as shown in Fig. 5.5, and assume that other tire characteristics are not affected much by this change in the normal load (in reality the maximum available friction coefficient is reduced somewhat with increased downforce).

The curve labeled by $F_z = 200$ *kg* in Fig. 5.5 represents a vehicle's normal weight distribution and load on a particular tire, and the cornering force created at a certain condition is marked by point *A*. If, due to aerodynamic loads, the normal force is increased by 50% (to $F_z = 300$ *kg*), then the same side force can be created at about 50% less side slip (shown by point *B*). This means that a vehicle using aerodynamic downforce will preserve its tires and reduce their heating due to friction (slip). On the other hand, if for maximum performance the largest possible force is sought, then point *C* represents a condition with the same tire slip as in *A*, but now the vehicle with the aerodynamic downforce is turning faster (or braking harder when longitudinal slip is considered).

Let us next consider a tire's performance during combined lateral and longitudinal slip (e.g., when cornering and braking). This can be demonstrated by

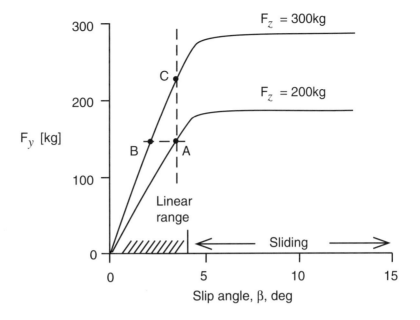

Fig. 5-5. *Dependence of tire's side force on normal force versus side-slip angle.*

the polar diagram shown in Fig. 5.6. The vehicle appears at the center of the diagram (and moving towards the left). The surrounding concentric circles (broken lines) measure acceleration in terms of $g = 9.814 m/\sec^2$ (which from the engineering point of view can be directly related to the adhesion coefficient, μ). So the farther the point is from the center of the circle, the larger the

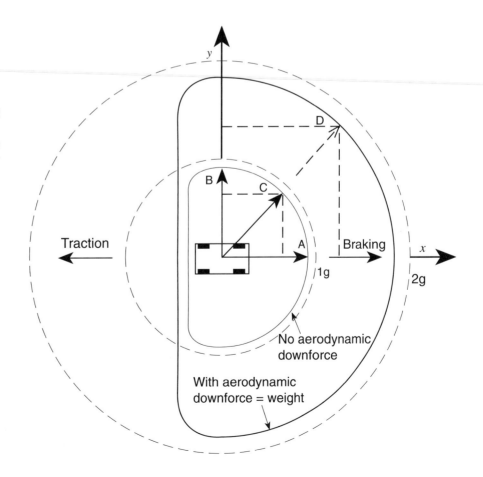

Fig. 5-6. *Effect of aerodynamic downforce on the polar diagram for a tire's maximum performance (sometimes called friction-coefficient circle). Note that the vehicle is travelling towards the left. Radial units are in terms of gravitational acceleration, g (9.814 m/sec²).*

acceleration, and the two circles represent the 1g and the 2g marks. The solid D-shaped lines describe the limits of the vehicle's performance in terms of braking (+X direction), acceleration (or traction, –X direction), and left and right accelerations (+Y and –Y, respectively).

Suppose the maximum friction coefficient of the tires is close to 0.95, then during straight-line braking we can expect a deceleration of μg. This condition is represented by point A on the inner D-shape boundary. When this vehicle turns to the right (without braking or accelerating) then its maximum lateral acceleration into the +Y direction is point B, and its magnitude should be the same as in point A. (Because of tire design and suspension geometry, these values are close but not the same.) Similarly, during combined braking and cornering (point C) the magnitude of the maximum acceleration is approximately retained, but as indicated by the dashed lines, the components into the X and Y directions are *reduced*. This means that when turning near the tires' limit and applying brakes or power, the available cornering capability is reduced, and the vehicle may enter an unplanned slide.

Thus, the line representing the "no aerodynamic downforce" case in Fig. 5.6 describes the envelope of maximum performance (in g-s) for a given vehicle without aerodynamic assistance (or at low speeds). This figure also indicates that at the traction side, the acceleration limit is far less than for braking and turning because in most cases the available driving power is far less than 1g. The second curve, with "aerodynamic downforce = weight," depicts a hypothetical situation when the normal load on the tires is doubled by aerodynamic downforce. For example, at point D at the boundary, the vehicle can turn much faster and at the same time outbrake the vehicle without downforce.

In conclusion, with the aid of aerodynamic downforce the tire performance envelope is enlarged and considerable improvements in a vehicle's braking and cornering can be expected. The small increase in vehicle traction, at high speed, represents the possible increase in engine power due to the ram-air induction effect.

VEHICLE DYNAMICS

The motion of a vehicle, or a vehicle's dynamics, is dictated by the forces acting on it: tire reactions, aerodynamics, and of course vehicle inertia. In this section, some of the more noticeable aspects of vehicle dynamics are presented briefly (more details on this highly advanced, and mathematical, science can be found in references such as Refs. 5.1–5.5).

Let us begin the discussion with the so-called "longitudinal plane" or side view shown in Fig. 5.7 and introduce the problems created by weight transfer during braking or acceleration. For simplicity let us ignore aerodynamic loads (or assume very low speed V). In this case the front and rear axle normal loads are shown by F_f and F_r, respectively. The ratio between the front and rear weight distribution, then, is a function of the location of the center of gravity (c.g.); that is, if l_f is less than l_r, then more weight will be carried by the front axle. During braking or acceleration, this ratio is changed by the inertial effect of the body.

For example, Fig. 5.7b indicates the large load transfer from the rear to the front axle under heavy braking. The higher the center of gravity (measured by h) the larger the weight transfer (when my neighbor's kid brakes hard on his

Fig. 5-7. Longitudinal weight transfer between the front and rear axles, without aerodynamic effects (e.g., at low speeds).

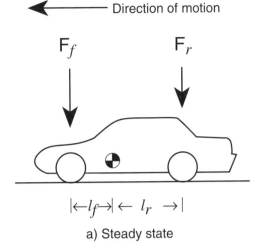

a) Steady state

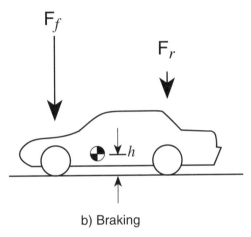

b) Braking

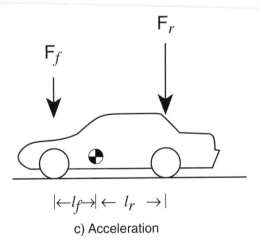

c) Acceleration

bicycle, he can lift the rear wheel). In acceleration the situation is reversed, as shown in Fig. 5.7c, and it is easy to understand why during first-gear acceleration, front-wheel drive vehicles create a noisy slide (while under similar acceleration a rear-wheel driven tire will experience increased normal force and can create more driving force, and is less likely to slide).

Weight transfer affects many aspects of vehicle design. For example, front brakes must be more powerful, and front/rear braking ratio should change with deceleration. Also, due to acceleration/braking the front/rear suspension loads are affected, creating vehicle pitch, which may interact unfavorably with aerodynamics (pitch sensitivity). In a steady turn, with a fixed front/rear braking ratio, weight transfer can first cause a slide of the front wheels under moderate braking, and a slide of the rear wheels under heavy braking.

Race car designers try to lower the center of gravity (reduce h in Fig. 5.7) as much as possible, and incorporate antidive characteristics into the suspension design in order to reduce the effect of load transfer on vehicle pitch. Furthermore, during high-speed braking of race cars, the aerodynamic downforce on each axle may be larger than the weight transfer effect, so the car is less sensitive to this problem (assuming no large variations in body pitch).

Next, let's consider lateral vehicle dynamics. In this category we can include side forces during cornering. Here, vehicle motion is best described from a top view. Let us start with the low-speed turning of an old-fashioned carriage, where the front axle turns about its center, as shown in Fig. 5.8. The front axle turning angle, δ, is called the Ackermann angle (named after Rudolph Ackermann, 1764–1834, the Anglo-German inventor of the movable carriage axle) and the carriage, in principle, should follow a coordinated turn along the bold curve, shown in the Figure. Effects due to weight transfer or suspension compliance can change the turn radius. In the case of a smaller radius, this condition is called oversteer. When the vehicle turns less than suggested by the Ackermann angle (the radius is larger than in the coordinated turn), then it has an understeer. If it follows the bold path it is labelled as neutral.

At this point we can focus on the side forces acting on the vehicle during, say, a turn to the left, as shown in Fig. 5.9. Such side forces are created by tire side slip during cornering. Because of this slip, the vehicle is actually moving at an angle, β, to the direction of heading (similar to the description in Fig. 5.3). In order for the vehicle to be in equilibrium, the moments about the center of gravity created by the front tires must be equal to the moments created by the rear tires. Let us explain the significance of this observation by presenting an example with a vehicle with a slightly forward-placed center of gravity.

Fig. 5-8. *Geometry of a turning vehicle with a solid front axle (top view).*

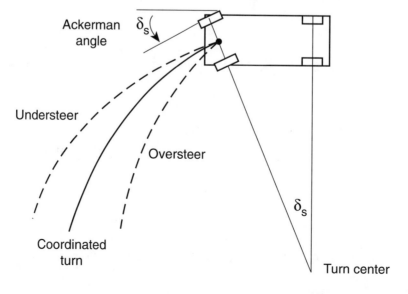

Fig. 5-9. Reaction forces created by the tires on a vehicle in a side slip β.

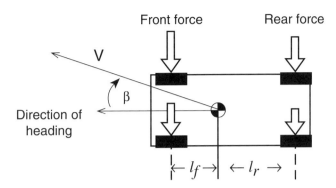

Front force   Rear force

V

β

Direction of
heading

$\leftarrow l_f \rightarrow$ $\leftarrow l_r \rightarrow$

In Fig. 5.9 l_f is less than l_r. The side force created by the rear tires during steady-state cornering will be less than the side force created by the front ones, due to the longer moment arm l_r (for the equilibrium case). If we assume that all four tires react similarly to a change in the angle β (have the same cornering stiffness), then the lower level of rear side force will result in less rear slide, compared to the front. Therefore, this vehicle will turn less than intended, or will understeer. This condition can be cured by using different tires in front or by altering suspension geometry. However, the important conclusion is that the location of the center of gravity is important, and a front weight bias usually leads to understeer while a rear weight bias (remember the old Corvair) leads to an oversteer. To further complicate the matter we can add braking or acceleration to change those characteristics, but it should be clear that with aerodynamic downforce we can change (for better or worse) the natural behavior of a vehicle.

To conclude this part of the discussion on vehicle dynamics, let us raise the issue of vehicle stability, and use the example in Fig. 5.10. Consider a rolling wheel attached to a long rod which is either pushed or pulled by a force F_x. Suppose that while the wheel is pushed forward (A), a small disturbance creates a slide angle β. This side slip creates a side force F_y, which tends to increase the angle β and eventually turns the rod backward. On the other hand, when the wheel is pulled (B), a similar disturbance in the side-slip angle will create a restoring force F_y which now acts to reduce the angle and keep the wheel parallel to the direction of travel V. We can conclude that the first case (wheel pushed) is unstable, while the second case (wheel pulled) is stable.

A quite impressive demonstration of instability is demonstrated in Fig. 5.11, where the unplanned "lift-off" of a top-fuel dragster occurs. As the vehicle accelerates forward, a small disturbance (combined with the huge torque of the rear wheels) may momentarily lift the front wheels. If at the time of this disturbance the vehicle is moving forward fast enough, and the angle α is more than a few degrees, an aerodynamic lift can be created by the long frontal body section. This lift will increase with the angle α, and combined with the rear wing's lift will create a destabilizing moment about point A. Incidentally, the mechanism creating the lift on the body is similar to the vortex lift described in Chapter 4, and at larger angles α even the small front wing will be lifting (upward). To make the situation worse, the inertial effects due to vehicle acceleration create a moment helping lift-off. So instead of a restoring moment about point A, we have a situation where the destabilizing moment increases with incidence angle (as in Fig. 5.10A), and a large pitchup is in most cases inevitable.

Fig. 5-10. In an unstable case (A), any small lateral disturbance can magnify and divert the vehicle (wheel in this figure) from its original direction. A stable situation is when, in spite of a small disturbance during the motion, the vehicle maintains its original direction (B).

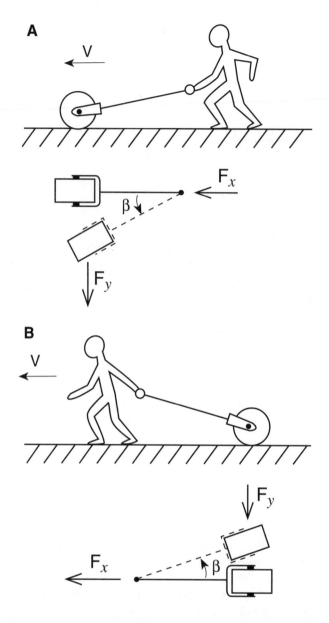

Now we can return to Fig. 5.9 and explain how the simple roller example of Fig. 5.10 is related to vehicle stability. For example, in the case of the forward center of gravity, the moment arm of the rear tires is longer so the vehicle in Fig. 5.10 resembles the stable case and we can conclude that vehicles with understeer are laterally stable. Along the same line, a vehicle with natural oversteer is laterally unstable. (However, a closer observation of the dynamic equations, as in Ref. 5.1, p. 63, reveals that such vehicles are stable at low speeds and become unstable only above a certain critical speed, which is fairly high for most passenger cars.)

Combining our knowledge about tires and vehicle dynamics we can see that when a tire operates in the linear range, the effects of oversteer or understeer are less pronounced. But even when following a straight line, an unstable vehicle will demand more driver effort and concentration to keep it straight, whereas a too-stable car will be difficult to steer. Also, a stable car with natural understeer and rear-wheel drive can be forced to oversteer during cornering by reducing rear tire adhesion through acceleration (remember Fig. 5.6).

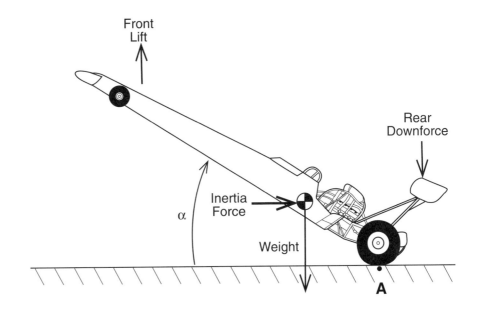

Fig. 5-11. Schematic description of the force balance leading to a blow-over (lift-off) of a top-fuel dragster. Note that once the front is lifted, both aerodynamic and inertial forces create moments helping the lift-off.

When adding the effects of aerodynamics at higher speeds, many passenger cars will develop rear lift and front downforce, which leads to a laterally unstable condition. This is usually corrected on passenger-car-based racers by increasing rear downforce with rear-deck spoilers or small wings. Also, in race cars, one must remember that those vehicles operate near the tires' maximum friction coefficient. Any small disturbance between the front/rear balance can cause complete sliding of either the front or the rear tires (since the tires will operate outside of the linear range). Such incidences can occur in a high-speed turn where loss of rear downforce can create a large oversteer, sending the vehicle into a spin; a similar loss in front downforce can cause a heavy understeer that can result in a missed turn (and a hitting of the retaining wall).

Finally, note that vehicle roll and lateral weight transfer are present during cornering, and play a very important role in vehicle handling (for the sake of brevity, this was not discussed here). The difference in the normal force between the left and right tires, as well as suspension compliance (due to vehicle roll), usually has a strong effect on a vehicle's stability (or the lack of it).

THE EFFECT OF AERODYNAMICS ON PERFORMANCE

The previous sections clearly suggest that a vehicle's handling and stability can be changed by altering the tire-generated forces, which in turn can be changed by varying the normal force on the tires (e.g., by controlling the front/rear ratio of the aerodynamic downforce). Thus the importance of aerodynamics on the high-speed performance of race cars is not limited only to reducing air resistance, but also affects areas such as a vehicle's braking, handling, and stability. The rest of this chapter is devoted to examples demonstrating the significance of aerodynamics to race car performance. We begin with simple longitudinal effects and towards the end of this section expand into lateral effects, as well.

Maximum Speed   The maximum steady-state speed of a vehicle is achieved when the maximum available driving force at that speed equals the resistance force due to aerodynamic drag and tire rolling resistance. This balance, in terms of power (force times speed) for a generic sports car is depicted in Fig. 5.12. Let us first examine the available driving power. Typically, the maximum engine output (in terms of horsepower, HP) initially increases with engine RPM, and the maximum engine output (with a no-slip clutch) can be related, through the overall gear ratio, to the vehicle's speed. This maximum available driving power is shown schematically for two gear ratios, HP_4 and HP_5, corresponding to 4th and 5th gears (overdrive) of a passenger car.

Fig. 5-12. Maximum available power in fourth gear, HP_4, and in fifth gear, HP_5, and total vehicle drag power versus speed.

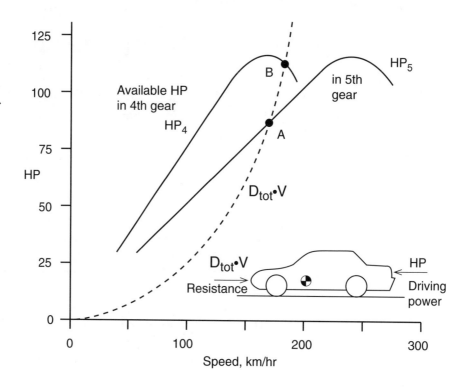

The total drag on the vehicle, D_{tot} (a sum of tire rolling resistance and the aerodynamic drag), increases rapidly with speed, and its power requirement $(D_{tot} \cdot V)$ is shown by the broken line in the figure. Usually, the increase in tire rolling resistance is marginal compared to the rapid increase in the aerodynamic drag (as shown by Fig. 2.20).

So for example, if the vehicle in Fig. 5.12 is traveling at a steady 100 km/hr, then in both gears there is more power available than is required to overcome the drag power, $D_{tot} \cdot V$. In the lower gear more power is available, but when traveling in steady state only part of this power is used (by partial throttle opening). With maximum throttle the maximum available power is generated at the top of the curve and the maximum speed is obtained when the engine output is equal to the drag power (points A and B in the figure). Careful gear ratio selection allows a higher maximum speed in the lower gear (B), while the highest gear ratio is usually designed for good fuel economy (but it avoids reaching the maximum output range of the engine, as clearly indicated by point A). The primary conclusion is that total resistance (mostly aerodynamic) increases rapidly with speed, as shown by the broken line (that changes with V^3), and selection of the proper gear ratio for maximum vehicle speed requires engine, tire, and aerodynamic data. Along the same lines, less aerodynamic drag presents the potential for higher maximum speed and for better fuel economy (at lower speeds). For a race car, gear selection must be made so that point A in Fig. 5.12 is at the engine maximum power.

Straight-Line Braking

To continue this discussion about the effect of aerodynamics on performance let us focus our attention on one of the simplest cases, the effect on straight-line braking. We can further divide the discussion into the case when the vehicle develops high levels of downforce, and the case where the reduction is obtained by increasing drag, as by the wing-spoilers on a landing airplane.

As we've already seen, a race car can develop large levels of downforce. The tire data presented earlier indicates that the maximum friction force created by the tire increases with increased normal (down) force. During high-speed travel, large levels of aerodynamic downforce can increase or even double the normal force on the tires, considerably increasing braking performance. It is not unheard of that at speeds near 300 km/hr a race car can brake more than $2g$ (twice the gravitational acceleration).

Typical calculations showing the effect of aerodynamic downforce on braking distance are presented in Fig. 5.13. The braking distance is estimated from an initial top speed, shown on the abscissa, to zero speed, with various values of aerodynamic downforce C_L. Clearly, with increasing aerodynamic downforce, shorter braking distance is required. For example, if vehicle initial speed is 250 km/hr, then with a downforce of $C_L = -2.0$, a 30 m shorter braking distance is required than for a vehicle without aerodynamic downforce (e.g., with $C_L = 0.0$). The interesting observation about high-speed braking is that as the race car slows down, the normal force and the corresponding braking force are reduced, and the driver should gradually ease the brakes.

The simplest method for reducing vehicle speed by aerodynamic means is to increase its drag. High-speed race cars, such as the dragster shown in Fig. 5.14, deploy parachutes at the end of their near-300-mph run to rapidly reduce their speed. The high drag coefficient of the parachute, which is close to $C_D \approx 1.2$ (see drag of circular plate in Fig. 2.21), can develop large levels of air resistance

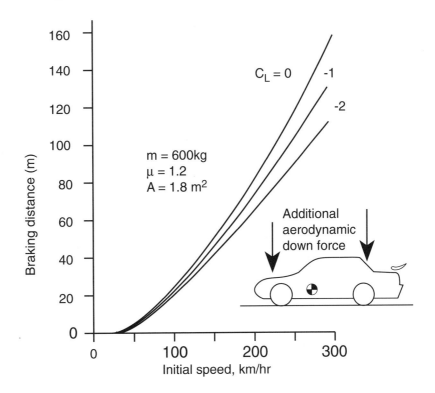

Fig. 5-13. *Effect of aerodynamic downforce on the braking distance versus vehicle speed.*

Fig. 5-14. *Deployment of the parachute at the end of a 300 mph (483 km/hr) run is a graphic example of the use of aerodynamic braking. Courtesy of Les Welch Photography (shot in Gainsville, FL, March 1994, with the late Jimmy Nix at the wheel)*

at higher speeds, creating an effective first-stage braking without overheating the brake pads. In the past, movable flaps were used to assist high-speed braking in other forms of racing. You won't find such devices on more recent race cars, though, since almost any movable aero-device is now banned. Such restrictions do not apply to road vehicles, however. The McLaren F-1 sports car has a moveable, brake-activated rear spoiler. It increases rear downforce during braking to counteract the effects of weight transfer. Motorcycle riders use the same trick at high speed by raising their shoulders to slow down. In terms of estimating the effect of drag force on deceleration, Eq. 3.2 can be used, exactly as it is for coast-down tests as described in the discussion on Fig. 3.5.

Maximum Turning Speed

The previous two examples dealt with the longitudinal aspects of vehicle performance. As the simplest example for the effect of aerodynamics on vehicle lateral performance let us consider the steady-state turning of a race car on an unbanked road. The forces acting on the vehicle are the tire forces, which increase with aerodynamic downforce, and the centrifugal forces, which increase with cornering speed (for a given radius). In Fig. 5.15 (taken from Ref. 5.6) the vehicle is treated as a point mass following an unbanked turn. The curves show the maximum speed versus road-curvature radius R for three values of the lift coefficient C_L (for all cases a maximum tire friction coefficient of $\mu = 1.0$ is assumed). The magnitude of this effect can be observed by, say, selecting a road-curvature radius of 200 m. In this case, with a maximum tire friction coefficient of $\mu \approx 1$ the wingless vehicle (assuming $C_L \approx 0$) can safely turn at a speed close to 150 km/hr. However, by increasing the normal load on the tires through aerodynamic downforce (without increasing the mass of the vehicle), turning speeds can be increased by about 100 km/hr in the case of $C_L = -2.0$.

Closed Circuit Lap Times

In the real racing world, having the fastest maximum speed is often not relevant, and each track requires a different aerodynamic setting. For example, on high-speed tracks without serious acceleration (and sharp turns) low drag is required, while on high-speed unbanked turns high downforce is the virtue. In fact, race car performance is ultimately measured by closed-circuit lap times.

Prior to estimating the effect of aerodynamics on lap times we must remember that an increase in the negative lift of a road vehicle is accompanied by an increase in drag, so a vehicle's straightaway top speed will be reduced. In order to evaluate the net effect of increased downforce, the variation of drag versus lift must be included in any analysis of race car performance on a given track.

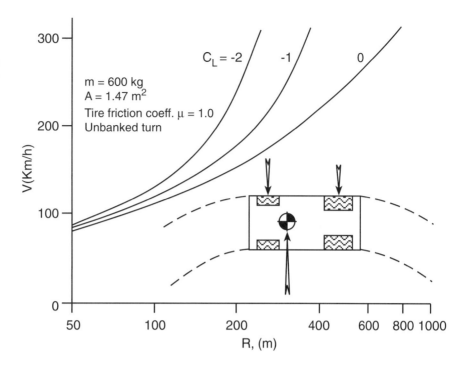

Fig. 5-15. Effect of aerodynamic downforce on maximum cornering speed. Reprinted with permission from SAE Paper 920349 (Ref. 4.11), Copyright ©1992 SAE, Inc.

Vehicle Drag and Downforce
In Chapter 3 we saw that when a finite wing's lift increases, the drag will increase as well. This induced drag increases with the square of the lift, as depicted by Eq. 4.8. In order to evaluate the net effect of increased downforce on a race car we can start with a similar correlation for the vehicle's drag. Indeed, when a large body of data is examined, its pattern was found to fit the following trend:

Eq. 5.2

$$C_D = k\,(C_L - C_{L_0})^2 + C_{D_0}$$

Here C_D is the vehicle's drag, and C_L its lift, which is negative for downforce. The minimum drag coefficient (without aerodynamic add-ons) is C_{D_0} and the corresponding lift at this condition is C_{L_0}, while the polar coefficient k multiplies the square term

Such a simple formulation is presented in Eq. 5.2, and for the present simulation a minimum drag coefficient (for the wingless car) of $C_{D_0} = 0.3$ is assumed, with a corresponding lift coefficient of $C_{L_0} = +0.2$. For the polar coefficient, which accounts for the added drag due to the added downforce, the range of $k = 0.03 - 0.04$ is used (which is reasonable for modeling the performance of a generic prototype car, such as IMSA GTP or FISA group C). Thus for the calculations in Fig. 5.16 a value of $k = 0.04$ is used.

The effect of aerodynamics on lap time is then calculated by incorporating Eq. 5.2 into a vehicle-dynamics simulation program, which calculates the vehicle speed around each point on the race track (a list of such simulation codes is given in Ref. 5.7). This simulation accounts for effects such as track curvature (track shape is shown on the inset to Fig. 5.16), elevation, banking, surface friction coefficient, and tire characteristics, along with the engine and gearbox

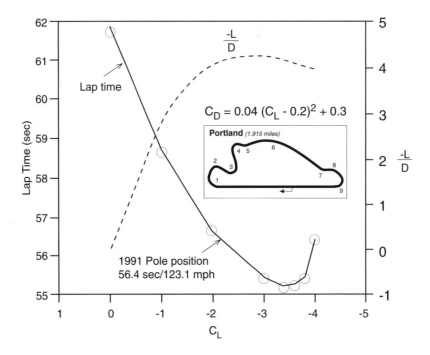

Fig. 5-16. *Effect of aerodynamic downforce on lap time, for a generic prototype race car (road course shape is shown in the inset). Reprinted with permission from SAE Paper 920349 (Ref. 4.11), Copyright ©1992 SAE, Inc.*

(with optimal gear change strategy). Based on such a computer simulation the diagram shown in Fig. 5.16 was created, and it clearly indicates the large initial effect of increasing a vehicle's downforce ($-C_L$) on lap time.

For very large negative lift coefficients, though, the resulting drag increase and the corresponding reduction in straightaway performance overcomes the benefits of improved cornering, and for each track an optimum aerodynamic setting probably exists. The lift-over-drag characteristic of this generic vehicle is also plotted on this figure and the interesting observation is that optimum performance (on this track) is obtained with more downforce than required for the most efficient configuration (i.e., with the largest downforce over drag ratio). The arrow in the lower part of the figure depicts the lap time for the pole position in 1991, and some of the slower cars had lap times which are higher than 62 seconds. This means that the vehicle modeled here could move from the last row to the pole position by simply changing its aerodynamic downforce from $C_L = 0$ to –2.0.

Effect of Side Winds

Up to this point, the effects of winds were assumed to be small. However, in case of strong side winds the direction of the free stream, relative to the vehicle heading, may be significant. It is usually measured by the angle β_w. This side wind condition, as illustrated in Fig. 5.17, results in an aerodynamic sideforce Y, and its effect on the vehicle is demonstrated by examining two representative situations.

The first case is likely to occur on open roads with strong, steady side winds, and is referred to as the "steady-state" problem. The second case is a result of entering or leaving a region with side wind, where the sudden change in airspeed direction (sometimes called *gust*) can cause steering reactions leading to lateral vehicle oscillations.

Returning to Fig. 5.17, it shows the aerodynamic load Y and the airflow angle β_w, as viewed from the top. (Note that for positive β_w the force Y points into the negative y direction, based on Fig. 2.19). In principle, by using an approach

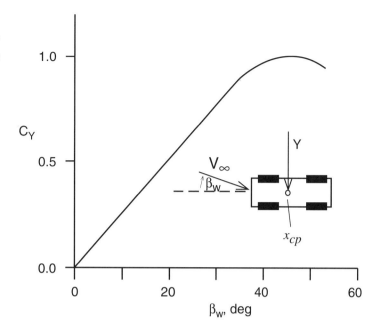

Fig. 5-17. *Variation of aerodynamic side force with side wind angle β_w.*

similar to that in Chapter 4 (and in Fig. 4.12), the added effect of the vehicle's surface pressure distribution (such a pressure distribution is depicted in Fig. 6.16), as viewed from the top, can be exchanged by a resultant force, Y, acting at the center of pressure x_{cp}. When increasing the airflow side-slip angle β_w the side force Y increases, resembling the lift versus angle-of-attack behavior of a symmetric wing. In this case, however, the flow separates at the sides of most vehicle shapes, and the resulting drag increase is large. For the larger angles of side slip, the increase in side force flattens out.

The resemblance to the symmetric airfoil case can be stretched a bit further by observing that, similar to an airfoil, many passenger car shapes have their center of pressure forward of the vehicle's geometrical center (from top view). The location of the center of pressure (cp) relative to the location of the center of gravity (cg)[1] becomes important only at higher speeds when aerodynamic forces become noticeable. Typical, and quite different, locations of these two points are depicted in Fig. 5.18. For example, a rear engine pick-up truck with a forward cabin will certainly have its center of pressure ahead of its center of gravity. Incidentally, this resembles the laterally unstable case shown in Fig. 5.10A, since at high speeds, any lateral disturbance (e.g., road irregularity) that causes a small initial side slip will tend to generate an aerodynamic side force which points in the direction of increasing side-slip angle. Without driver intervention the side slip will grow, but with a driver at the steering wheel, a noticeable driver effort is required to keep the vehicle moving along a straight line.

Because of this undesirable effect, most high-speed race cars will have their center of pressure behind the center of gravity. The addition of large fins at the aft section of the vehicle or end plates on the rear wings contributes to the backward shift of the center of pressure, and such devices can considerably increase a vehicle's high-speed stability. Such stabilizing fins appeared on many passenger and race cars, and their use increased in the mid 1960s. Fig. 5.19 de-

---

1. The symbol ◓ is used to mark the location of the center of gravity.

Fig. 5-18. *Typical locations of the center of pressure, x_{cp}, and center of gravity, x_{cg}.*

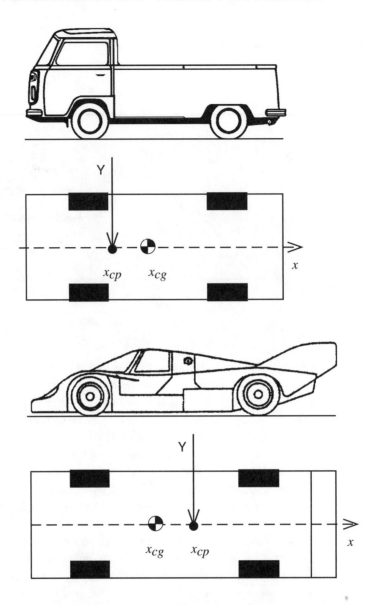

picts two examples. The earlier photo shows the Matra-Simca MS670 prototype using two fins on both rear fenders. Incidentally, with this car Graham Hill won the 1972 LeMans 24-hour race. The use of a single vertical fin is shown in the second photo on the 1994 Penske PC23 Indy car. This design dominated that year's race season. An even earlier application of such fins, on the Peugeot LeMans race car, is shown later in Chapter 7.

The distance between the center of gravity x_{cg} and the center of pressure x_{cp} is called the *static margin*. The relative location of the center of pressure requires special attention. For an aerodynamically stable vehicle (airplanes included) the center of gravity must be *ahead* of the center of pressure. Additionally, a larger static margin means a more stable vehicle. It must be pointed out that the discussion in this paragraph deals with aerodynamic loads only; total vehicle performance is primarily controlled by the tire forces. Therefore, at low speeds the aerodynamic forces can have only an annoying effect on driveability, but at race car speeds they can seriously influence handling and stability.

Fig. 5-19. *Utilization of vertical fins to increase lateral stability are found throughout the history of high-speed racing. One early example (top) is the Matra-Simca MS670 prototype. A more recent example (bottom) for the resurrection of the vertical fin is the Penske PC23. In the latter case, instead of the traditional two fins, only one fin mounted behind the driver is used. Top: Courtesy of Randy Barnett. Bottom: Courtesy of Marlboro Racing News Service .*

The next step is to demonstrate the effect of aerodynamics on the performance of a complete vehicle (including aerodynamic and tire forces). Let us start with the steady-state case in Fig. 5.20, where a vehicle moves forward along a straight road. If a steady side wind exists, then a side force Y will act at the center of pressure, causing a side slip of the tires and resulting in a motion which is inclined at an angle β to the direction of heading. (In order to be mathematically correct, note that a positive side wind angle β_W causes a force in the negative y direction, leading to a negative side slip of the tires, $-\beta$.) Therefore, a vehicle traveling in heavy side winds will have to turn slightly into the wind direction, so that the forces created by the side slip of the tires will counteract the wind forces. Motorcycle riders know this well, since under similar conditions they must lean into the wind to generate the required side force.

The location of the center of pressure has an additional effect on this problem, as shown in Fig. 5.21. When the center of pressure is ahead of the center of gravity, the front wheels must create a larger portion of the reaction to the aerodynamic side force Y, and the steering wheel is turned into the wind by an additional angle δ_s (Fig. 5.21B). In the case of an aft-located center of pressure,

Fig. 5-20. *Vehicle side slip caused by an external force Y.*

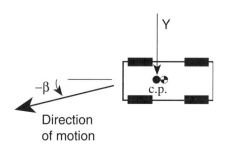

Fig. 5-21. Realignment of a vehicle, moving in strong, steady side winds. The front tires of a vehicle with aft center of pressure should create less side force (A) than those of a vehicle with a forward center of pressure (B).

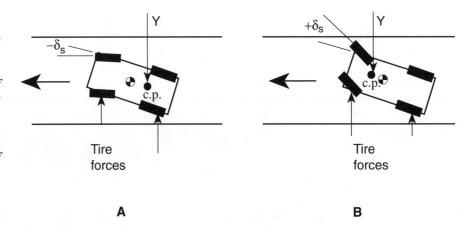

A   **B**

the opposite happens and the steering wheel is turned away from the wind, as shown in Fig. 5.21A.

Let us now examine the transient effect resulting from a sudden change in the aerodynamic conditions. Such a situation is described in Fig. 5.22, where a vehicle traveling in a calm, windless area behind tall buildings and walls suddenly faces strong side winds. If a vehicle with a forward center of pressure moves from section 1 to section 2 without any response from the driver, then the vehicle with a fixed steering wheel position will gradually turn away from the wind direction (Fig. 5.23). The other, less sensitive option is when the center of pressure is behind the center of gravity, and when reacting to the aerodynamic side force the vehicle will steer itself into the wind direction.

Typical driver reaction to correct the first change in the direction of travel (Fig. 5.23A) is to steer into the wind, and the lateral oscillation history of such

Fig. 5-22. A possible situation of a vehicle entering a gust.

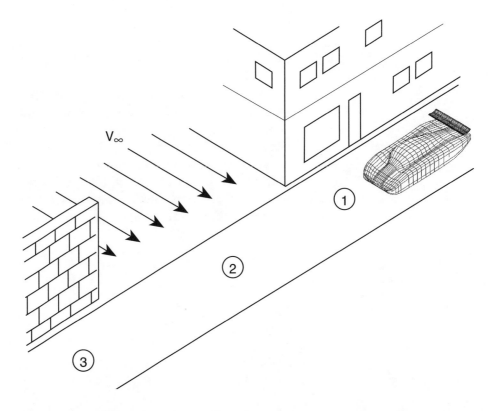

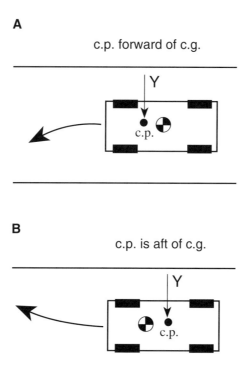

Fig. 5-23. *Fixed steering-wheel reaction of vehicle to a gust: with a forward (A) and an aft located center of pressure (B).*

an incident is shown by the dashed line in Fig. 5.24. To counteract the sudden aerodynamic loads in a vehicle with an aft center of pressure, the driver should steer slightly away from the wind. In this case the time history of the lateral oscillation is usually less dramatic, and more damped (solid line).

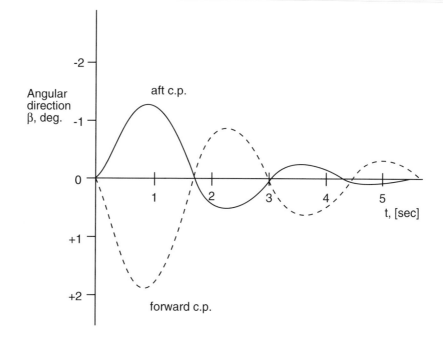

Fig. 5-24. *Typical transient side-slip history of a vehicle entering a gust.*

Lateral Stability

The lateral stability of a vehicle is affected by a number of factors, such as the location of the center of gravity, tire characteristics, suspension compliance, and aerodynamics. For the purpose of the present demonstration, let us select one aspect of this problem, and use Fig. 5.25 to depict the effect of the front/rear lift ratio on vehicle handling.

At the top of Fig. 5.25 the vehicle slips sideways at an angle β, exactly as was presented in Fig. 5.9, and at low speeds the aerodynamic effects are negligible. This side-slip condition can be a result of a momentary disturbance or a result of the vehicle turning to the left. The side force created by the tires is proportional to the normal load, and in the low-speed case is a result of the weight W_f and W_r on the front and rear axles, respectively (recall Eq. 5.1: $Y_f = \mu W_f$, and $Y_r = \mu W_r$). For a stable vehicle, the rear tire side force Y_r multiplied by the distance from the center of gravity l_r is larger than the same product for the front tires: $Y_f \times l_f$. When this condition is met, then the moments (in top view) tend to rotate the vehicle into the slip direction (understeer) and by using the previously defined terminology, the vehicle is considered to be stable.

Fig. 5-25. Lateral forces created by the tires during side slip: without aerodynamic effects (A) and with aerodynamic lift at the rear axle (B).

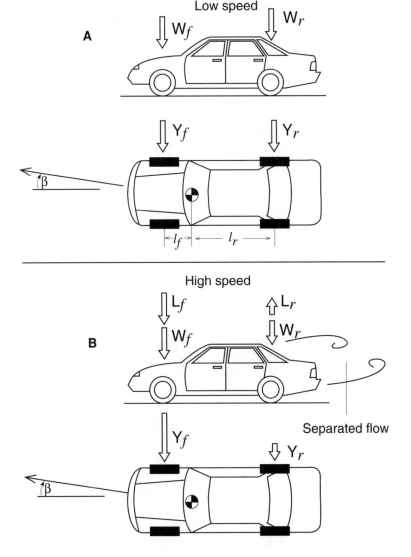

Next, let us construct the same force description, but for a high-speed case where the aerodynamic effects create some front downforce and some rear lift (due to aft-flow separation). This situation may be encountered by production sports cars with a lowered front hood and less streamlined rear window area. The vehicle encounters a side-slip situation, as before, but now the tire reaction to this side slip in the front, Y_f, is much larger than at the rear, Y_r, due to the aerodynamic load difference. The vehicle in this case will be turned away from the direction of the side slip (oversteer), and will be considered unstable. This terminology becomes more clear when the vehicle in Fig. 5.25B turns to the left and the larger side force in the front turns it more into the turn, hence the term "oversteer" becomes more meaningful.

The above described phenomenon affects the stability (usually referred to as handling) for many passenger cars that generate more lift at the rear than on the front axle. The driver usually feels that large effort is required to keep the vehicle along a desirable path, even when driving in a straight line along a straightaway.

Suspension and Pitch Sensitivity

The previous examples have demonstrated that for a laterally stable vehicle design, namely a good race car, the moments about the center of gravity created by the rear tires must be larger than those created by the front ones (during a fixed-steering side slip). Maintaining this requirement for various maneuvers, when the vehicle rolls and suspension geometry varies, is not a small task. Before aerodynamic downforce devices became popular, most race car design efforts to ensure predictable handling went into suspension compliance and tire design. But as racing speeds have increased, stability problems such as those described in the previous section were faced, and sometimes large rear fins were used to cure that problem.

The breakthrough in the mid-1960s was the realization that by adding rear aerodynamic downforce, and thereby increasing the rear tires' cornering stiffness, the vehicle could be made more stable and controllable at high speeds. However, one aspect of this breakthrough is far less pleasant, and this is that with increased speed the vertical loads on the tires rapidly increase. This requires much stiffer springs (and vibration-resistant drivers) and, more recently, active suspension to avoid large changes in suspension geometry (in the 1993 F-1 seasons many teams used the active suspension system to create active aerodynamics by changing vehicle ride height and pitch along different portions of the track).

Vehicle attitude and ride height will clearly vary as aerodynamic downforce changes with speed, having a major effect on suspension compliance and on vehicle's lift and drag. Thus, suspension compliance, spring and damping ratios were suddenly dictated by aerodynamic requirements as well, and as a result there were many new problems, with a combined suspension/aerodynamic nature. As an example, one of the simplest suspension/aerodynamic interactions, the pitch sensitivity, is described in the following paragraphs.

The term *pitch sensitivity* is often used, say, by one team engineer to describe the weaknesses of the cars built by the competitors. But in reality, the influence of vehicle attitude change (pitch) on handling is based on well-founded mathematical principles (the formulation usually describes the change of aerodynamic forces and moment versus vehicle's angle of attack, and how this affects vehicle's tendency to over/understeer). Some of the principles can be found in Refs. 5.1–5.3.

In this section, an effort is made to present the simplest part of this problem using two previously mentioned aspects. The first is the dynamic aspect, which indicates that an increase in the cornering stiffness of, say, the front tires, will reduce stability (whereas the same increase at the rear will increase stability). The second aspect is the variation in the lift of wings placed near the ground. Fig. 5.26 presents similar information for the ground effect of an open-wheel race car's front wing. The important point here is that the lift can be nearly doubled if ground clearance changes from 15 cm to 5 cm. Furthermore, the front wing of an open-wheel race car is placed ahead of any major flow distortion that could be created by the vehicle's body and wheels, and its undisturbed boundary layer is thin, so the wing's lift keeps increasing as its ground clearance decreases—down to very small ground clearances.

Fig. 5-26. *Effect of ground proximity on the lift of an open-wheel race car front wing.*

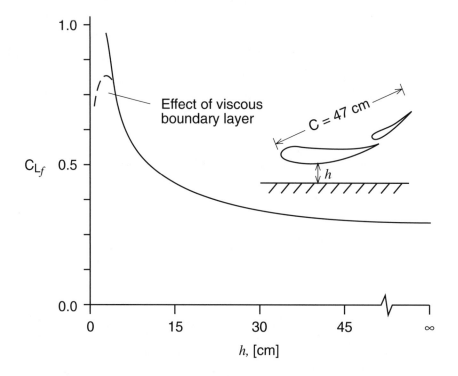

So, by combining those two observations it becomes clear that lowering a race car's front wing will increase its front downforce; this will make the vehicle less stable, and more driver effort will be required to control the vehicle, even when following a straight line.

Next, let us observe how race car engineers find ways to generate large values of downforce (working under certain regulations aimed at doing exactly the opposite). For example, F-1 cars (after 1983) have flat bottoms, as illustrated in Fig. 5.27, to reduce downforce which, prior to 1983, had been created by the body's ground effect. The downforce initially was obtained by two wings, one far in the front and the other way in the back. With time, though, it was discovered that a small Venturi effect can be created behind the rear axle, where the regulations did not specify a flat bottom. With an additional lower wing that boosts the flow into this area, the airflow emerges between the body and the rear wheel and creates a vortex under the upward bent rear plate, which creates sizable downforce. However, the front and rear downforce is be-

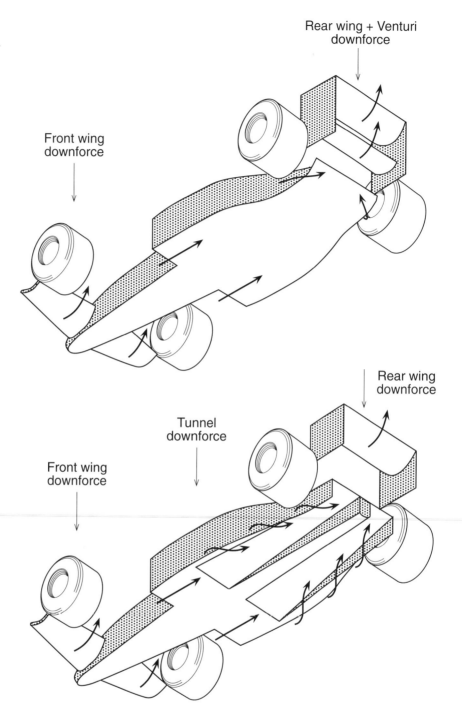

Fig. 5-27. *Primary contributions to a flat-bottom, open-wheel race car downforce (F-1), and to one with underbody channels (tunnels) (Indy).*

Rear wing + Venturi
downforce

Front wing
downforce

Rear wing
downforce

Tunnel
downforce

Front wing
downforce

ing generated at the two far ends of the vehicle, and this is where the pitch sensitivity becomes important.

Suppose, that due to variable road conditions or momentary suspension motion, such a vehicle is pitched forward. As a result, the front wing downforce will dramatically increase (due to the ground effect). In addition, the reduced gap between the ground and the front wing will limit the flow beneath the car toward the rear diffuser, reducing the rear downforce. The combination of these two changes clearly makes the car less stable. Fig. 5.28 illustrates the steady-state part of this problem and indicates the large increase in downforce

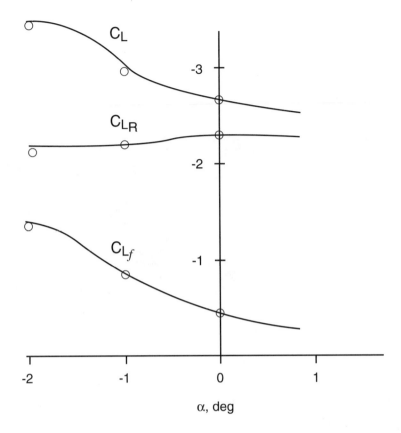

Fig. 5-28. *Static pitch sensitivity of a generic open-wheel race car pitched about its center of gravity (and raised by 3 cm). Positive pitch is defined as nose up.*

at the front axle C_{L_f}, while pitching down the vehicle's nose (incidentally, at 1° pitch the nose of many race cars will hit the ground). As a result of such forward pitch, the rear wing downforce increases a bit too, but due to the front wing ground effect the downforce at the rear axle C_{L_r} will be somewhat reduced. Now, if the driver of this race car is turning and using maximum tire friction coefficients, then in the worst case a disturbance increasing the vehicle pitch can cause oversteer and even vehicle spin. This can be corrected by making the suspension extremely stiff or active, to avoid sudden sinking of the front wing. So in principle, the pitch sensitivity is a problem created by the change of downforce distribution (which causes the center of pressure to move) and in low-mounted front wings it becomes a front ground-clearance problem.

It is interesting to compare Indy with F-1 design, since in the first case the regulations allow underbody tunnels (lower part of Fig. 5.27). Here, large values of downforce can be obtained by these tunnels, and the resultant aerodynamic downforce is placed closer to the vehicle center. The additional negative lift created by the two wings is less crucial in this case, since wing-generated negative lift is only a fraction of the total downforce, and also most of the vehicle's lower surface is not as close to the ground as the flat bottom of typical F-1 cars. Consequently, such race cars can create more downforce and can have softer suspension (and, in principle, can be made less pitch-sensitive).

Similar problems can be seen on certain enclosed-wheel, prototype race cars. It is very tempting to use a highly cambered front wing, which can generate large levels of downforce. However, the front wing diverts the flow from under the nose, so that the flow under the vehicle continuing into the rear tunnels is now very limited. The high downforce tunnels then become pitch-sensitive since their front-flow supply originates under the front wing. Therefore, at the

Fig. 5-29. *Primary contributions to the downforce of an enclosed-wheel race car with a distinct front wing, and one with raised nose.*

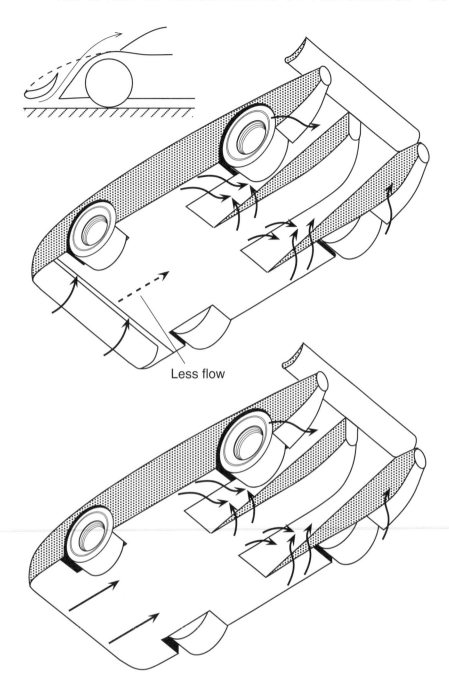

Less flow

lower front clearance cases the flow into the tunnels is obstructed, and they are fed mainly by the airflow from the sides, as shown at the upper part of Fig. 5.29. By nature, this front wing is quite pitch-sensitive since the wing lift is created at the front, and the tunnel center of pressure is located more rearward.

A more traditional design, which is less pitch-sensitive, is described in the lower part of this figure. Here the vehicle nose is raised somewhat to allow sufficient flow to feed the tunnels in the back (which are fed from the sides, as well). This method creates downforce near the vehicle nose, too, but most of the downforce is created over the whole lower surface and near the tunnel entrance; thus the vehicle is less sensitive to small changes in pitch (or loss of front ground clearance).

**Multivehicle
Interactions**

The nature of aerodynamic effects can be quite complicated, especially when more than one vehicle is involved. An interesting aspect is when one of the vehicles is much larger, as in the case of a bus overtaking a small passenger car, or a motorcycle following the fluctuating wake of a large truck (Fig. 2.17). Another important variable would be the effect of side wind, say when one vehicle is passing another which may be larger or smaller than the overtaking vehicle. Since the available data on most of these interactions is very limited, especially when race cars are concerned, the following discussion will focus on two basic maneuvers: passing and drafting of similar vehicles.

The passing condition between two similar-size sedans is shown in Fig. 5.30, with resulting aerodynamic forces plotted in Fig. 5.31. In this case, both vehicles move in a steady speed but vehicle 2 moves faster than vehicle 1. When vehicle 2 is behind vehicle 1 (e.g., at point A, or where Δx is positive in Fig. 5.31) both lift and side force are being increased somewhat by the accelerated flow over vehicle 1 (that is, the local velocity is larger than V_∞). As vehicle 2 moves closer (e.g., its nose is at point B), then the inflow behind the leading car pulls it inside (negative side force) and drag is reduced because of the drafting effect.

Fig. 5-30. *Schematics of the aerodynamic interaction during overtaking.*

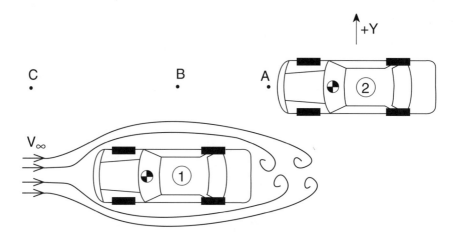

Once vehicle 2 passes vehicle 1, those trends are reversed and lift, drag, and side force increase sharply, probably because of the faster flow created by the presence of the other vehicle. Once the passing vehicle is ahead of vehicle 1 (point C), then the outflow created by vehicle 1 exerts a positive side force, which diminishes with increasing distance. Also the local dip in the lift and drag data, near $\Delta x/L = 0$, is probably a result of the complicated separated-flow region behind the rear window and luggage compartment of these two sedans.

The effect of increasing lateral separation $\Delta y/L$ is to reduce the magnitude of the interaction, as indicated by the three sets of data for each force coefficient (e.g., for lift, drag, and side force). The data is based on 1/10th scale testing of two three-box-type sedans, and the aerodynamics of passing may be different at full scale and for other types of vehicles. Similar data on open-wheel race cars is scarce, if nonexistent, and may be different because the two strong vortices of the rear wing (see Fig. 2.18) may change this behavior. Also, lift variation on a high downforce vehicle may be significant, with the trailing vehicle losing some of its lift due to the disturbed streamlines ahead.

Fig. 5-31. *Generic variations in the lift, drag, and side force of the overtaking vehicle (based on 1/10-scale data).*

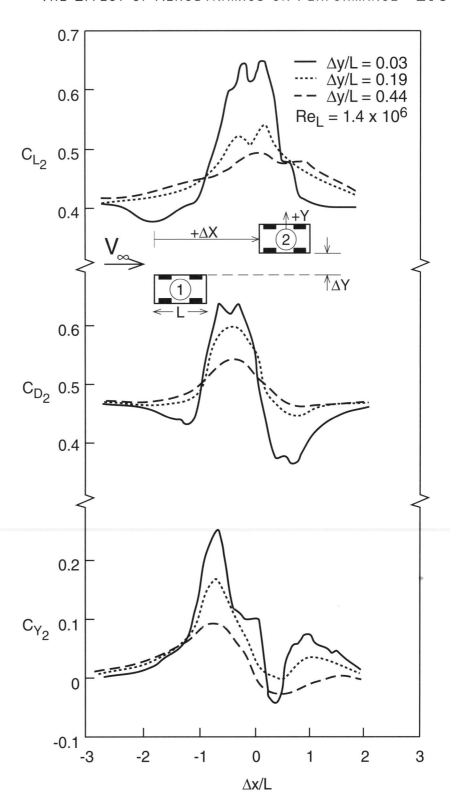

The second interesting aerodynamic interaction between two vehicles occurs when one closely follows the other (drafting). This condition is often seen in high speed (e.g., oval circuit) stock car racing where the drivers utilize the drag benefits of the lead car. Such drafting is depicted by Fig. 5.32. When the following vehicle (No. 2) comes close to the leading vehicle (No. 1), the free-flow streamlines do not impinge (and form a high-pressure stagnation point) on the front of the drafting vehicle, so its drag is expected to be less, as indicated by the data of Fig. 5.33. The flow visualization of two drafting NASCARs is shown in Fig. 5.34, which reinforces the hypothesis of Fig. 5.32.

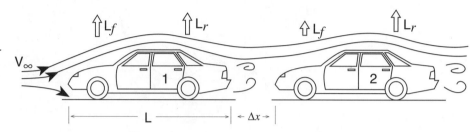

Fig. 5-32. *Schematic description of the aerodynamic interaction during drafting.*

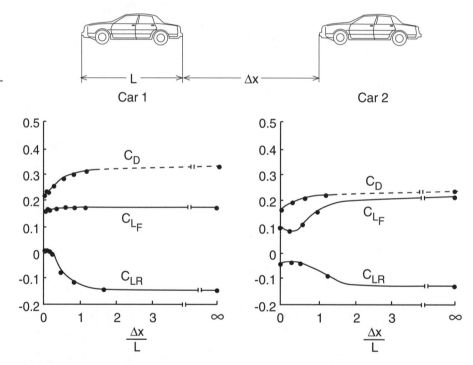

Fig. 5-33. *Lift and drag variation for the two cars during drafting. Reprinted with permission from SAE Paper 710213, Copyright ©1971 SAE, Inc.*

The effect of drafting on lift is a little more complicated, and according to Ref. 5.8 the rear lift of the leading car will be reduced, since the flow does not turn downward behind the rear deck, while the change in its front lift is hardly detectable. Since the following car stays inside the wake, its front lift is reduced, whereas its rear lift increases (less downforce), due to stronger flow separations there. These trends (apart from the rear lift of the leading car) were also recorded on a more recent test of drafting NASCARs reported in Ref. 5.9.

So, based on the terminology adapted in this chapter, the stability of both vehicles is reduced (more oversteer), and the effect is larger for the trailing vehicle. Again, similar data for open-wheel race cars is not available, but the lift of the front wing or the flow into the underbody tunnels of a trailing car are expected to be reduced when a car follows within the wake of another vehicle.

Fig. 5-34. *Visualization of a smoke particle line above two Jackson NASCARs at the Lockheed wind tunnel. There is some indication that the free-stream flow does not impinge on the front grill of the following car, thus reducing its aerodynamic drag. Courtesy of Automotive Aerodynamics, Inc.*

Therefore, most high-downforce race cars (including prototypes) are expected to lose downforce and performance when following another car.

To close the discussion, I will mention one other point relevant to race cars running very close to retaining walls. According to Ref. 5.10, an investigation into the aerodynamics of stock cars, both lift and drag are strongly affected by the proximity to a wall, and the effects are reduced if the wall is inclined. Ref. 5.10 also reports that when the vehicle approaches the wall the resulting side force pushes the vehicle away from the wall.

CONCLUDING REMARKS

The most important conclusion from this chapter is that vehicle dynamics and handling are primarily dictated by the performance of the tires. However, tire performance can be changed considerably by aerodynamic loads. This leads to major increases in cornering speeds and improved braking performance, without an increase in the vehicle's weight (this point was made before, but only in this chapter is it proved). Therefore, vehicle aerodynamics is far more significant than the old concept of drag reduction for improved fuel economy. In fact, proper aerodynamic settings can seriously improve vehicle handling and reduce lap times for a race car, and reducing lap times is the essence of most forms of racing.

REFERENCES

5.1   Ellis, J. R., *Vehicle Dynamics*, London Business Books Ltd., 1969.

5.2   Genta, G., *Meccanica Dell'Autoveicolo*, Libreria Editrice Universitaria Levrotto & Bella, Torino, 1981.

5.3   Pater, A. D., and Pacejka, H. B., *1st Course on Advanced Vehicle Dynamics*, International Center for Transportation Studies, Rome, 1982.

5.4   Gillespie, T. D., *Fundamentals of Vehicle Dynamics*, SAE, Inc., 1992.

5.5   Wong, J. Y., *Theory of Ground Vehicles*, John Wiley and Sons, Inc., 1993.

5.6   Katz, J., "Investigation of Negative Lifting Surfaces Attached to an Open-Wheel Racing Car Configuration," SAE Paper 85-0283, Feb. 1985.

5.7   Kortum, W., and Sharp, R. S., "A Report on the State-of-Affairs on 'Application of Multibody Computer Codes to Vehicle System Dynamics'," *Vehicle System Dynamics*, Vol. 20, No. 3-4, 1991, pp.177–184.

5.8   Romberg, G. F., Chianese, F., and Lajoie, R. G., "Aerodynamics of Race Cars in Drafting and Passing Situations," SAE Paper 71-0213, Feb. 1971.

5.9   Duncan, L.T., "The Effect of Deck Spoilers and Two-Car Interference on the Body Pressures of Race Cars," SAE Paper 94-2520, Dec. 1994.

5.10 Wallis, S. B., and Quinlan, W. J., "A Discussion of Aerodynamic Interference Effects Between a Race Car and a Race Track Retaining Wall (A Wind Tunnel NASCAR Case Study)," SAE Paper 88-0458, Feb. 1988.

6 AERODYNAMICS OF THE COMPLETE VEHICLE

INTRODUCTION

Just as racing success is measured in terms of time, so can the difference between the brilliant and less competent designs be measured by time: The winners are usually those who are the quickest to properly implement a new idea, i.e., by taking fewer iterations to arrive at the right solution. Resources or large budgets are equivalent to time, so a large budget is often exchangeable with wisdom. Given sufficient time, teams with bad designs or lack of support, or both, will eventually reach the right solution—but in the meantime the brilliant (or the over-supported) teams will be working on their next trick. A careful observer of the technological advances in the various forms of motorsport can clearly see the migration of good and bad ideas between the various teams.

This short prologue is aimed at explaining the large number of black-magic tricks that appear as aerodynamic modifications—and why some of the weirdest of all came from the best-supported teams. Because those teams could (and still can) afford the largest number of trial and errors (mostly mistakes) they have seen the winner's circle more often—which does not necessarily mean that they always had the best aerodynamic design.

The preceding chapters focused our attention on the basic disciplines influencing vehicle design and aerodynamics. In this chapter this information will be used to examine both generic body shapes applicable to high-speed vehicle design, and some of the components aimed at improving the aerodynamic performance of various race cars. Later on I will focus on those tricks that did work, and for the sake of brevity will ignore those that did not (e.g., double floors, three wings, with one above the driver, etc.).

In order to simplify this initial discussion, the numerous shapes of race cars are grouped into three generic categories:

- Sedan-based race cars: IMSA GTU, GTO, NASCAR, European Touring, etc. These cars bear strong resemblance in their outer lines to their passenger car sibling, and only minor aerodynamic modifications are allowed. Fig. 6.1 shows one such a vehicle (1993, IMSA GTS Class) with open windows, but no opening doors (which is a widely used concept).
- Enclosed-wheel race cars: IMSA GTP, FISA group C, etc. These vehicles are basically the designer's dream since the body shape is mostly unrestricted. Most leagues allow underbody tunnels (venturis) and complex wing shapes. Fig. 6.2 depicts an example.
- Open-wheel race cars: Indy, Formula 1, 2, etc. These vehicles have four exposed wheels, a narrow body which may have underbody tunnels (Indy cars), and two large wings mounted at the front and rear ends of the vehicle for aerodynamic downforce. These race cars are single seaters while the previous two categories, in principle, must have a wider seating area. Fig. 6.3 shows an example.

Fig. 6-1. A typical production-based race car; the 1992/3 Nissan 300ZX Twin-Turbo (only the exterior resembles, vaguely, the production vehicle). Dennis Ashlock photo.

Fig. 6-2. A typical prototype race car: the 1992 Jaguar XJR-14. Courtesy of TWR USA.

Fig. 6-3. A typical open-wheel race car: 1992 Williams FW14B, Formula One. Richard Dole photo.

The discussion that follows begins with several basic aerodynamic observations relevant to the three vehicle categories. These fluid dynamic phenomena then can be used as building blocks in a hypothetical, conceptual vehicle design. More detailed geometrical concepts aimed at improving vehicle aerodynamics are presented later in the chapter. In general, the sedan-based and prototype race cars have a more promising potential for an efficient aerodynamic design. This is because the aerodynamic components of an open-wheel race car are within the disturbed flow field created by the four large, exposed wheels and their wakes.

BASIC VEHICLE BODY CONCEPTS

The discussion on the effect of aerodynamics on vehicle performance (Chapter 5) clearly indicates that the typical objectives of a good aerodynamic design are 1) to reduce drag, and 2) to increase the downforce (not to mention reduce the sensitivity of the front/rear downforce ratio to pitch, yaw, roll, etc.). With these objectives in mind let us investigate how some very generic changes in a body's geometry can effect its aerodynamic lift and drag. The information found on this topic in the open literature can be further divided into two subcategories. The first group identifies typical flow fields over generic bodies with quite sharp corners, resembling a variety of road vehicles. The second category includes additional generic shapes, more relevant to race cars, which have the potential to generate downforce with reasonably low drag. The following two subsections describe these two groups of generic body shapes.

Flow Field over Generic Ground Vehicles Shapes

Recall the aerodynamic data presented in Chapter 2, Fig. 2.22, on two basic ellipsoid shapes with dimensions reminiscent of the ratios used on road vehicles. The important conclusion to be drawn from this Figure is that both positive and negative lift can be generated by bodies when placed close to the ground. Drag, however, is primarily a result of the blunt rear-end shape, which creates local flow separation, as shown in Fig. 2.3 (note that skin-friction drag is usually small, as indicated in Table 2.4). While the first type of design in Fig. 2.22 will focus on highly streamlined shapes, with minimum rear-end flow separations, flow separations may appear in different locations on vehicles with more angular geometries, and vortex dominated flows can exist on a variety of road

Fig. 6-4. *Typical separated-flow patterns found on some automobile-related shapes.*

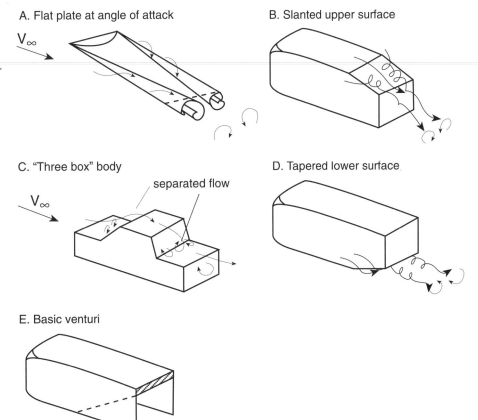

A. Flat plate at angle of attack

B. Slanted upper surface

C. "Three box" body

separated flow

D. Tapered lower surface

E. Basic venturi

vehicles. In order to reintroduce this concept of vortex-dominated flows, let us return to the discussion of a flat-plate lifting surface (described in Chapter 3, and shown again in Fig. 6.4). In this case, a thin, low-aspect-ratio flat plate is placed in a free stream at an angle of attack larger than 10°. The main aspect of this flow field, relevant to the present discussion, is the formation of two concentrated side edge vortices which dominate the nearby flow field. Those two vortices induce a large velocity on the plate (under the vortices), creating strong suction forces which considerably increase the lift of the flat-plate wing.

Interestingly, a similar situation develops when slanting the rear, upper surface of a generic body (Fig. 6.4B). This vortex-dominated flow is present in a slant-angle range of $10° < \theta < 30°$, as indicated by the lift and drag data in Fig. 6.5 (region I). At larger angles θ, the flow over the whole rear base area is separated, as on a typical bluff body.

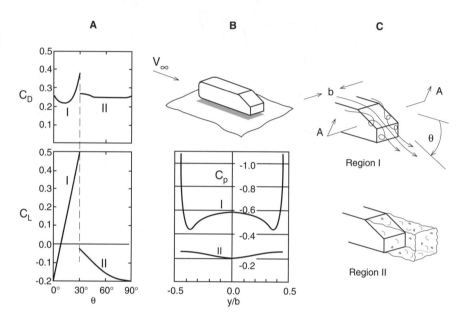

Fig. 6-5. *Drag, lift, and lateral pressure distribution along the sloping rear end (section AA) of the generic body shown in the inset (After Ref. 6.1).*

This fully separated case is indicated as region II, and Fig. 6.5B shows that the corresponding pressure distribution (along a lateral line AA) is evenly distributed. In region I, the two concentrated side vortices attach the flow near the body's longitudinal centerline (Fig. 6.5C), effectively creating a lifting flow. The pressure distribution for this case shows the large negative pressure peaks created by the vortices at the side of the slanted rear surface (Fig. 6.5B, region I) resulting in a force acting normal to the slanted surface (which can be resolved into lift and drag).

As the slant angle is increased from zero, a positive lift will develop, which increases up to $\theta = 30°$. At slant angles larger than 10° the rearward projection of this negative pressure causes quite a large increase in drag, as shown in this Figure. The most interesting feature of this data is that above a critical angle (close to $\theta = 30°$) the vortex structure breaks down and the drag and lift contribution of the slanted surface is much smaller. This fact has an effect on hatchback automobile design, where rear window inclination angle should be more than 35° or less than, say, 25°. Also, note that in this case, the basic body (with θ = 0°) has negative lift due to ground effect, similar to the case with the ellipsoid, shown in Fig. 2.22.

Another typical pattern of flow-separation frequently found on three-box-type sedans is depicted in Fig. 6.4C. In this case a separated bubble, with locally recirculating flow, is observed in the front, at the break point between the bonnet and the windshield. The large angle created between the rear windshield and trunk area results in a second, similar flow-recirculation area. Data on the effect of those parameters on the drag can be found in Ref. 2.6, Chapter 5.

When inverting the body so that now the lower surface of the body is slanted (Fig. 6.4D), a similar trend can be expected. This principle can be utilized for race cars since for moderate angles (usually less than θ = 15°) an increase in the downforce is observed (see also Ref. 2.6, pp. 143–144). However, a far more interesting case is when two side plates are added to create an underbody tunnel, sometimes called venturi (Fig. 6.4E). This geometry can generate very large values of negative lift, with only a moderate increase in drag, as shown in Fig. 6.6 (after Ref. 6.2). Furthermore, the downforce created by this geometry increases with smaller ground clearances (and probably larger values can be obtained by adding skirts along the sides of this particular body).

Fig. 6-6. *Lift and drag variation versus ground clearance for a model with generic underbody tunnel (or venturi), after Ref. 6.2.*

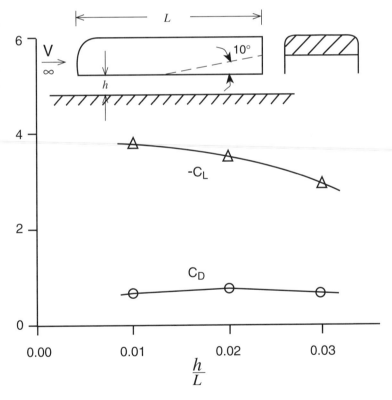

Race Car Oriented Basic Aerodynamic Shapes

The previous section dealt with some aerodynamic features of boxy shapes in ground proximity, whereas in this section the target is to present basic body shapes that can create downforce without creating large drag force. With these earlier basic shapes in mind it is possible to define a limited number of conceptual race car configurations, and some are presented in Fig. 6.7.

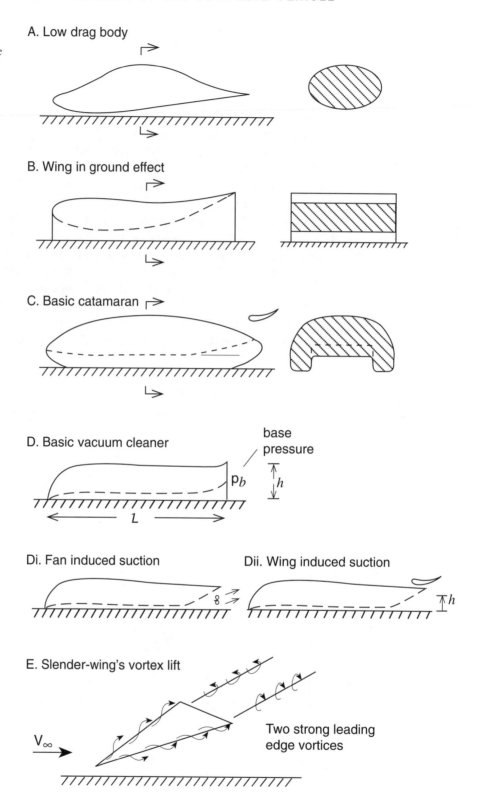

Fig. 6-7. *Several basic conceptual shapes (building blocks) for race car aerodynamic design.*

A. Low drag body

B. Wing in ground effect

C. Basic catamaran

D. Basic vacuum cleaner

base pressure

Di. Fan induced suction

Dii. Wing induced suction

E. Slender-wing's vortex lift

Two strong leading edge vortices

The first generic shape in Fig. 6.7A is aimed at a very low-drag configuration, and such configurations were studied by Morelli, in Ref. 2.4, pp. 70–98. The basic intention is to create a vehicle body with very low drag, and at the same time

BASIC VEHICLE BODY CONCEPTS **185**

to be able to generate lift or downforce with the body. The above cited article indicates that with such configurations, drag coefficient values of less than $C_D = 0.1$ are obtainable, while lift can be varied by slightly pitching the body. The lift coefficient can range from $C_L = 0.25$ at a positive pitch of 6°, down to about $C_L = -0.75$ for a negative pitch of 6°. Such low-drag configurations are usually applicable to speed-record cars that run along long straightaways, without any turns. Such vehicles usually require low levels of downforce, primarily to improve their high-speed stability, and usually do not have additional lifting surfaces (wings). An example is presented in Fig. 6.8, the Oldsmobile Aerotech Aurora V-8, which broke 47 speed-endurance records in December 1992.

Fig. 6-8. *Typical design for high-speed vehicle with low drag (Oldsmobile Aerotech Aurora V-8, that broke 47 speed-endurance records in Dec. 1992).*

On most racing circuits with medium- to high-speed turns, vehicles with high downforce can run faster lap times (see Chapter 5). If an aerodynamicist is asked to recommend a configuration for such a circuit with high downforce and relatively low drag, then very likely his choice will be based on an inverted wing in ground effect, as shown in Fig. 6.7B. (Recall the large increase in the lift or downforce of a wing when placed near the ground—ground effect.) The addition of side fins to seal the airflow from the sides considerably increases the downforce (since the lift of a two-dimensional airfoil is larger than that of a low-span wing).

Applications of this principle were incorporated into the "skirt era" race cars, and an example is shown in Fig. 6.9. In this Lotus 79 F-1 car the lower surface of the side pods resembled an inverted airfoil, while the side skirts (sliding on the road) effectively created the high downforce (more information on this important concept is presented later in this chapter and in Chapter 7).

A more realistic shape that can be related to prototype race cars is the "catamaran" concept (Fig. 6.7C.) The need to cover the wheels at the two sides of

Fig. 6-9. *Schematic description of the inverted airfoil shape of the side pods on the Lotus Type 79. In practice, only the sliding skirts were visible (see Fig. 7.11).*

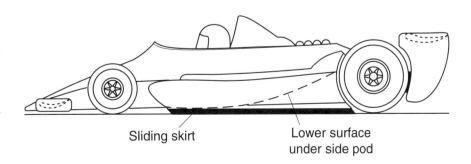

Sliding skirt

Lower surface
under side pod

the vehicle resulted in a shape with a fairly high central tunnel ending with a moderate upward, rear slope (venturi). The ability to channel the momentum of the undisturbed free stream under the car reduces the area of flow separation on the back of the central body, creating an ideal high-downforce and low-drag configuration. Some modern prototype race cars are partially utilizing this principle. As an example, a generic model for such a vehicle is depicted in Fig. 6.10, with which L/D values of over 6 were obtained.

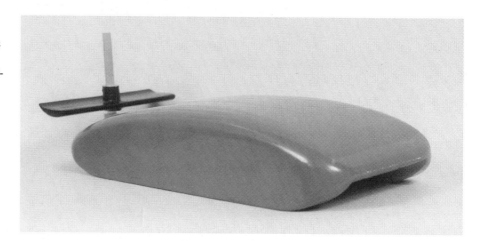

Fig. 6-10. *1/5th scale wind tunnel model of a high lift/drag configuration, based on the catamaran concept. The unusually tall rear wing mount was used to study the effect of wing-body interaction.*

A far more popular concept is the "vacuum cleaner" car (Fig. 6.7D). In this case every effort is made to seal the gap between the front and the two sides of the vehicle and the ground, to minimize or entirely eliminate any airflow there. Because of the flow separation at the base, the base pressure p_b is very low, and by leaving the rear section of the car open so that this pressure prevails under the car, a strong suction force (downforce) is created. The suction force can be increased by a small spoiler, and the lift/drag ratio (due to this pressure) can be fairly well approximated by the length/height ratio (e.g., $L/D \sim L/h$). A logical improvement on this concept is the addition of a fan that on one hand creates vacuum under the car, and on the other hand blows the air out at the base, filling the separated flow bubble behind the car and reducing drag.

This idea was discovered very early, and the Chaparral 2J, shown in Fig. 6.11, was the first race car to utilize this principle. The success of this concept led quickly to the banning of active aerodynamic devices, such as fans or variable

Fig. 6-11. *The first race car to utilize the fan-aided vacuum cleaner concept: the 1969 Chaparral 2J. Illustration by Brian Hatton.*

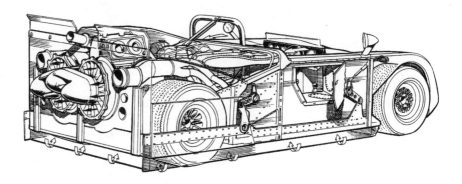

angle wings, on race cars. The remaining alternative is to reduce the base pressure by using a wing, while at the same time reducing the height of the rear bodywork h for drag-saving considerations. The prototype race car shown in Fig. 6.12 can be used as an example for this design philosophy; however, the high rear deck in this case probably resulted in an undesirable increase in drag.

Fig. 6-12. *Example for using the rear wing to reduce the pressure under the vehicle, in order to generate downforce (1992 Chevrolet Intrepid GTP). Richard Dole photo.*

The principle of vortex lift (see Chapter 3) on slender wings can also be used to create downforce. In the particular case depicted in Fig. 6.7E, the inverted delta wing shown can create downforce on the order of $C_L \sim -1.3$ (based on wing surface area) at a negative pitch of about 30°, with a downforce/drag ratio of about 1.7. This principle was tested on a generic open-wheel race car, shown in Fig. 6.13, where the drag of the open wheels reduced the downforce/drag ratio to about 1. One of the disadvantages of this concept is that the side edge vortex-wake of the delta planform considerably reduces the effectiveness of a conventional rear wing when placed behind it, so when using a rear wing, the main delta-wing plane must be set at a much smaller angle of attack. Of course, numerous applications of this principle can be seen in the form of the small dive plates (at an angle of attack) which are attached to the nose or aft sections of many race cars (as shown later).

Fig. 6-13. *Full-scale experimental model of an open-wheel race car using the inverted delta-wing concept.*

AERODYNAMICS OF THE COMPLETE VEHICLE

In the preceding section the influence of the vehicle shape on aerodynamics was investigated; in this section it is assumed that the vehicle geometry has already been fixed. The typical parameters affecting the aerodynamic performance of existing vehicles are usually side-slip angle, body's incidence, and ride height. The effect of these parameters on vehicle aerodynamics will be demonstrated on two types of vehicles: a sports sedan and an open-wheel race car. The aerodynamic coefficients depend strongly on a vehicle's shape, and can change considerably from one configuration to another. Therefore, the following two examples demonstrate the generic trends, but are not necessarily accurate for any particular vehicle.

For the first example, let us examine a generic sports sedan. Its top view is shown in Fig. 6.14 (this data is for a 20% scale model, at $Re_L = 3.0 \times 10^6$, with smooth underbody). The graph depicts the effect of wind side-slip angle β_W on the aerodynamic coefficients. In order to explain the source of these aerody-

Fig. 6-14. Lift, drag, and side force coefficient variation versus side-slip angle, for a generic sports sedan.

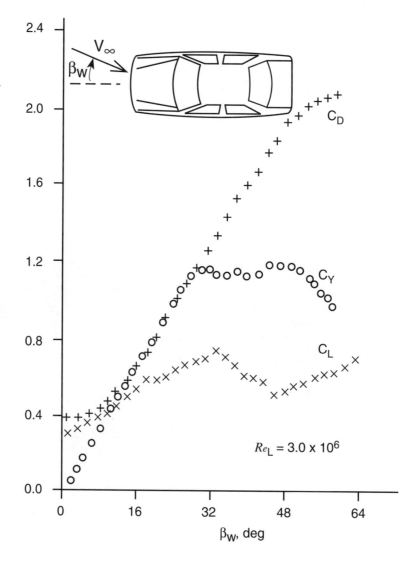

namic loads let us observe the generic flow field depicted in Fig. 6.15. Basically, for the small, near-zero side-slip conditions the flow is attached on the vehicle's sides, and the pressure distribution (from a top view) resembles the pressure distribution on a thick airfoil.

Fig. 6-15. Top view of the flow field at small side-slip angles (attached flow) and for large side-slip angles (separated flow).

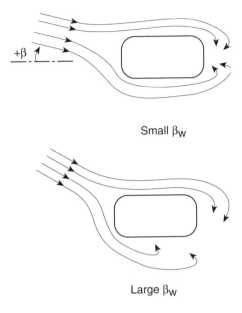

Small β_W

Large β_W

The pressure distribution data of Fig. 6.16 (after SAE paper 73-0232) reinforces this comparison. This analogy to the airfoil case explains the almost linear increase of side force, C_Y, with side-slip angle β_W which eventually stalls at about $\beta_W \sim 25°$ (see also Fig. 5.16).

Returning to Fig. 6.15, you can see that at the larger side-slip angles the flow separates at the side of the vehicle, and when combined with the separation at the back, creates a much larger separation bubble. Because of the low pressure inside this separated zone, and the increase of the frontal area with increasing β_W the drag coefficient increases sharply, as shown in Fig. 6.14. Usually, the larger separation bubble created by the side slip increases the velocity above the vehicle, resulting in a smaller increase in the lift. At very large side-slip angles (of over 35°), the separated area behind the rear window is reduced by the momentum of the side flow, causing a reversal of this trend in the lift (e.g., a local reduction in the lift).

Another important parameter that has a strong aerodynamic influence is the incidence of the complete vehicle. This effect is demonstrated in Fig. 6.17. Most vehicles will react to a change in their attitude in a manner similar to wings, that is, the lift will increase with increased angle of attack. The lift slope is very large for this particular vehicle, which has a smooth underbody, but in principle, for most road vehicles the pitch sensitivity is clearly noticeable and follows the same trends presented in Fig. 5.28. The drag coefficient usually increases slightly when the vehicle's lower surface angle is changed from zero, due to possible increase in the boundary layer thickness.

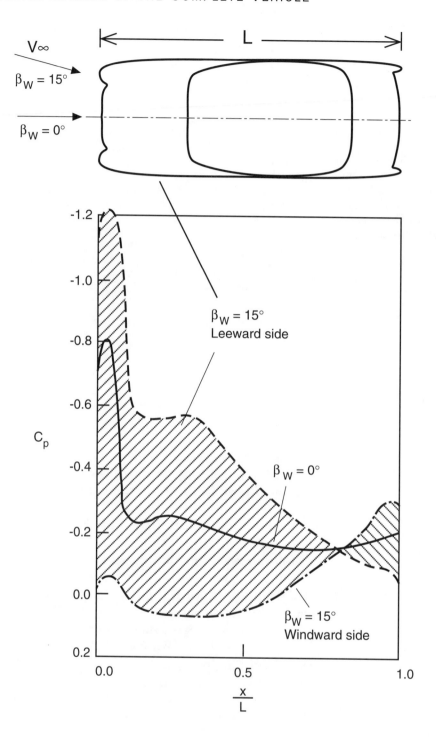

Fig. 6-16. Top view of the pressure distribution on the sides of a vehicle (along a horizontal line above the wheels), at $\beta_W = 0$, and at $\beta_W = 15°$. Reprinted with permission from SAE paper 730232, Copyright ©1973 SAE, Inc.

The effect of ground proximity was shown to have a strong influence on the aerodynamic coefficients of generic bodies (Fig. 2.22). For enclosed-wheel vehicles, with reasonably clean underbody flow, drag and lift usually decreases with decreasing ground clearance, as shown in Fig. 6.18 (see also Fig. 3.38). The increase in the downforce can be attributed to the higher speeds under the car, with decreased ground clearance, as shown in Fig. 2.22 (for the ellipsoid). The drag reduction in automobile shapes with major rear flow separations is

Fig. 6-17. *Lift and drag coefficient versus angle of attack for a generic sedan (based on 1/5-scale wind tunnel test and model with smooth underbody and fixed ground plane).*

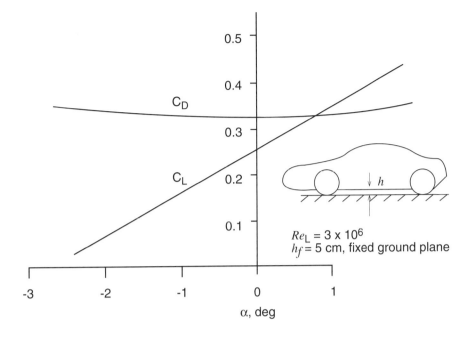

$Re_L = 3 \times 10^6$
$h_f = 5$ cm, fixed ground plane

Fig. 6-18. *Lift and drag coefficient increments as a function of ground clearance (based on 1/5-scale wind tunnel test and model with smooth underbody and fixed ground plane).*

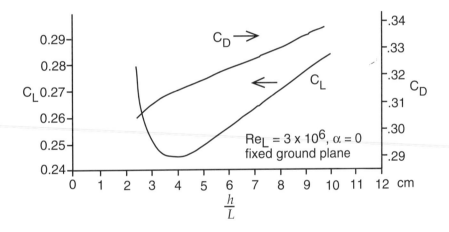

$Re_L = 3 \times 10^6$, $\alpha = 0$
fixed ground plane

partially a result of this faster airstream emerging from under the vehicle, which reduces the size of the rear flow separation.

Another effect that causes this trend is the reduction in the frontal exposed area of the wheels (as they slide into the body), which decreases drag with the reduced ground clearance. In regard to lift, the interesting observation is that the trend (that less ground clearance equals less drag and less lift) is reversed at a certain small distance. This is a result of the viscous effects (thick boundary layer) of the too-small ground clearance blocking the flow between the road and the vehicle underpanel. Thus, in this case of very small ground clearance the flow resembles the case of the semi-ellipsoid and not that of the ellipsoid (Fig. 2.22). In Fig. 6.18 the critical distance for the lift reversal is close to 3.5 cm, but for full-scale race cars with smooth underbody, moving on the track, this distance can be as small as 0–5 cm.

Similar data for race cars is sparse in the open literature. Therefore, the following set of data presented for an open-wheel, flat-bottom race car (which was collected from the scattered data in various publications) is not representative of all race car configurations. In the case shown in Fig. 6.19 for a flat-bottom car, the drag increases with side slip, too, but since the flow is not blocked between the wheels, the increase in the separation areas is far less than in the case of the sports sedan (Fig. 6.14).

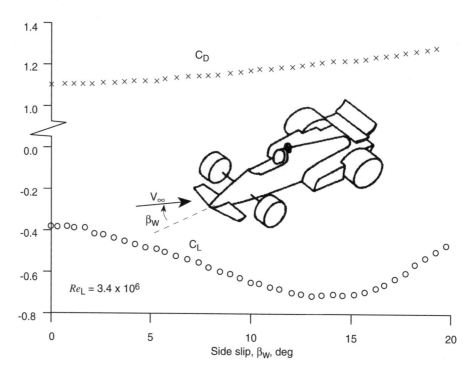

Fig. 6-19. Lift and drag coefficient variation versus side-slip angle, for a generic open-wheel race car. Reprinted with permission from SAE paper 850283, Copyright 1985 SAE, Inc.

The lift for this vehicle, without side fins, is actually reduced with increased side-slip angle. This is probably a result of the increased flow rate under the vehicle, which is boosted by the flow coming from the side. The importance of this data is in indicating that for such vehicles the effect of side slip is not very large. (For open-wheel race cars with underbody tunnels and large side fins on the rear wing, the downforce is slightly reduced with increased side slip. Because of the reduced downforce the drag may decrease, resulting in behavior opposite to that shown in Fig. 6.19.)

The effect of pitch and ground clearance was obtained from a different source (Ref. 6.3—an open-wheel race car with underbody tunnels) and the first effect, shown in Fig. 6.20, is similar to the data of Fig. 6.17. Because of the low ground clearance of this vehicle, for incidence of less than –1°, the viscous effects block the underbody flow and stop the increase in downforce (usually a small negative incidence is desirable to compensate for the boundary layer growth, but such that no part of the body will be too close to the ground). Note that this is an early ground effect vehicle (circa 1980) with side skirts.

The effect of ride height in Fig. 6.21 is similar to the previously presented data. That is, the ground effect will increase the downforce with reduced clearance, until a critical limit is obtained. Usually, a race car with underbody tunnels can be lowered more than a car with a flat bottom. Therefore, the

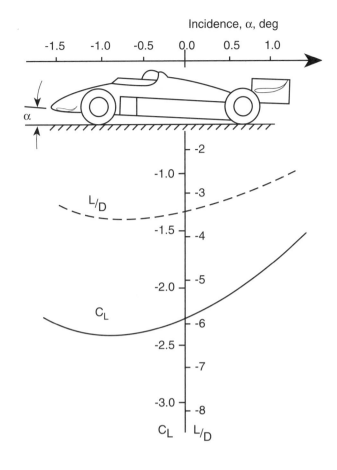

Fig. 6-20. *Lift and drag coefficient versus body's angle of attack for a generic open-wheel race car with underbody tunnels (after Ref 6.3).*

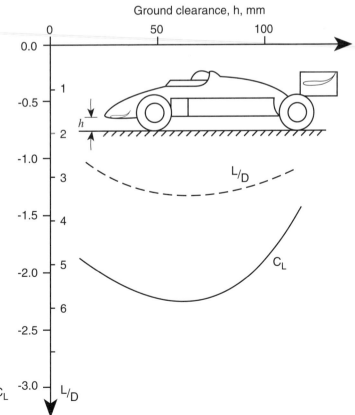

Fig. 6-21. *Lift and drag coefficient increments as a function of ground clearance for a generic open-wheel race car with underbody tunnels (after Ref 6.3).*

ground clearance limit for the former is probably near 0–5 cms, while for the latter, near 0–10 cms.

The important conclusion to be drawn from these two figures is that downforce reaches a maximum level at a certain ground clearance (which depends on vehicle pitch, as well). Also, note that the C_L scale on Fig. 6.20 and 6.21 was changed compared to the scale in Ref. 6.3. This was done since the original data was reduced by using the planview area (of 7.53 m^2) and not the frontal area (of 1.68 m^2), which is the practice followed in this text.

FLOW OVER WHEELS

The wheels are one of the most influential components affecting vehicle aerodynamics (particularly for open-wheel race cars); this is why the discussion on vehicle components begins with this topic. The flow over wheels was mentioned briefly in Chapter 3 in regards to the effect of wheel rotation, wheel placement in the wind tunnel, and the Reynolds number on wheel lift and drag. Thus, one of the most important aspects of wheel aerodynamics is understanding the influence of the above effects on the aerodynamic coefficients of a complete vehicle. This can often help explain differences between wind tunnel results based on reduced-scale, simplified models (e.g., with nonrotating wheels) and actual race track data. In this section, however, the features of the flow over isolated wheels is revisited (assuming that the reader is familiar with Chapter 3), primarily to show the large separated flow regions, created by isolated wheels, which dominate the aerodynamics of open-wheel race cars.

First, consider the simple flow over a cylinder. The smoke traces of the streamlines in this case are shown in Fig. 6.22. The streamlines separate behind the body, creating a long periodic wake, filled with alternating vortices (see also Fig. 2.17). When the cylinder is placed against a ground plane (which is basically what a wheel on the road is), the periodic wake shedding is somewhat reduced, but the large region of separated flow is still present. Also, the presence of the ground forces a zero speed condition near the tire's contact patch, which will create lift on the cylinder/wheel. The primary reason for presenting this generic flow visualization is to emphasize that the separated flow caused by open wheels may generate periodic wakes that can affect other parts of the vehicle, and that open wheels will have positive lift.

The next step is to observe the flow over actual wheels. As shown in Fig. 6.23, the nature of the flow does not change much from that shown in Fig. 6.22, but the location of the separation point is more representative of race car wheels. The effect of rotation on the location of the frontal (upper) separation point is emphasized by this figure. In a stationary wheel the separation seems to be behind the wheel's highest point (near $\theta \sim 160°$; see definition of θ in Fig. 6.24). However, for the rotating wheel, the upper separation point moves forward, as shown in the figure.

The effect of this behavior on the pressure coefficient is described in Fig. 6.24 (based on results of Refs. 6.4 and 6.5). For a rotating wheel, the forward separation point causes a close-to-constant pressure distribution behind this point, which translates to drag and lift. When this point moves backward (for a nonrotating wheel), then the pressure coefficient becomes more negative on the upper surface (due to higher speed resulting from the locally attached

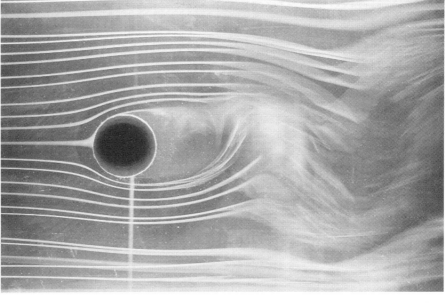

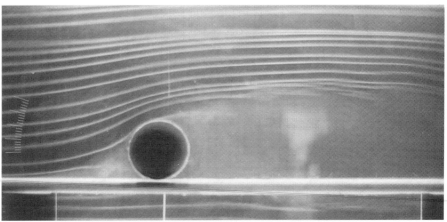

Fig. 6-22. Visualization of the flow over a cylinder in a free steam (top), and on a cylinder near the ground (bottom). Reynolds No. = 0.2 x 10^6.

Fig. 6-23. Visualization of the flow on a rotating (left) and stationary (right) wheel. Reynolds No. = 0.53 x 10^6. After Ref. 6.4, Copyright ©1977 AIAA, Reprinted with permission.

flow), causing more lift, while the additional negative pressure behind the wheel causes more drag. So based on these observations, it is expected that rotating wheels will have lower lift and drag coefficients than stationary wheels

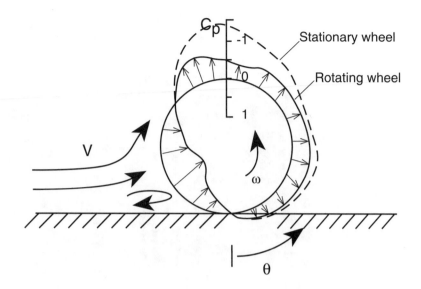

Fig. 6-24. *Schematic description of the centerline pressure distribution on a stationary and a rotating isolated wheel.*

(an observation which is supported by the experimental result presented in Table 6.1). Note that ahead of the wheel, near the front stagnation point, a high-pressure area exists, which can be seen as a small flow recirculation area in the lower frame in Fig. 6.22. Mounting a plate near this area, ahead of the wheel and parallel to the ground, can pick up this high pressure on its upper surface, and one may use it to create downforce (see later Fig. 6.49).

Because of the large separated flow regions on such isolated wheels, large deviations can be expected in the available experimental data on their total aerodynamic coefficients. These deviations can be a result of the Reynolds number effect (see Fig. 3.42), different tread pattern, or wheel width to diameter ratios. As an example, some of the typical results found in the open literature are summarized in Table 6.1:

**Table 6.1 Sample Lift and Drag Coefficient Values
for an Isolated Open Wheel**

Width/Diameter	C_D	C_L	Re Number	Ref.
0.28	0.180 (0.272)	0.579 (0.593)	1.1×10^6	3.9
0.50	0.40 (0.95)	0.65 (0.75)	0.2×10^6	6.5
0.612	0.48 (0.76)	0.56 (0.77)	5.3×10^5	6.4
0.658	0.32	0.60	5.3×10^5	6.4

Values are as reported in the literature. Coefficients are based on wheel frontal area, and the numbers in parentheses are for nonrotating wheels; otherwise the wheels rotate at zero slip.

The flow field near wheels enclosed by various types of body work can be very complicated. However one aspect of this interaction, shown in Fig. 6.25, is fairly typical to most enclosed-wheel vehicles. Usually the tire drives the air flow between the wheel and the wheel well in the manner indicated in the figure. This flow pattern can be used to channel cooling flow, or to move flow from the bottom of the car in order to generate additional downforce.

Fig. 6-25. *Schematic description of the flow induced by a wheel rotating inside the front fender.*

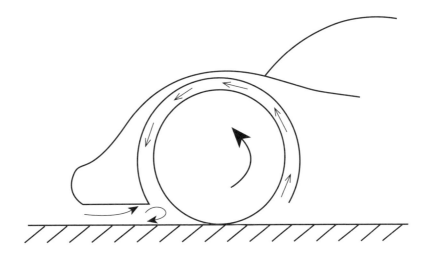

Based on the above information it is clear that the drag of the wheels can dominate the drag coefficient of an open-wheel race car, and when not covered properly can create large drag on enclosed-wheel cars, as well. Therefore, many efforts have been made to reduce the aerodynamic drag of wheels and some of them are listed in the following paragraphs.

One of the most logical solutions would be to cover the wheels inside a streamlined body, a method which is used by many land-speed-record vehicles. Even a streamlined fender can provide some visible drag reduction results. Of course this is not allowed in most forms of open-wheel racing, and then only a limited number of add-ons can be used. For example, a smooth rim cover (hubcup) can reduce wheel drag by about 16% (Ref. 3.9), and many Indy cars use smooth outer rims on the high-speed tracks, because of this reason.

Reduction of the drag on a bluff body can be obtained by injecting the momentum of the free stream into this area, thereby reducing the area of flow separation. Various baffles and turning vanes can be used for this purpose, and some of them are shown in Fig. 6.26 and 6.27.

Fig. 6-26. *Flow deflector mounted behind the front wheel of a 1986 Zakspeed F-1 race car (note the small horizontal plate, mounted exactly under the rearview mirror, to comply with "flat bottom" regulations).*

Fig. 6-27. Deflector plates, used between the front wheels and the cooling intakes (with a potential to reduce wheel drag, and improve cooling intake flow). Part B of the Figure shows that an addition of a horizontal plate under the higher pressure region can also generate some downforce.

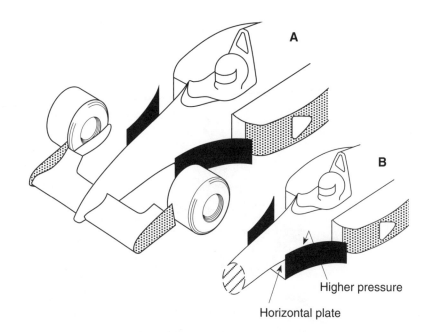

The first type on the 1986 Zakspeed is a simple effort to turn the flow, with the main objective to reduce front wheel drag. A larger turning plate of this kind was used during and after the 1993 season in F-1 (Fig. 6.27) and in this case the longer plate serves to direct the flow into the cooling inlets as well. When these side plates are held by a horizontal plate, then some downforce increments also can be gained. This is a result of the higher pressure created near the cooling inlet, above the horizontal plate. The high pressure is formed near the concave curvature of the body (as explained in Fig. 2.14 and 2.15) and also by the cooling inflow slowing down ahead of the inlets.

The second device, shown in Fig. 6.28, is an effort to channel the high-speed flow from under the front wing into the lower separated flow area behind and under the wheel, in an effort to reduce the wheel's drag. In this latter case the end plate of the front wing is extended so that it also serves to block the disturbances originating at the rotating wheel, which may reduce the efficiency of the front wing (operating in extreme ground effect).

Fig. 6-28. Extended end plate on the front wing of a 1993 Indy car.

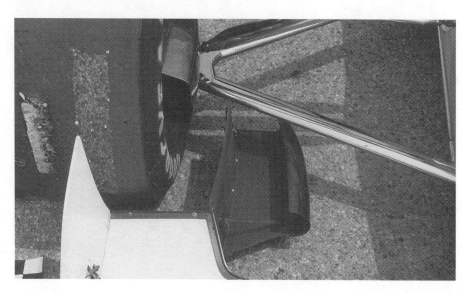

Another effect that can be achieved by such devices is a better positioning of the front-wing-tip vortices, so that they won't interfere with the cooling intakes in the side pods. Such devices can reduce the vehicle's drag, but when they obscure the flow of the front-wing-tip vortex, the interaction may send this strong vortex to numerous undesirable locations, such as cooling intakes, or even the rear wing (where a loss in rear downforce may result). This high sensitivity to proper positioning, and some of its unpredictable aspects, probably caused the ban of this device in F-1 at the middle of the 1994 racing season.

Because of the limited body work allowed near the rear wheels of open-wheel race cars, shielding efforts are very limited. A typical example of the bodywork near the rear wheel of an Indy car is shown in Fig. 6.29. Here the diagonal plate not only creates some downforce, but also partially directs the flow above the wheel in order to somewhat reduce its drag. The lower horizontal plate is influenced by the high pressure prevailing near the forward lower region of the tire, and contributes to the vehicle downforce.

Finally, the rotation of the wheels, and especially the rims, can be used for various aerodynamic chores. A properly shaped rim can serve as an excellent air pump, which can suck the flow from under the car, while at the same time provide cooling flow for the brakes. Unfortunately, most racing regulations do not allow the exploitation of such wheel-rim-driven devices.

Fig. 6-29. *Typical body work near the rear tire of an Indy car (1993 Lola).*

Sliding Seals and Skirts

One of the points made about the generic shapes presented in Fig. 6.7 was that some of the shapes benefit by sealing the gap between the vehicle body and the ground. Two body concepts, the inverted wing and the vacuum cleaner, using such seals were incorporated into actual race car designs in the past. The seals used were either flexible or rigid (sliding up and down) and they were called by the generic name "skirts." The most obvious and first application of such seals was found on vacuum cleaner cars such as the Chaparral 2J (Fig. 6.11, and 7.6) or the Brabham BT46B (Fig. 7.7), which used flexible seals to prevent the airflow from penetrating the low pressure area under the car. These two concepts did not last long because regulations eliminated this type of downforce generation method.

A far more successful, and fairly long-lived, skirted car period in race car evolution began when the basic inverted airfoil concept was rediscovered. It is clear to any aerospace engineering student that such a configuration can generate very large lift/drag ratios, as long as the flow is kept close to being two-dimensional (see Eq. 4.7). Such a two-dimensional flow is created when the end plates at the two tips of the airfoil are very large, compared to the airfoil itself, and the seal between the end plates and the ground is perfect. However, leaving even a small gap between the ground and this side plate will allow the air to flow from outside, under the airfoil, creating a three-dimensional flow, resulting in less lift and more drag.

Another small detail worth paying attention to is the fact that the center of pressure of an airfoil is close to its forward part (see Chapter 4). Since most of the downforce is needed in the back, utilization of this principle should be applied to parts of the body placed more toward the rear (e.g., the side pods and not the nose, as depicted in Fig. 6.30). Also, in this case the rear wing was placed low to create low pressure near the exit of the underbody flow, which enhances this flow (note the importance of the wing/body interaction in addition to the individual downforce of the rear wing).

The first car to be designed with this concept in mind was the Lotus Type 78 F-1 car (Fig. 7.9) that raced in the 1977 season. The basic idea was to use the side pods as inverted airfoils, as depicted in Fig. 6.30. The sides of the car had to be sealed by the skirts as shown, and because of the very low pressures created under the car, the seals had to be rigid (they were actually sliding on the ground with a vertical degree of freedom, to allow for suspension movements and road irregularities).

Fig. 6-30. Sliding skirts used to seal the side flow on the inverted airfoil-like side pod of the late 1970s Formula One cars.

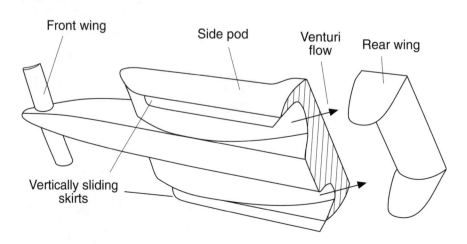

The sensitivity of this configuration to a gap between the skirt and the road is illustrated by two different sets of data (Fig. 6.31 after Ref. 6.3, and Fig. 6.32 after Ref. 6.6). The first Figure clearly illustrates the sudden reduction in downforce when a gap between the skirt and the road is created. Fig. 6.32 describes the effect of this gap on the pressure coefficient at the car's lower surface (possibly center of side pod), which again indicates the large variations with any slight increase in the skirt-to-road clearance.

The skirted ground-effect race cars (both open- and enclosed-wheel type) of the late 1970s and early 1980s were based on the above principles and generated very large values of down force ($C_L \sim -2.6$ for an F-1 car, according to Ref. 2.6, p. 285), which led to the tremendous increase in lateral accelerations (see later Fig. 7.14) and also to a considerable increase in suspension stiffness. This was not only a result of the much increased vertical load on the suspension but also due to the limited suspension travel dictated by the moving skirts. These constraints led to quite uncomfortable cars from the driver's point of view. Also, the possibility of a failure in the skirts' sealing ability (say due to a bump in the road) could lead to a severely unsafe situation.

As a result of the above concerns the skirts were banned in most forms of racing by 1983. To demonstrate these positive and negative virtues two supporting photographs are presented. Fig. 6.33, for example, shows the 1979 Ligier negotiating a high-speed turn with perfectly sealing skirts. Vehicle roll is quite limited and clearly the seals work well on both sides. On the other hand, this small incident that happened to the side skirt of the 1979 Arrows in

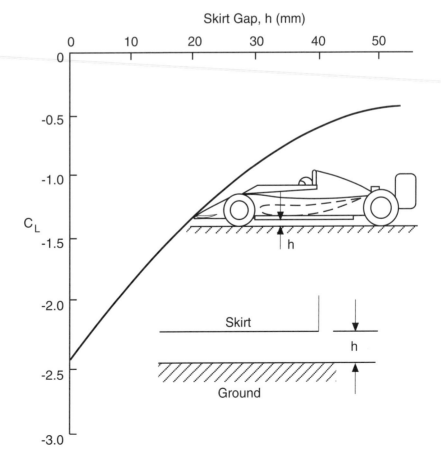

Fig. 6-31. *Effect of side skirt gap on the downforce of a late 1970s open-wheel race car (after Ref. 6.3).*

Fig. 6-32. Effect of side skirt gap on the pressure distribution under the side pod of a late 1970s, open-wheel race car (after Ref. 6.6). Due to standard Italian practice of not showing numerical values on the ordinates of figures appearing in the open literature, the author has inserted the pressure coefficient values on this figure, based on his own speculations.

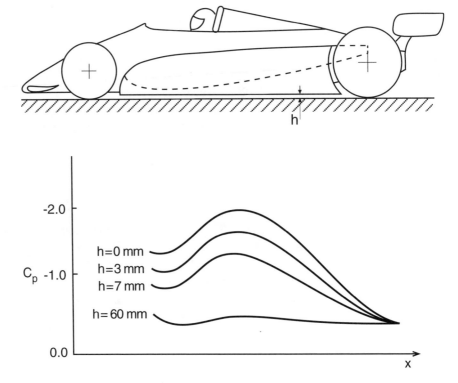

Fig. 6-33. Ground effect at work while cornering at high speed. This photo shows clearly the extended skirts of the Ligier F-1 car sealing perfectly during the 1979 Argentinian GP. (Incidentally, the Ligier driven by Jacques Laffite won that race). Phipps Photographic.

Fig. 6.34 indicates the danger of a stuck skirt. This malfunction clearly reduces downforce, and if it occurs suddenly during a turn, then the unplanned maneuver can be quite dangerous!

Interestingly enough, banning this concept did not end the high aerodynamic downforce era, but rather led to underbody tunnels, which were incorporated even onto the flat-bottom cars. Those cars were supposedly less sensitive to ground clearance and the basic concept is described in the next section.

Application of the sliding side skirt principle (after banning their use on the side pods) to seal the sides of an inverted airfoil was used on the front wings of many open-wheel race cars, as shown in Fig. 6.35. For this application, the flexible skirts were mounted on the end plates of the front wing. The use of such skirts extended into the early 1990s.

Fig. 6-34. *Typical example of a sliding seal malfunction. This photo shows the 1979 Arrows with the front end of its skirt stuck in the Up position. Phipps Photographic.*

Fig. 6-35. *Flexible skirts on the front wing (under the side fin) of an open-wheel race car.*

UNDERBODY CHANNELS (VENTURIS)

The earlier discussion about the flow over generic vehicle shapes indicates that by properly channeling the flow under the car, significant levels of downforce can be obtained. This idea is best demonstrated by the basic concept of an airfoil in ground effect (Fig. 6.7B), which has the potential to generate very large values of downforce with relatively low drag penalties. Since the bodywork of most vehicles should leave a reasonable ground clearance (minimum requirements vary from 5–10 cm and up) and heavy components such as the gearbox need to be placed as low as possible, the lower surface of some race cars will have longitudinal, slanted underbody channels (instead of a neat inverted airfoil shape). The size of these channels is usually limited by racing regulations. Typical examples on an open-wheel and on an enclosed-wheel race car are shown in Fig. 6.36.

Because of the low pressure created inside these channels, the flow from the sides of the vehicle (in between the front and rear wheels) enters the channels from the sides, creating strong concentrated vortices as shown in the Figure. The vortices in turn keep the flow attached inside the tunnels, and actually stabilize the underbody flow. Therefore, the tunnel edges (especially the outer

Fig. 6-36. *Typical underbody channels on two types of race cars.*

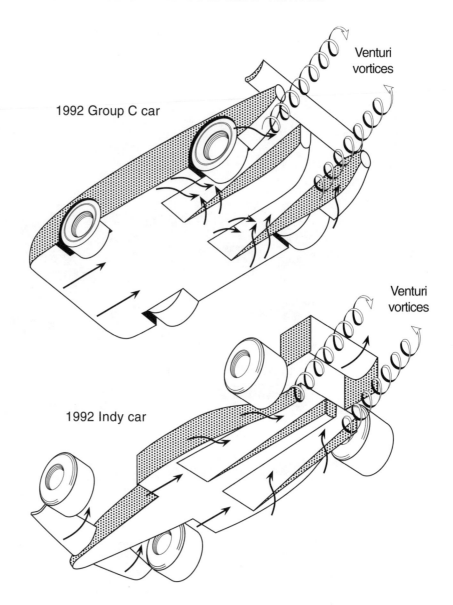

Venturi vortices

1992 Group C car

Venturi vortices

1992 Indy car

ones) should be kept sharp to increase the rolled vortex strength (similar to the vortex pattern of slender wings in Chapter 4). Also, in most cases a closely mounted rear wing is needed to help pump the flow under these vehicles.

At this point it's worth clarifying some terms. In many circles the above described channels are called *underbody tunnels*, *diffusers*, or most frequently *venturis*. The origin of the latter term was related in Chapter 2, where I mentioned that the underbody tunnels do not exactly resemble a venturi tube. Here, let us speculate about possible similarities between the underbody flow and the venturi flow, as shown in Fig. 6.37.

The left-hand side of this figure shows the lower surface pressure distribution along the centerline of a generic body (after Ref. 6.2), while the right-hand side shows the pressure distribution along the centerline of a venturi tube. The converging part of the venturi tube increases the flow speed, and hence is called the *nozzle*, while the diverging section, which reduces flow speed, is called the *diffuser*. There is clearly some similarity between the two pressure distributions even though the venturi flow is internal (inside tubes). Also, in

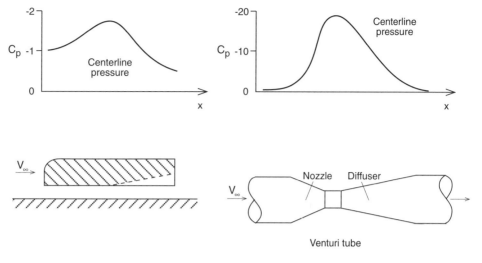

Fig. 6-37. *Pressure distribution along the centerlines of a generic body with slanted lower surface, near the ground, and along a venturi tube.*

both cases the lowest pressure is obtained at the narrowest flow passage, which in a ground vehicle can be utilized to generate downforce. So, in conclusion, we will accept the terms *underbody channel/tunnel*, *diffuser*, or *venturi* as synonymous.

The following figures will demonstrate the actual effect of underbody channels on the pressure distribution for a variety of vehicle shapes. Fig. 6.38 de-

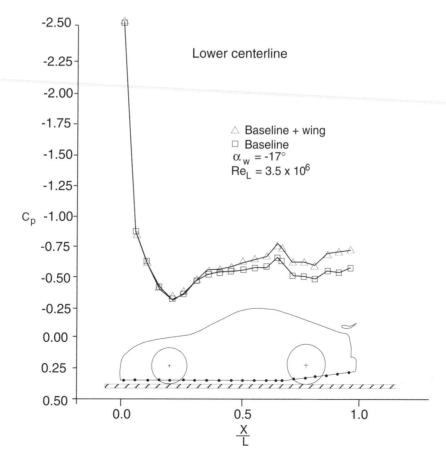

Fig. 6-38. *Effect of rear wing on a vehicle's slanted lower surface, centerline pressure distribution (wing height above rear deck = 0.75c). Reprinted with permission from Ref. 2.7.*

picts the case of a passenger car-based racer with a smooth underbody. In this case the use of indented tunnels was not allowed, but a slightly slanted-up lower surface created a small venturi. The small suction peak at the entrance to this venturi, at about $X/L = 0.6$, is clearly an indication to the downforce generated by the lower surface. This figure also indicates the strong effect of a rear wing on this type of flow. In this case the wing-induced low pressure under the car almost doubles the downforce (Ref. 2.7, and later Fig. 6.67).

The effect of this rear slant on the drag and rear lift of a generic sedan is presented in Fig. 6.39. Lift at the rear axle is clearly reduced with increasing slant angle. Drag is reduced up to a slant angle of 4°, above which it increases again (probably due to the side vortex effect described by Fig. 6.4D).

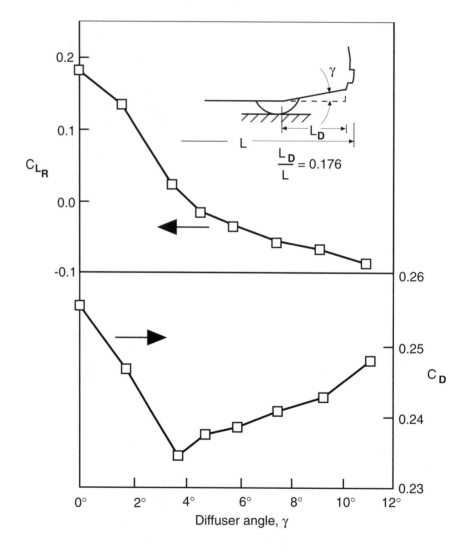

Fig. 6-39. *Effect of rear diffuser angle on drag and rear axle lift (data points based on results from Ref. 2.6, p. 144).*

The method of generating downforce by underbody tunnels seems to work for almost any type of vehicle. In the case of Fig. 6.40 the pressure distribution along the channel centerline is depicted and the suction peak at the channel entrance is similar in nature to the one shown in Fig. 6.38, but now the magni-

Fig. 6-40. Effect of tunnel angle on the tunnel centerline pressure distribution for a generic prototype race car. Reprinted with permission from Ref. 2.9.

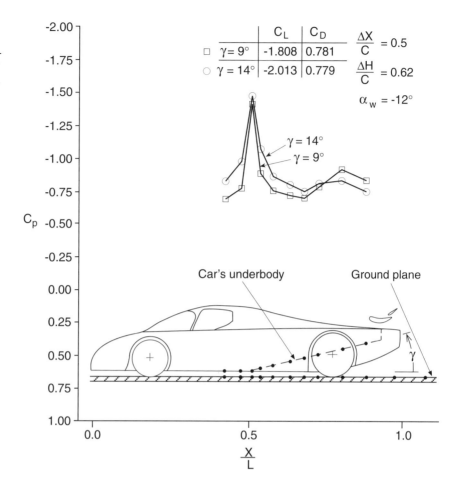

tude of the peak is larger. This figure also demonstrates that for larger slant angles (γ) at the channel, more suction and more downforce can be created (within practical limits).

The same phenomenon appears on open-wheel race cars, and even without the help of the side skirts large suction values can be obtained. This is shown in Fig. 6.41. Again, note the difference in the lower surface pressure distribution for the wing-on and wing-off cases. This clearly demonstrates that most rear wings can be used to augment the flow under the car to increase the body's contribution to the downforce. Further experimentations, aimed at improving the effectiveness of the underbody tunnels, have shown that the insertion of flat plates or turning vanes can improve their performance. Fig. 6.36 indicates that most tunnels are fed initially by strong lateral flows, which leads us to think that by proper placement of the turning vanes, the underbody flow can be increased (of course along the same lines, a misaligned vane can hurt the flow as well). As a result, most of these plates are mounted only after careful development in the wind tunnel. A typical arrangement on the rear diffuser of a prototype race car with two sets of turning vanes is shown in Fig. 6.42 (the actual car is shown later in Fig. 6.78).

Fig. 6-41. *Effect of rear wing on an open-wheel race car's underbody pressure distribution, along the tunnel centerline (1987 March Indy car). Reprinted with permission from SAE paper 890600, Copyright ©1989 SAE, Inc.*

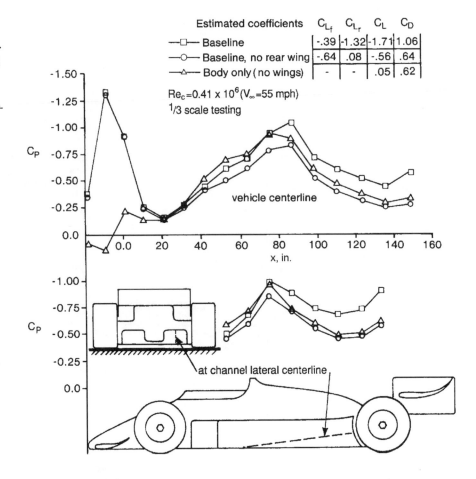

Estimated coefficients	C_{L_f}	C_{L_r}	C_L	C_D
Baseline	-.39	-1.32	-1.71	1.06
Baseline, no rear wing	-.64	.08	-.56	.64
Body only (no wings)	-	-	.05	.62

$Re_c = 0.41 \times 10^6 (V_\infty = 55 \text{ mph})$
1/3 scale testing

vehicle centerline

at channel lateral centerline

Fig. 6-42. *Underbody panel of a 1992 IMSA prototype racer (Toyota). Note the large and small turning vanes in the entrance of each tunnel.*

SIMPLE ADD-ONS: SPOILERS, STRAKES, AND WICKERS

Under this category we can include simple devices that alter the aerodynamic balance of existing vehicles. For example, spoilers made of simple sheet metal clearly qualify, whereas rear wings which must be based on well-matched airfoil sections do not, and therefore are discussed elsewhere. Also, since these devices are added onto existing vehicles, their use is quite popular on passenger-car based sports cars and racers.

The first and most popular device is the spoiler, which can be used on the front or rear of the car. In the former case it is often called a front underbody dam. In passenger cars, the underbody flow is disturbed by the various driveline and plumbing components hanging from the body. By diverting some of the underbody flow, spoilers can actually reduce the vehicle's drag. Furthermore, the pressure behind the dam is lower, and this can help cooling flow across a front-mounted radiator, and at the same time the front lift is reduced as well.

Fig. 6.43 shows the performance of a typical front spoiler for a generic passenger car. The figure indicates that both lift and drag initially improve with increased spoiler height. When the height becomes larger than about 100 mm, the drag increases and the effectiveness of the device is reduced.

Fig. 6-43. Effect of front spoiler height on the lift and drag coefficients of a generic sedan automobile. Reprinted with permission from SAE paper 770389, Copyright ©1977 SAE, Inc. (Ref. 6.7).

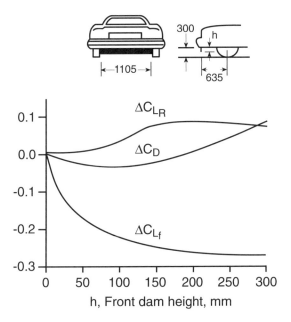

The addition of a front spoiler to race cars with a smooth underbody (primarily based on sedan shapes), usually results in increased drag, but at the same time long front dams can create the vacuum cleaner effect shown in Fig. 6.7D, which increases downforce.

Another very popular and interesting device is the rear-deck spoiler, shown in Fig. 6.44. Its performance depends on rear-deck geometry, and in many cases the separated flow area on the rear window can be reduced, resulting in a drag reduction. The general effect of a rear-mounted spoiler is to elevate the rear stagnation line (or point) and create more downforce. In fact, a well-placed rear spoiler can increase the flow under the vehicle, and the magnitude of the downforce versus spoiler's length is shown in this figure. The low base pressure behind this device increases the drag, and for the longer spoilers the drag increment due to such a rear spoiler is quite visible. For certain race car shapes the height of a spoiler is limited, so its inclination angle becomes more important. Such data is presented in Fig. 6.45 for a sedan-based racer. Clearly, both downforce and drag increase with increased spoiler angle. A large body of data on both the front and rear spoilers can be found in Ref. 2.6, pp. 166–176.

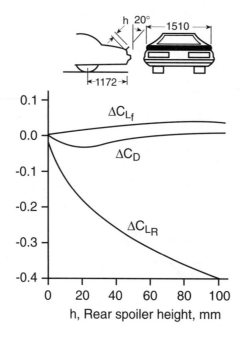

Fig. 6-44. *Effect of rear spoiler height on the lift and drag coefficients of a generic sedan automobile. Reprinted with permission from SAE paper 770389, Copyright ©1977 SAE, Inc. (Ref. 6.7).*

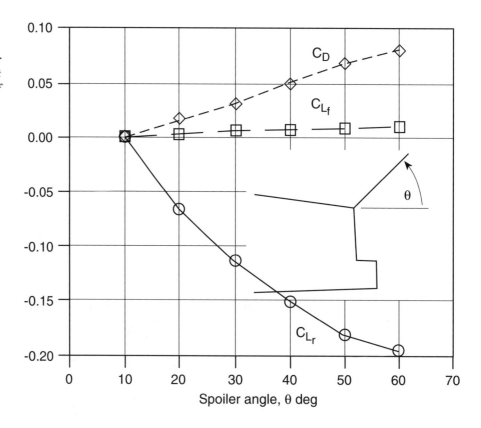

Fig. 6-45. *Effect of rear spoiler angle on the lift and drag coefficients of a sedan-based race car (after Ref. 6.8).*

The vortex lift created by flat plates at an angle of attack was introduced in Chapter 4 (Fig. 4.27–4.30), and in this chapter (Fig. 6.7E). Such flat plates, when placed close to the free stream, are very effective; their lift can be estimated by Eq. 4.11 and their drag in terms of the lift can be approximated as $D = L/\tan\alpha$ (from Eq. 4.12). Typical mounting locations are shown in Fig. 6.46.

Fig. 6-46. Typical application of small, flat-plate downforce devices, used on various race cars.

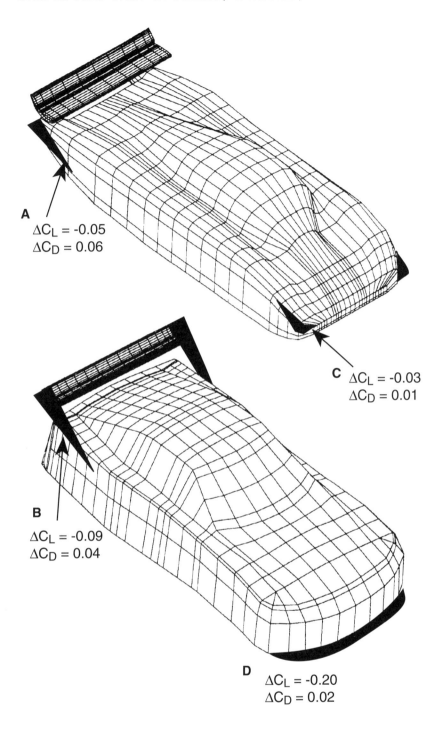

A
$\Delta C_L = -0.05$
$\Delta C_D = 0.06$

C $\Delta C_L = -0.03$
$\Delta C_D = 0.01$

B
$\Delta C_L = -0.09$
$\Delta C_D = 0.04$

D $\Delta C_L = -0.20$
$\Delta C_D = 0.02$

The first case (A) depicts a strake mounted at the back of a prototype race car, where the increment in downforce (for strakes at both sides) is close to the value of Eq. 4.11. However, in this case the base pressure is strongly affected and the drag increase is very large. A more efficient placing is shown on a passenger-based racer (B), where the strake interacts with the rear-mounted wing, and the incremental lift/drag ratio is much better.

Such strakes can also be mounted at the front of a vehicle (called *dive plates*), and in the case of cars without front wings, can be used to trim the front/rear downforce ratio (C). A mutation of this approach is when the plate is mounted horizontally (D), creating only a small drag increment. If the stagnation point is above this plate, then the high pressure above it will create downforce, and by controlling the length of the plate, the front/rear downforce ratio can be controlled. It must be pointed out that such a device may not work for vehicles with a highly streamlined nose section. Also, the initial effect of this plate is close to the values shown in the figure, but too-long splitter plates usually tend to increase drag, only without additional (to the values shown in the figure) downforce benefits.

When listing simple, effective (and cheap) devices, wickers added on the trailing edges of wings, sometimes called *Gurney flaps*, should be mentioned. The effectiveness of these trailing edge flaps was demonstrated for an Indy car wing in Chapter 4 (Fig. 4.40). The schematic flow field near such a flap is shown in Fig. 6.47. The small vortex formed behind the flap, usually helps to turn the streamlines so that the suction side boundary layer (lower side in this figure) becomes thinner, apparently increasing the wing's effective camber (more circulation in aerodynamic jargon).

Fig. 6-47. *Schematic description of the streamlines in the vicinity of a wing's trailing edge with a normal flap.*

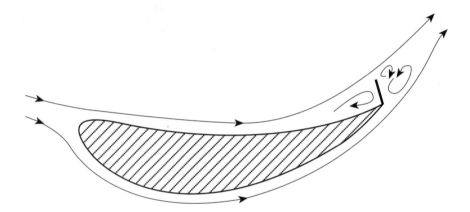

Contrary to the multi-element, small aspect-ratio wing in Fig. 4.40, the data presented in Fig. 6.48 is for a single-element, high aspect ratio wing mounted on the rear of a sports car-based racer. When varying the height of the flap, a very short extension will have a noticeable effect on lift, with a small increase in drag. In fact, when the wing is partially separated without such a flap, drag can be reduced by adding one to the wing trailing edge. Extending the length of those flaps beyond 20 mm usually will not increase downforce, but will increase drag, and is therefore not recommended.

The idea of mounting a horizontal plate under a high-pressure stagnation zone was raised earlier and again in Fig. 6.46D. The most tempting aspect of these devices is the impression that because of their horizontal placement their contribution to drag is negligible (which may not always be the case). Fig. 6.49 depicts two areas on a 1993 F-1 car where similar horizontal flat plates are used. The application in front of the rear tire was discussed before, but the plate behind the front axle is unique to such open-wheel race cars. The insets in this Figure depict the higher pressure (+) prevailing above the plate and the lower pressure (–) under the plate. Also, the device shown in Fig. 6.27B may partially belong to this group, since in that case, too, the high pressure above the plate was created by the body's curvature.

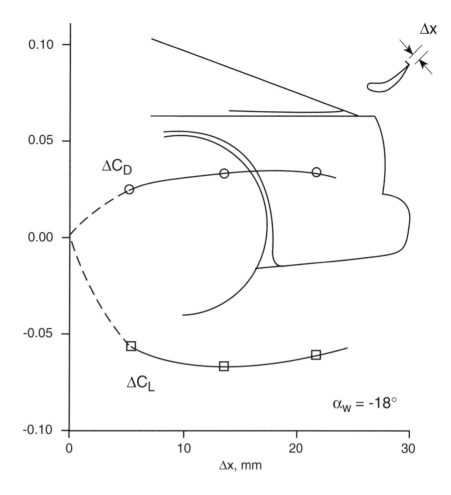

Fig. 6-48. *Effect of 90° flap length on the lift and drag increments of a sedan-based race car.*

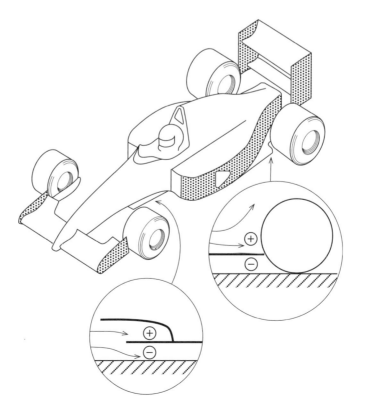

Fig. 6-49. *Typical location of horizontal, downforce-generating flat plates on open-wheel race cars.*

INTERNAL FLOW

Fluid flow-related problems in road vehicles are not limited to external flows. They have a strong influence on vehicle cooling system shape, induction air intakes, interior ventilation, and even on engine intake, exhaust manifold, and cylinder head design. From the engineering point of view, some of these problems are highly complex since they involve viscous flow effects such as boundary layers and flow separation, which may be complicated by the possible effects of heat transfer. In this section, an effort is made to demonstrate some of the features of such internal flows by using some simple examples.

The most common internal flow system, found on most race cars, is a cooling system that transfers the heat rejected by internal radiators to the external flow. Such a system is shown in Fig. 6.50. In the upper part of the figure, the free-stream flow enters the vehicle through its nose intake. The incoming stream is slowed down by a short duct (diffuser), then passes through the heat exchanger, and is ejected outside into a low-pressure area (behind the front wheels). There are numerous other arrangements of various cooling systems, but most of them will have the elements depicted in Fig. 6.50B.

The static pressure coefficient variation along this schematic cooling system is shown in Fig. 6.50C. The primary function of the diffuser is to slow down the

Fig. 6-50. *Basic elements of a typical cooling system.*

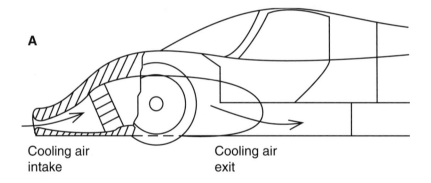

Cooling air intake

Cooling air exit

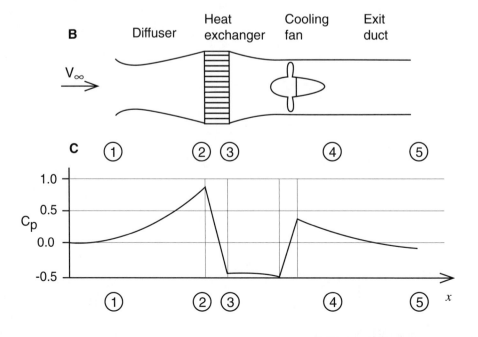

incoming flow and increase the static pressure ahead of the heat exchanger (recall the Bernoulli Eq. 2.5). As the flow passes through the heat exchanger, the static pressure drops due to the heating and friction effects inside the radiator core. In most automotive systems a cooling fan is included which creates the pressure jump that drives the flow through the system. In the absence of such a cooling fan, the exits must be placed in an area of sufficiently low static pressure (e.g., where $C_p \sim -0.5$), so that the pressure difference between the two ends of the cooling duct will drive the flow across. In most race cars, a cooling fan is not allowed by regulations and the cooling of the various components must rely on the above principle. The primary drawback is that the pressure difference between the two ends of the cooling system is a function of the vehicle speed, and at zero speed the cooling is zero, too (as many drivers of enclosed cockpit cars have noticed while sitting in the pits).

The addition of a cooling installation usually results in an increase in the external drag of a vehicle (see Eq. 3.10 and Fig. 3.47). The range of this increase for a variety of passenger cars is depicted by Fig. 6.51 and Fig. 6.52. The data in the first figure were generated for passenger car shapes by blocking the cooling inlets and measuring the drag of the vehicle with and without the cooling flow. Even though such data on race cars is limited, the data in these two figures depicts the range of expected drag increment ΔC_D due to the cooling installation. The important conclusion from Fig. 6.51 is that the worst system may increase the drag by $\Delta C_D \sim 0.07$, but with a good system, cooling drag close to zero is also possible.

This fact of very low or even negative cooling drag is known to airplane designers. By proper design of the cooling ducts and by using the added momen-

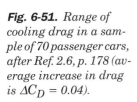

Fig. 6-51. *Range of cooling drag in a sample of 70 passenger cars, after Ref. 2.6, p. 178 (average increase in drag is* $\Delta C_D = 0.04$).

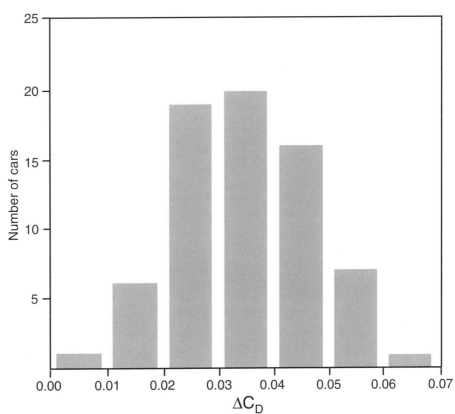

tum of the heated air, the total installation drag can be reduced to a value close to zero (or even negative, at least in principle). Fig. 6.52 shows the drag increments in various ducting arrangements as measured on passenger cars. The important conclusion here is that a positioning of the inlet or exit ducts with their axis normal to the free stream (as in side or top intakes/exits) does not necessarily guarantee lower cooling drag.

Matching the various components of the cooling system with each other and with the external flow is probably more important than optimizing the performance of any one component (e.g., using a better radiator). In many occasions, repositioning of an exit in a lower pressure area can have a larger effect than increasing inlet or cooler sizes.

As an example, for matching the components let us investigate the performance of the inlet in Fig. 6.53. Let us assume that the race car with this inlet is properly designed for a certain speed. The streamlines entering the cooling system at that speed are shown at the center of the figure. The remarks in the

Fig. 6-52. Various cooling system arrangements and the associated cooling drag. Note that V_R is the cooling air velocity ahead of the heat exchanger, which is considerably lower than the free-stream speed, V_∞. Reprinted with permission from SAE paper 810185, Copyright 1981 SAE, Inc.

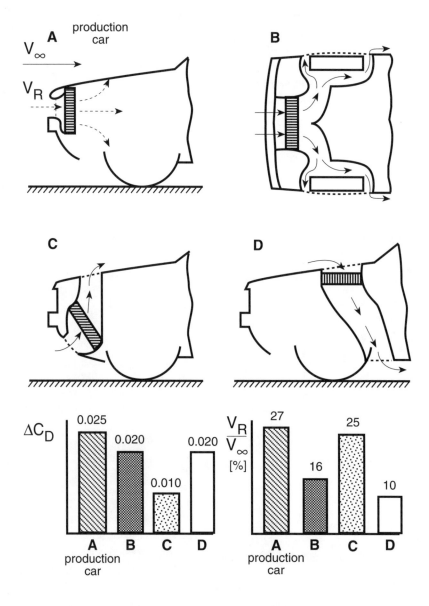

Fig. 6-53. *Effect of speed on the flow near the intake of a cooling system.*

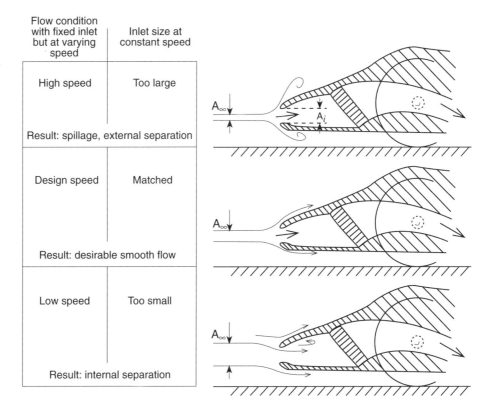

Flow condition with fixed inlet but at varying speed	Inlet size at constant speed
High speed	Too large
Result: spillage, external separation	
Design speed	Matched
Result: desirable smooth flow	
Low speed	Too small
Result: internal separation	

left column describe the conditions faced by the vehicle when moving above or under the design speed. At higher speed the inlet (with area A_i) will be too large and only a small fraction of the incoming streamlines can enter the intake. This results in a spillage, or some local outer flow separations (note that at higher speed the flow through the radiator increases too, but because of the larger heat transfer and friction in the heater cores, the increase is less than in the external flow). This condition usually increases the local boundary layer thickness and can cause earlier flow separation on outer parts (usually toward the back) of the vehicle, resulting in an indirect drag increase.

An even worse condition appears at speeds lower than the design speed. In this case the capture area A_∞ is larger than the inlet area A_i and the flow must accelerate ahead of the inlet to meet the cooling requirements. This is possible in cases when a cooling fan is used, but in a race car without a cooling fan the cooling will be less than designed. Additionally, the converging streamlines at the intake lip may separate inside the internal diffuser, further reducing the effectiveness of the installation. It must be noted that engine cooling requirements will increase with speed, and usually the cooling system is designed for maximum speed conditions in hopes that at lower speed the cooling needs will drop faster than the cooling ability of the system. Also, in most effective designs some external diffusion is used, that is, the capture area A_∞ is somewhat smaller than the inlet area A_i.

The above flow conditions can be related directly to inlet size (at constant speed) instead of a fixed inlet at three different speeds. Thus, the inlet shown at the top of Fig. 6.53 is oversized, and the external flow separation adds to vehicle drag. If, however, the inlet is too small, as depicted at the lower part, then inner flow separation is likely—reducing cooling system performance.

In spite of the sensitivity to inlet size, the cooling intake is probably the most neglected element on a race car in terms of proper aerodynamic design. A proper design should be based on the integration of both external and internal parts (diffuser), and this process resembles in many aspects an airfoil design (but is more complicated because of the three-dimensional inlet geometry). Most of the information appearing in the literature concentrates either on the internal flow (e.g., Ref. 2.6, Chapter 9) or on the external flow, because of the complexity. Therefore, the sample data presented in the following figures depict the type of information available on the external and internal performance of various intakes (for a more advanced design, a designer probably should use some of the now available three-dimensional computational methods).

The most common intake location is at the front of the vehicle, near the front stagnation point, where the pressure coefficient value can be close to $C_p = +1.0$. Another type of cooling inlet is sometimes used for brake cooling, induction air, or ventilation air inlets, and must be mounted in less attractive locations. A large variety of such inlets were tested by Ref. 6.9, and one of them is shown in Fig. 6.54. A typical raised airscoop will have a streamlined top view and must be elevated above the boundary layer near the wall. The internal diffuser must be well matched with the external flow, and in order to avoid internal flow separations, some internal guide vanes must be used. Typical drag increments due to such an installation are in the range of $\Delta C_D \sim 0.12$–0.30, based on the scoop frontal area.

Another common intake is the flush-mounted NACA duct depicted in Fig. 6.55. (see Refs. 6.10 and 6.11 for additional experimental data on the performance of these inlets). The drag penalty of such an intake is usually very small, but for proper operation it usually must be mounted at the front of the vehicle where the boundary layer is still very thin.

Fig. 6-54. *Typical raised cooling intake with internal turning vanes ($\Delta C_D \sim 0.12$– 0.30, based on scoop frontal area!).*

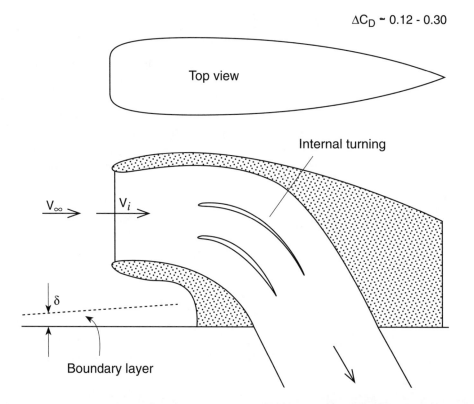

$\Delta C_D \sim 0.12 - 0.30$

Top view

Internal turning

V_∞ V_i

δ

Boundary layer

Fig. 6-55. *Typical submerged NACA duct (intake).*

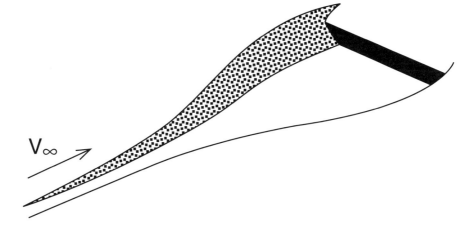

The typical total pressure recovery behind such inlets is shown in Fig. 6.56. In principle, if the flow moves through the inlet without any friction losses, then the coefficient $(p_{tot} - p_\infty)/\frac{1}{2}\rho V_\infty^2$ is equal to 1.0. However as the inlet speed V_i (an average speed at the inlet) is increased, the friction losses increase due to the inner boundary layer and internal flow separations. Incidentally, with the use of Eq. 3.6 it can be shown that this velocity ratio is the inverse of the inlet area ratio shown in Fig. 6.53 (that is: $V_i/V_\infty = A_\infty/A_i$). Fig. 6.56 also indicates that the submerged NACA duct is usually less efficient at the higher inlet flow rates, when compared to the raised air scoop, because of the boundary layer ahead of the inlet.

The performance of the internal part of the intake, the diffuser, is very sensitive to external flow conditions and to internal geometry. A large body of data

Fig. 6-56. *Total pressure recovery of typical inlets.*

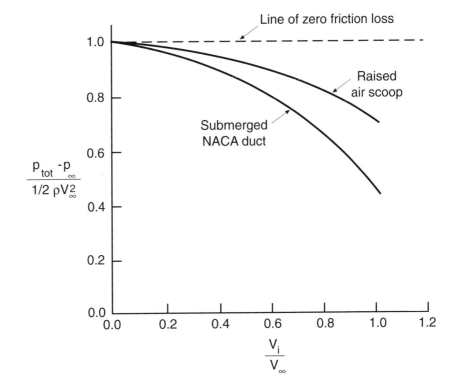

on simple diffuser shapes are presented in Ref. 6.12. Fig. 6.57 is an example for the performance of a two-dimensional diffuser. The length/width ratio of a proper design must fall in the region under the line limiting the range of internal stall, as shown in the Figure. The interesting observation here is that shorter diffusers can have larger diffuser angles θ, but angles larger than 15° cannot be used, according to this diagram. Also, the addition of splitter vanes (shown in the inset) can usually improve the performance of a diffuser which operates near the borderline of stall.

Fig. 6-57. Performance limits (due to internal stall) of straight, two-dimensional diffusers (based on data from Ref. 6.12, p. 274).

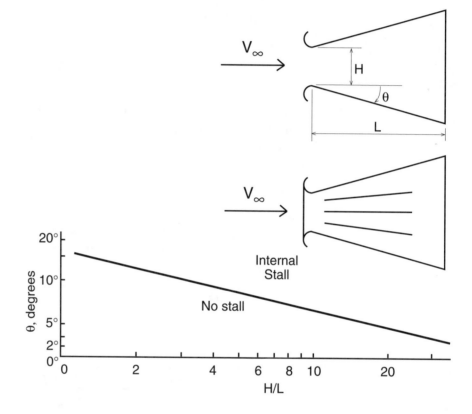

Performance data similar to that presented above for the inlets can be found for a variety of exits (see Ref. 2.20, Chapter 9). Those exits usually should be placed in a low-pressure coefficient area to increase the pressure drop across the cooling system. The possible increment (negative) in the pressure coefficient due to such devices, along with the drag increase (based on their exposed frontal area) is shown in Fig. 6.58. Most of these devices will increase the boundary layer thickness behind them, increasing the likelihood of flow separation on the surface they have been attached to.

The above examples indicate that the integration of the cooling system into the overall vehicle design is very important and even small miscalculations can lead to considerable drag increments. It is possible, however, to use some of the momentum left in the cooling air and eject it into areas of massive flow separation, which exist behind most vehicles. This idea was tested on a sedan in Ref. 2.3, and measurable drag benefits were reported. A possible implementation of this approach for a Formula One vehicle is to locate the cooling flow exit at the back where the flow is separated anyway. See Fig. 6.59.

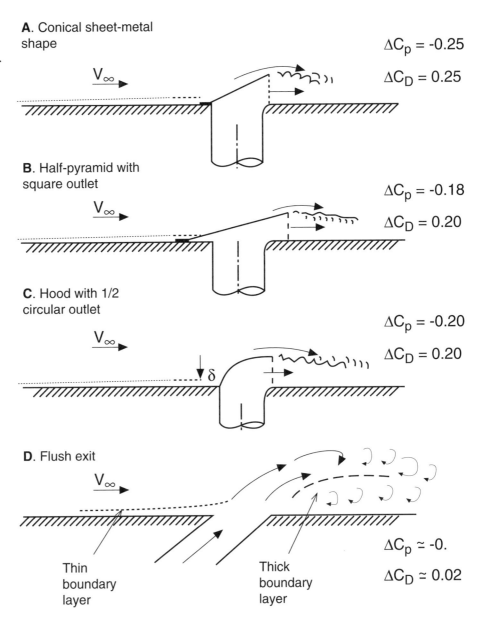

Fig. 6-58. Variety of cooling-flow exits, their drag increment, and typical pressure coefficient values at the exit plane (C_D is based on exposed frontal area).

A. Conical sheet-metal shape

$\Delta C_p = -0.25$

$\Delta C_D = 0.25$

B. Half-pyramid with square outlet

$\Delta C_p = -0.18$

$\Delta C_D = 0.20$

C. Hood with 1/2 circular outlet

$\Delta C_p = -0.20$

$\Delta C_D = 0.20$

D. Flush exit

$\Delta C_p \simeq -0.$

$\Delta C_D \simeq 0.02$

Thin boundary layer

Thick boundary layer

Not only is the rear separation zone filled with the cooling flow (less drag), but the low pressure at the back can also increase the cooling system mass-flow rate. Continuing with the ideas about system integration (from the aerodynamic point of view), one should think about the waste of the residual momentum left in the engine exhaust gases. One application which is seen on many race cars is to use the higher speed exhaust jet to increase the flow inside the venturis, under the car (shown at point B, in Fig. 6.59). The effect of the faster jet on a slower airstream can be utilized by the ejector concept, described schematically in Fig. 6.60.

Here the high-speed internal jet mixes with the outer flow and increases its speed. The additional momentum can delay flow separation, as in the case of point B in Fig. 6.59, or it can even be used to augment an airfoil's lift, as shown in Fig. 6.61 (say, for the lower rear wing of an F-1 car). This super-circulation

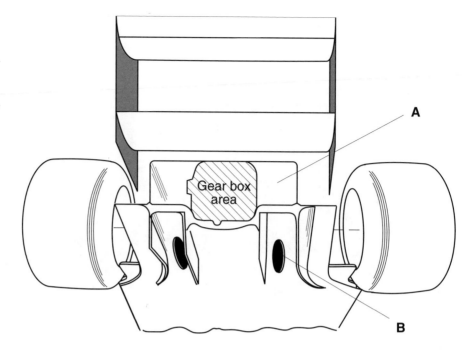

Fig. 6-59. *Exit of the cooling flow into a separated region behind the vehicle (A), and use of the exhaust flow to augment the flow in the rear venturi (B).*

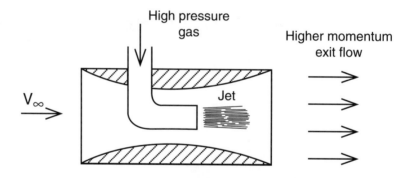

Fig. 6-60. *A typical ejector using a high-speed jet to move a larger airstream.*

effect due to an injection of a faster jet at the trailing edge of an airfoil was described briefly in Chapter 4 (Fig. 4.32). One major problem with this use of the exhaust gases is that lift may be reduced unexpectedly when the accelerator pedal is released, which may explain why this idea has not been used yet. However, in cases when the rear wing size is limited by regulations, using a super-circulating wing, with low levels of blowing (even at the dynamic pressure level), can lead to measurable benefits.

Finally, there are many other internal flow-related problems, such as internal cooling and ventilation, deposition of dust from the road and water from the rain, etc. As closing remarks for this section the following two examples are presented, due to their importance to several forms of auto racing. The first is the open window effect, shown in Fig. 6.62, which typically increases the drag due to internal flow recirculation. The increment for the sedan due to opening its four windows is much larger than for the 1991 IMSA GTO race car, which did not have windows (recall regulations). In this latter case the effect of the open window was obtained by closing smoothly the window openings on both sides.

Fig. 6-61. *Use of high-energy jet to augment the downforce of the rear wing.*

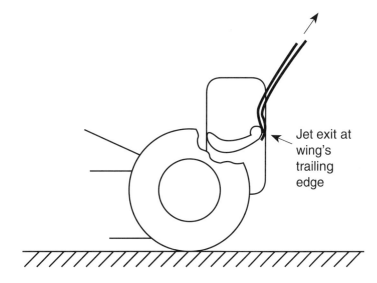

Jet exit at wing's trailing edge

Fig. 6-62. *Effect of open windows and open cockpits on vehicle aero-dynamic coefficients.*

			ΔC_D	ΔC_L	Ref.
Effect of open window	Sedan	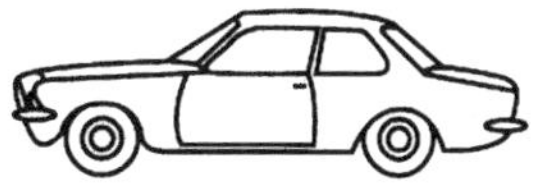	0.067	N/A	2.3
	Group B race car	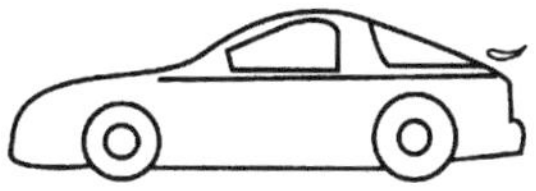	0.025	0.005	
Effect of top	Convertible sports car		0.09	N/A	2.6, P. 194
	Group C race car	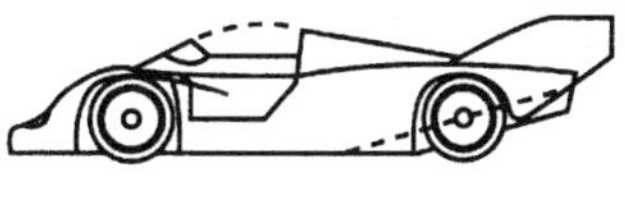	0.05	0.05-0.10	1/5 scale experiment
Effect of venturi			0.05	0.6	

Another frequently asked question is the drag increment between an open and an enclosed cockpit car, as depicted by the last two examples in Fig. 6.62. The increase in the drag of the convertible sports car is a result of the flow separation behind the windshield, due to the increased pressure caused by internal recirculation, and by the flow impinging on the aft section of the passenger compartment. In the open-top race car, the drag penalty is less than for the convertible because of the more careful treatment of the cockpit aft section. In this 1/5-scale wind tunnel test the flow recirculation, in the case of the open cockpit, increased the lift coefficient of the car by 0.05 to 0.10, depending on ride height and body incidence. Incidentally, the objective of this particular test was to evaluate the effect of changing IMSA prototype cars into the WSC type in 1994. The WSC formula required a flat underbody, and the effects of closing the underbody tunnels (shown by the broken line) was to increase the lift coefficient by about 0.6 and the drag coefficient by 0.05 (and the increase in drag was probably a result of the largely increased base area).

RACE CAR WINGS

The first question that comes to mind when reading the title of this section is: Why cover wings again, especially when Chapter 4 was devoted entirely to the same topic? The simple answer is that Chapter 4 dealt with the traditional point of view on wings, which is based on data accumulated in designing airplane wings. However, a race car wing, in addition to its airplane wing-type properties, has some quite different aspects. Those differences can be summarized briefly as:

- The interaction of a race car wing with other body components is very important; in fact, the downforce induced by the presence of a wing on the body can be as large as the downforce of the wing itself. Furthermore, the interaction changes the shape of the pressure distribution on the wing, and designs which were perfected without taking into account this interaction may not work well on the vehicle.

- Some race car wings have a very small aspect ratio, particularly the rear wings of open-wheel race cars. The interesting observation is that the pressure distribution along the airfoil shape is entirely different from the two-dimensional one, which was usually borrowed from an airplane-type design. The second aspect of the low-aspect-ratio feature is the delayed stall, which means that the angle of attack of such wings can be increased more than expected, without facing a sudden loss of lift.

- Some race car wings operate in extreme ground effect, meaning that their downforce is considerably larger than the downforce of the same wing when placed far above the ground. This can lead to sudden changes in downforce during suspension motion, a factor that can alter the car's handling. Also, a too-low front wing can divert the airflow from going under the portion of the vehicle body immediately behind the wing. This may reduce the effectiveness of underbody tunnels or other ground effect devices.

Additional, but less important, differences are the fact that race car wings are designed for a single operation point, contrary to airplane wings which face a large range of operation in terms of speed, angle of attack, and flap deflections. So, from the aerodynamic design point of view, a race car wing design should be easier to accomplish. Its worth noting, too, that Reynolds number effects become important in race car aerodynamics only when significant speed variations exist along a certain track (e.g., in drag racing) or when small-scale wind-tunnel tests are used to simulate the flow field on the actual vehicle. Thus, quite often, in such small-scale tests the wing chord-based Reynolds number is close to (or less than) 0.2×10^6, and wing performance will be strongly affected by this low Reynolds number (see Fig. 3.41 and discussion).

Some of the above points were mentioned earlier, especially in Chapter 3, and therefore the following sub-sections will focus on aspects of wing aerodynamics that are unique to automotive and race car applications.

Wing Placement and Interaction with Other Components

Once the idea of using lifting surfaces to generate aerodynamic downforce is accepted, then the question still remains about the number, shape, and placement of such devices. A fairly generic study on this issue (Ref. 5.6) investigated basic rectangular and delta wing combinations for an open-wheel race car application. Some of the configurations tested and their aerodynamic coefficients are presented in Fig. 6.63 (only a few were tested in full scale). The primary conclusion at the time was that centrally mounted wings (e.g., between the two wheel axles) are less efficient than a far-forward or a far-aftward mounted one. In terms of controlling front/rear downforce ratio, the two-wing concept (No. 7) seemed to be the most easy to adjust. The central wing (No. 4) seemed not to work well because of the unfavorable interaction of the wing with the body. In addition, the wake of the central wing reduced the efficiency of the rear wing causing a too-forward location of the center of pressure (of the whole vehicle). The delta wing concept (Nos. 3 and 6) seemed to work only when used without a rear wing. With a wing placed behind the large delta (as in 6), the rear wing was completely ineffective because of the delta wing's vortex wake.

After selecting the approximate location of a lifting surface, its best position relative to the other body components must be investigated. This fine tuning is unique to each vehicle, and the following examples serve primarily to illustrate this generic wing/body interaction. One of the strongest interactions appears

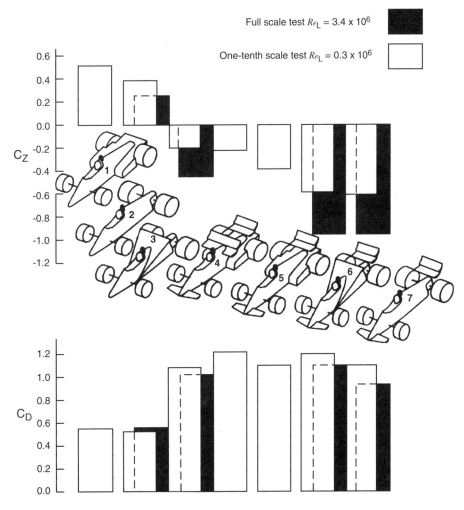

Fig. 6-63. *Lift and drag for a variety of open-wheel race car and negative-lift wing combinations (only four configurations were tested in full scale). Reprinted with permission from SAE paper 850283, Copyright ©1985 SAE, Inc.*

when mounting a rear wing on a race car with a smooth lower surface (undertray). A schematic description of the effect on the flow field is depicted in Fig. 6.64. With a generic ellipsoid, near the ground, the flow is usually attached over most of the front section, but toward the rear end some limited flow separation region may exist. When an inverted wing is added at the back, the flow under the ellipsoid accelerates as a result of the lower base pressure induced by the wing. This higher speed causes more downforce on the body, apart from the downforce created by the wing itself. Furthermore, in many occasions, the high-speed flow created near the wing partially reattaches the flow on the body, reducing the area of flow separation (see Ref. 4.11).

Fig. 6-64. *Schematic description of the effect of a rear wing on the streamlines nearby a generic body.*

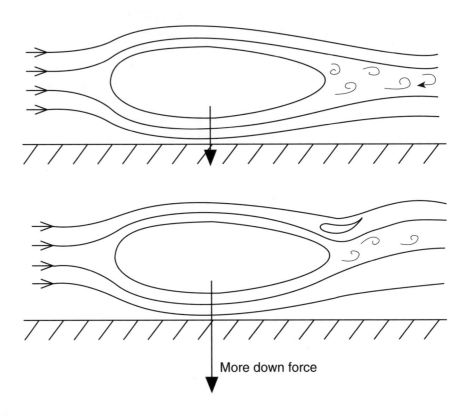

More down force

The effect of the wing/body interaction on the pressure distribution at the lower surface of a generic prototype race car is shown in Fig. 6.65. Also see Fig. 6.38 and Fig. 6.41 for similar data on sedan-based and open-wheel race cars. The vehicle in Fig. 6.65 had underbody tunnels, and the suction peak in the pressure distribution clearly identifies the tunnel entrance area. With the rear wing in place, there is a clear increase in the magnitude of the negative pressure coefficient along the whole lower surface. Thus, the contribution of the wing/body interaction to the vehicle's downforce is created over most of the lower surface and results in a reasonable distribution of the downforce between the front and rear wheels.

The total effect on the aerodynamic loads, due to the wing/body interaction, can be demonstrated by observing the change in the lift and drag versus the wing height h (measured between the wing trailing edge and the rear deck). Fig. 6.66 demonstrates this effect for the generic prototype car shown in Fig. 6.65,

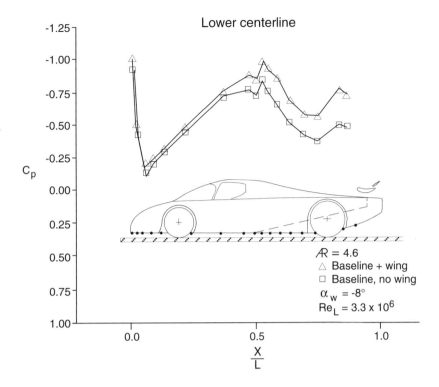

Fig. 6-65. *Effect of a rear wing on the pressure distribution along the lower surface centerline of a prototype race car with ground effect tunnels. Reprinted with permission from SAE paper 920349, Copyright ©1992 SAE, Inc. (Ref. 4.11).*

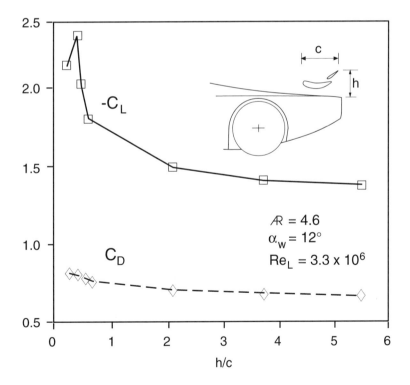

Fig. 6-66. *Effect of rear wing proximity to vehicle's body on lift and drag (for a generic prototype race car). Reprinted with permission from SAE paper 920349, Copyright ©1992 SAE, Inc. (Ref. 4.11).*

while Fig. 6.67 depicts the effect on a sedan-based race car (shown also in Fig. 6.38, or the lower part of Fig. 6.46). Both figures indicate, clearly, the large change in the lift on each vehicle whereas the changes in the drag coefficients are smaller. The magnitude of the increase in the downforce, in the prototype car, is much larger due to the streamlined upper surface and the pumping ac-

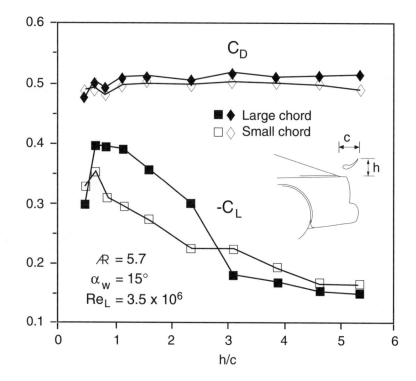

Fig. 6-67. *Effect of rear wing proximity to vehicle's body on lift and drag (for a generic sedan-based race car). Reprinted with permission from SAE paper 920349, Copyright ©1992 SAE, Inc. (Ref. 4.11).*

tion of the wing on the flow coming through the underbody channels (or in other words, the low pressure induced by the wing at the tunnel exit reduces the flow separation inside the tunnels and increases the flow rate there).

Fig. 6.67 shows that adding a wing to a passenger car-type vehicle can dramatically increase the downforce, too. When wing proximity is less than $h/c = 0.5$, the boundary layer originating at the rear window blocks the flow between the wing and body and the interaction becomes less effective. This minimum distance may differ for the various vehicle configurations, but its order of magnitude is close to the boundary layer thickness on the vehicle rear, upper surface. The data in Fig. 6.67 shows that the effect was investigated for two different rear wings having the same airfoil shape and span of 1.53 m, but with different chord lengths (full-scale chord was $c = 0.21$ m for the small chord and $c = 0.27$ m for the large chord). The larger wing did produce larger values of downforce.

The above data demonstrate that the aerodynamic wing/body interaction is large and important, and that the downforce obtained by the interaction may exceed the negative lift of the isolated wing. Also it must be reiterated that the above race cars had smooth underbodies; for passenger cars with exposed underbody components this effect may be much smaller.

The effect of this interaction on the pressure distribution on the wing is even more important, especially in view of the guidelines established for a desirable pressure distribution (Chapter 4) required for an effective airfoil design. The source of the problem is that the streamlines are distorted by the presence of a vehicle's body, and the basic undisturbed free-stream assumption (Chapter 4) is no longer valid. Fig. 6.68 depicts the centerline pressure distribution on the wing of the sedan-based race car (of Fig. 6.38, or at the lower part of Fig. 6.46; for a real car see Fig. 7.15).

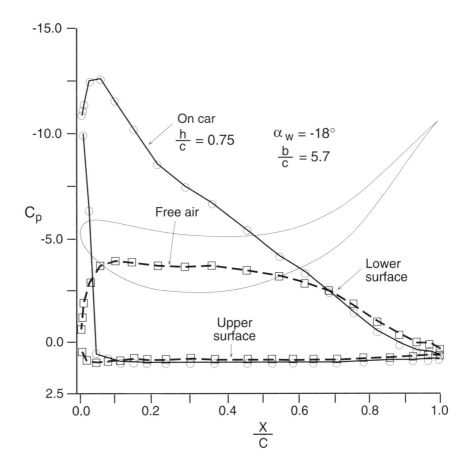

Fig. 6-68. *Effect of wing proximity to vehicle's body on the chordwise pressure distribution of a race car's rear wing. Reprinted with permission from SAE paper 920349, Copyright ©1992 SAE, Inc. (Ref. 4.11).*

The pressure distribution marked "free air" represents the case for the wing without the vehicle body effect, while the curve marked "on car" shows the data with the wing on the car. Note the large difference in the shape and magnitude of the two pressure distributions. This is primarily a result of the change in the flow direction near the rear window area. Instead of a horizontal flow, the air flows in the downward direction, so the wing is subject to an effectively larger angle of attack. Also, the suction peak for the on-car case is almost three times larger than in the free-air case, and the two pressure distributions are entirely different. Incidentally, on the actual vehicle the flow on the wing and the vehicle was attached, but such a large suction peak in a small-scale test will result in flow separation (and in a more conservative design).

Another interesting aspect of the three-dimensional flow caused by the vehicle's body is the change in the wing's spanwise loading due to the wing/body interaction, as shown in Fig. 6.69 (for the generic prototype race car). In this case, the flow over the rear wheel fenders increases the local angle of attack near the wing tips, while the flow of the underbody channel reduces the lift at the center of the wing (relative to the tips). Consequently, the spanwise loading resembles that of a twisted wing with higher angles of attack near the tips. The induced drag can be expected to be larger than that of a similar wing with equal lift but with an elliptic (ideal) spanwise loading.

In conclusion, Figs. 6.68 and 6.69 demonstrate that a race car's wing shape cannot be well designed without knowing the prevailing three-dimensional flow caused by the presence of the body. Proper computational or experimental

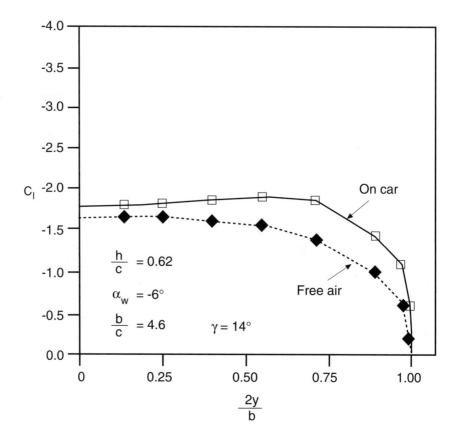

Fig. 6-69. *Effect of vehicle body on the spanwise loading of a prototype race car's rear wing. Reprinted with permission from SAE paper 920349, Copyright ©1992 SAE, Inc. (Ref. 4.11).*

tools are required for a race car wing which operates within the complex three-dimensional flow field created by the vehicle's body. These tools can be used to provide information on the wing's pressure distribution in its actual location. Then, by using well-developed Target Pressure Distribution (see Chapter 4) the wing shape can be reiterated until the target pressure distribution is met with the wing on the vehicle. More information on the wing/body interaction for the above two vehicle shapes can be found in Ref. 4.11.

Rear Wings   The previous discussion about the rear wing/body interaction demonstrates the importance of the rear wing and the sensitivity of the aerodynamic coefficients to its exact placement. Typical arrangements of rear wings on several types of race cars are shown in Fig. 6.70. The interaction in the prototype car, shown in the upper part of the figure, was presented in the previous section (Figs. 6.65, 6.66, and 6.69). In this case the wing should provide the suction for the flow leaving the tunnels, and this will generate the ground effect-type downforce by the body. In an effort to increase the downforce of the prototype race cars in 1992, a second, higher mounted rear wing was added (see Fig. 6.2, 7.18, and 7.20). The function of the rear wing was still the same, and the second wing was mounted as high as allowed by regulations, in order to reduce the biplane interaction of Fig. 4.43.

The role of the rear wing in the open-wheel-type race car (e.g., Indy car), as shown at the center of the figure, is similar to that described earlier. Therefore, those wings are usually placed sufficiently low to interact with the flow exiting the tunnels (in Indy cars only one rear wing is allowed). In the flat-bottomed car (e.g., F-1, shown at the lower part of the figure), only a small venturi is al-

Fig. 6-70. *Typical positioning of a race car's rear wing to exploit underbody venturi flow.*

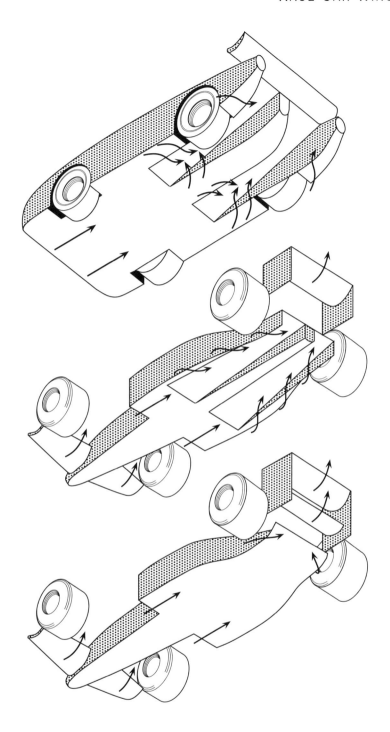

lowed behind the rear axle, and a low mounted wing serves the same purpose. In this case, however, the number of wings is not limited, and a second wing can be added as high as possible (as shown). Note that the two wings interact unfavorably (see Fig. 4.43); therefore their vertical separation is usually limited by the maximum height of the vehicle. In view of this it is worth investigating the benefits from increasing the number of planes of the rear wing, and the generic trend is shown in Fig. 6.71.

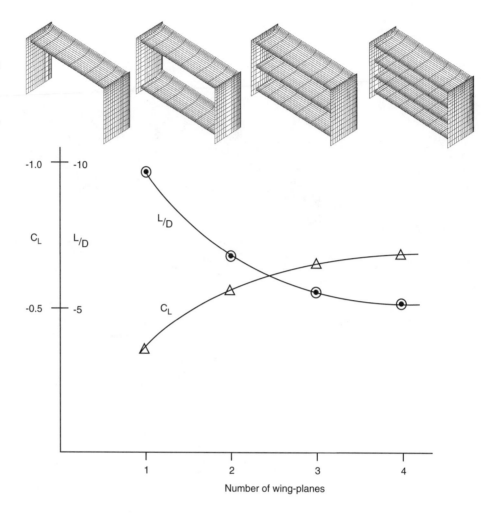

Fig. 6-71. *Effect of the number of planes in an F-1 type rear wing on vehicle downforce, and downforce-over-drag ratio (coefficients based on vehicle reference area).*

This figure is based on the ideal flow analysis of an isolated rear wing (without the rest of the body), and it is assumed that the lower and the upper plane positions are fixed by regulations (also, all planes are identical in terms of airfoil shape and angle of attack). In principle, the lift of the individual plane is reduced by the interaction described in Fig. 4.43, but the incremental lift to the vehicle ΔC_L increases with the added number of elements. However, the incremental downforce-over-drag ratio $\Delta L/D$ is reduced, and the use of more than two elements is usually not recommended. Increasing the number of wing planes, though, can increase the maximum lift and angle-of-attack range of the airfoil cascade and delay flow separation, because of the curved streamlines caused by the multiple airfoil (called *cascade*) interaction. So, if maximum lift is sought and drag penalties are disregarded, then more (wing planes) is better. Incidentally, the idea about augmenting the lift of a wing by trailing edge blowing, as shown in Fig. 6.61, can be easily incorporated into the lower wing element, shown in Figs. 6.70 and 6.71.

A typical multi-element rear wing of an Indy car is shown in Fig. 6.72. In this case the size of the wing is limited by regulations, and in order to generate more lift, several elements are used (multi-tier wing). The size of the side fins (apart from increasing lateral stability) is also very important, and their effect is shown by the data in Fig. 6.72. As mentioned before, the wing can be pitched

Fig. 6-72. *Effect of side fins on the lift and drag of an Indy car rear wing (coefficients are based on wing planview area). Reprinted with permission from SAE paper 890600, Copyright ©1989 SAE, Inc. (Ref. 2.13).*

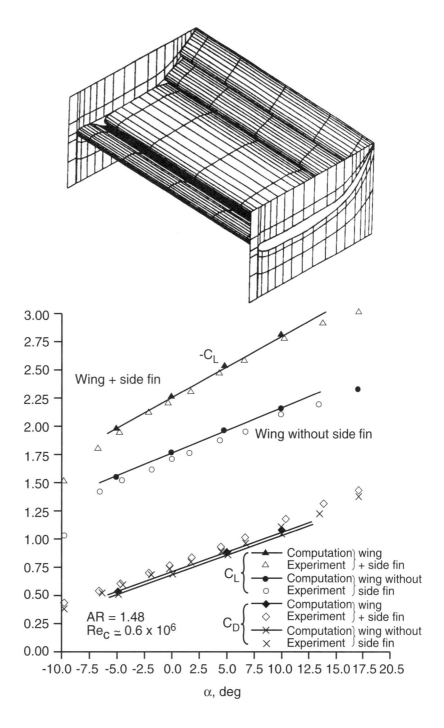

to very large angles of attack without stalling, as indicated by this data. Of course this particular wing will be legal only at zero angle of attack, due to the size limitations imposed on these vehicles. It is worthwhile to look at Fig. 4.36 and Fig. 4.40 since they provide more information on this particular wing. For example, the pressure distribution on this low-aspect-ratio wing is considerably different from the two-dimensional, airfoil-type pressure distribution (Fig. 4.36). Also, the lift of such wings quite often can be varied by changing trailing edge wickers (Fig. 4.40) and by not moving the flaps—keeping the wing geometry within the dimension limits dictated by the regulations.

To conclude this discussion about Indy car-type rear wings, where wing size is limited, the option of using a close-to-vertical flap at the wing trailing edge must be mentioned. This option is shown in Fig. 4.52 (the airfoil was designed for a 1988 Indy car). Minor deflections of the trailing edge flap can help to change its downforce, but will not cause the wing tip to extend above the maximum height limit. (Incidentally, vertical or even forward-turned trailing edges with attached flows are possible for such low-aspect-ratio wings.) For more information on various airfoil shapes that were considered for the rear wing of this 1987/8 Indy car, see Ref. 2.13.

On most open-wheel race cars the rear wing is influenced by the tires. One important function of the large end plates on those wings is to isolate the wing from the wheels, in order to reduce this effect. The available data on this interaction is quite limited, but small-scale results reported in Ref. 2.16 (p. 103) indicate that wheel rotation will reduce the wing's downforce.

Front Wings in Ground Effect

Front wings can be found on both open- and enclosed-wheel race cars. However, in the first case the front wing is clearly identified, and the discussion in this section will be limited to those wings only. Some of the "hidden" front wings found on enclosed-wheel race cars will be discussed in the next section.

A typical front wing of an open-wheel race car is seen in Fig. 6.73. These wings usually face the undisturbed free stream (similar to airplanes), and their airfoil shape can be similar to well-established airplane-type airfoils. The two major effects that control their function are the ground proximity effect and the presence of the front wheel.

The magnitude of the ground effect on the chordwise pressure distribution, at the semispan station of such a wing, is shown in Fig. 6.74. Note the large in-

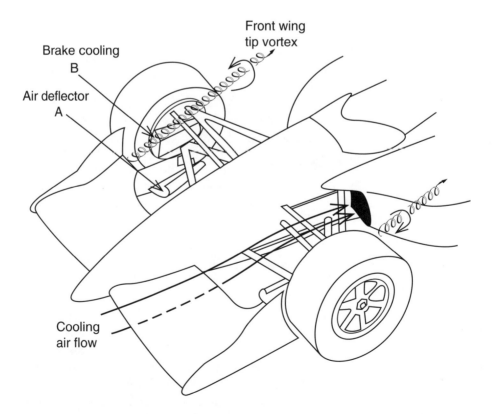

Fig. 6-73. *Typical front wing of a 1990s open-wheel race car.*

Front wing tip vortex

Brake cooling
B

Air deflector
A

Cooling air flow

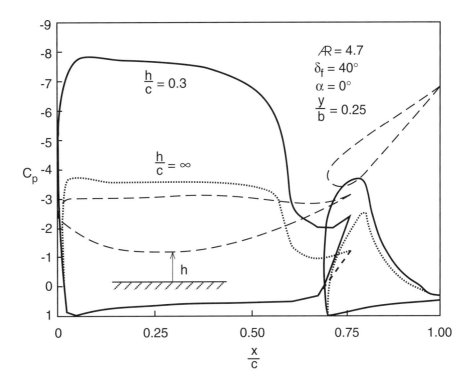

Fig. 6-74. *Effect of ground proximity on the chordwise pressure distribution of an open-wheel race car front wing. Results are based on potential-flow computations; the flow in the h/c=0.3 case is probably separated.*

crease in suction at the lower surface. The rapid increase in the downforce of such a wing, with decreasing ground clearance, was shown also in Fig. 5.26. One positive conclusion from Fig. 6.74 is that the shape of the pressure distribution does not change much near the ground (compared to other effects, such as in Fig. 4.36). Consequently, a well-developed airplane-type airfoil can be used for such front wing applications.

The planform shape of such wings was basically rectangular until a few years ago, with the highest possible span, and the wings were placed as forward as possible. However, with time, the effect of the front wing on the other parts of the vehicle was recognized. For instance, if the tip vortex (of the wake) of the wing hit the tire, it could have reduced the pressure behind the front wheel, increasing its drag. This led to the trend of narrower front wings, but with larger flaps (for more downforce). However, too-large flaps would divert air from the cooling inlets, so most front wings were cut out near their root (Fig. 6.73). This figure also indicates use of the wing structure to mount air deflectors for blowing air behind the front wheels to reduce drag (see also Fig. 6.28). Front brake cooling inlets should be placed such that they receive most of the free-stream momentum. Incidentally, the generic shape of such wings has an adverse taper (see Chapter 4). This means that near the tip the lift coefficient is not increased much by the larger chord and camber, and flow separations (or partial wing stall) is less likely.

Another interesting aspect of the front wing design is the so-called "wing body interference," an effect described schematically in Fig. 6.75. The lift of the basic wing, without the vehicle nose (case A), will generate the best performance. The spanwise loading (lift distribution) is shown at the upper part of this Figure. By adding the nose cone (case B), the lift at the center portion of the wing is partially lost, resulting in the dip shown in the spanwise loading di-

Fig. 6-75. *Various configurations of open-wheel race car front wings. The spanwise loading shown in the inset compares cases A and B.*

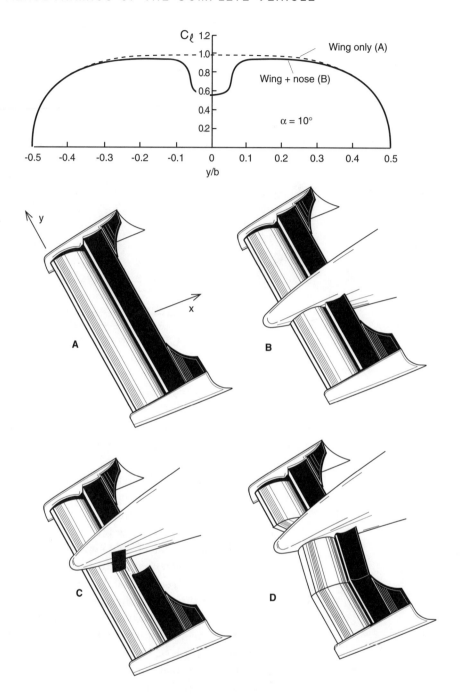

agram. As the importance of the flow under the car was recognized, the wings were raised and some of the ground effect was lost (but pitch sensitivity was reduced, and also more cooling flow from under the wing could reach the cooling intakes).

The additional flow under the vehicle can enhance the flow in the tunnels (venturis) toward the back of the lower body panel, which not only increases the downforce contribution of the body, but also can reduce the base drag. Two of the most frequently used methods to increase airflow at the front are shown by cases C and D. In case C (see Fig. 1.23), wing performance is better, and the lower surface of the nose cone must be used to divert the flow to the cooling intakes and under the body. In case D, an anhedral is used for the central portion of the wing to allow the larger flow under the nose cone. Wing aerodynamics is affected, in this case in a manner similar to case B, and wing performance is less efficient than in case C.

Hard-to-Recognize "Wings"

This section deals with the nose section of enclosed-wheel race cars (prototypes or sedan-based racers) where the designer is free to change the geometry as much as he wishes to in order to generate aerodynamic advantages. Some of the front nose designs (for some reason called *front wings*) are shown schematically on Fig. 6.76. The basic vehicle is shown at the upper part of the figure. If the underbody allows ample airflow under the car, as in a car with ground effect tunnels, then the flow will accelerate under the nose, much like around an airfoil's leading edge (see Fig. 6.65). Shaping the upper part of the vehicle nose as a concave surface will increase this effect, and it is known that a concave upper surface of the nose will create more front downforce (for more data on nose shapes see Ref. 6.13). Usually, the lower surface (ahead of the front wheel) will taper up, as an airfoil, creating a larger passage between the two wheels to re-

Fig. 6-76. *Various methods to generate front downforce on enclosed-wheel race cars.*

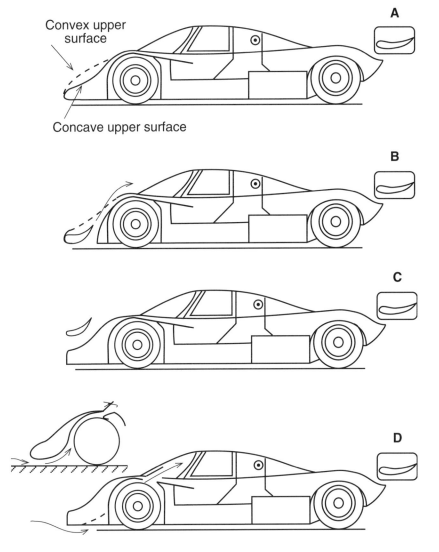

Convex upper surface

Concave upper surface

duce large local flow accelerations (recall the continuity equation, Eq. 3.6; this increase in the area by raising the underbody is also shown in Fig. 6.77).

A more clearly identified front wing is shown in Fig. 6.76B. Here a completely legitimate wing is squeezed ahead of the vehicle body. The wing usually works well, but it also diverts the flow upward, so that the underbody tunnels must rely primarily on air supply from the sides only (such a wing was used on the successful Jaguar XJR-14, Group C / IMSA GTP racer, shown in Fig. 6.2). This design is usually more pitch-sensitive, and a more conservative vehicle, such as Fig. 6.76A, with a properly designed nose can probably be better balanced and generate more downforce.

Another issue is the size of the rear tunnels (diffusers). If those are large, then more flow must move under the vehicle. If this flow is limited by very low ground clearance or by a front wing, then the size (or angle) of the rear diffuser must be reduced, resulting in less rear downforce.

The simplest addition of a front wing (from the installation point of view) is to mount one above the nose, as shown in Fig. 6.76C. The only problem is that when the wing is too close to the vehicle surface, then the pressure in the channel between the wing and the body is nearly the same on both surfaces. Thus the lift increment is mostly lost while the drag penalty remains (that is probably why this approach is not very popular).

Another alternative, often seen on passenger car-based racers, as well as on prototype cars, is a variation on the front wing as shown in Fig. 6.76D. Here the lower part of the nose is shaped as an airfoil, but the flow is channeled around the front wheels and exhausted out usually at the upper part of the fenders (where the pressure coefficient is low). A large flap on top of the wheel fender can assist the suction of the flow, but usually this is accomplished with consid-

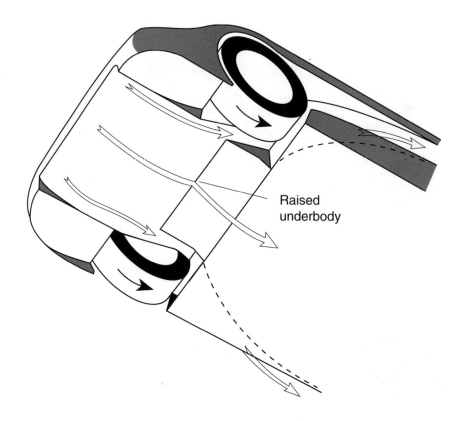

Fig. 6-77. *Example for channeling the flow from under the nose and exiting it behind the front wheels (as in the 1992/3 Toyota prototype race car). Note that wheel rotation assists the flow into the side channels.*

Raised underbody

erable drag increase. When the flap is mounted behind or ahead of the highest point of the front fender (as in Fig. 3.2), then the drag penalty is much less.

Another option (usually with less drag increment) is to create louvers on the upper fender that will ventilate the lower nose section, thereby reducing the pressure there (or creating more downforce). The effectiveness of this device may be reduced by the opposite flow driven by the tire rotation, as described in Fig. 6.25. A possible solution in this case would be to isolate the wheel by an internal shroud so that the flow upward, originating at the vehicle lower surface, would not be channeled near the surface of the rotating tire.

Another variation on the same theme is shown in Fig. 6.77, which resembles the approach used on the 1992/3 Toyota prototype car (Fig. 6.78). In this case the flow enters under the nose, in the usual way, but most of it exits at the sides through well-defined and low-resistance channels. This ensures high-speed flow under the car and reasonably high front downforce, even though the front nose must be raised to allow sufficient flow to feed the side channels. The interesting feature of this design is that the tire's rotation is helping the flow, rather than spoiling it. Also, in this figure the raised underbody panel between the front wheels is shown, which opens up the area for the flow moving toward the rear tunnels of the vehicle.

Fig. 6-78. The 1992 Toyota Eagle Mk3, winner of the 1992 IMSA Camel GT championship in the US. Courtesy of Toyota Motorsports.

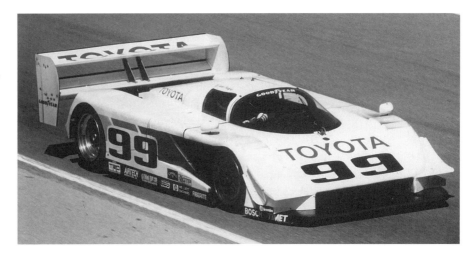

For completeness, the front strakes (dive plates) of Fig. 6.46C must be mentioned again. These devices are usually very effective and when their size increases they can qualify as small side wings. Because of their simplicity, they are used in many forms of motor racing. Fig. 6.78 shows one of them.

CLOSING REMARKS

The emphasis in this chapter was placed on relating vehicle geometry or the effect of local geometrical modifications to the aerodynamic performance of the race car. The many devices and methods that were listed cannot, naturally, be used on one particular vehicle, and the question that arises is: How can one improve an existing race car? In an effort to provide some advice, based on the data provided in this chapter, the following can be said about the various race car categories.

First, for most vehicles, the changing of ride height and pitch angle can create variations in the aerodynamic coefficients, as described in Figs. 6.17–6.21. Some of the other devices listed in this chapter need further attention and may be more effective for a particular type of race car, as described in the following paragraphs.

Let us start with production car-based racers. In this case, the first question that comes to mind concerns the possibility of covering the lower surface of the vehicle with a smooth floor pan. If the lower part of the vehicle must stay in its stock form (with exhaust tubes, wirings, fuel tank, drive line, etc.), then usually front air dams and side skirts can increase downforce with limited drag penalty. Rear spoilers are often needed to reduce rear lift, and as we know, rear lift can have an adverse effect on high-speed, lateral stability. Vehicle aerodynamic balance can be improved by using add-ons as described in Fig. 6.46. If the race car under consideration only needs to resemble the production car, and it can have a smooth under pan, then the importance of the airflow underneath the car increases. This allows a more successful utilization of a rear wing, which can interact with underbody venturis or tunnels (as shown in Figs. 6.36 or 6.39). The contouring of the vehicle aft section can have a strong influence on base drag, while the placement of the wing relative to the rear deck may have a noticeable effect, as suggested by Fig. 6.67. The control of the front downforce in such vehicles is somewhat more limited but some of the tricks shown by Figs. 6.46 and 6.76 may be applicable.

When considering an enclosed-wheel-type race car, its aerodynamic performance depends considerably on its initial design. For example, front hood shape or hidden wings (as in Fig. 6.76) can increase tremendously front downforce, while underbody tunnels can glue the rear tires to the ground. The wing-body interaction emphasizes the importance of integrating wing and body design. This implies that the rear end of such cars should be designed together with the rear wing cluster, as implied by the sketches in Fig. 6.76. The front/rear aerodynamic balance of an existing car can be altered, usually, by using tricks such as shown in Figs. 6.46 and 6.47. Finally, special attention must be paid to the underbody tunnel, to allow sufficient flow by increasing the flow area between the front wheels (which may require a limited elevation of the nose center section) and from the sides of the car, especially behind the front wheels. If this is not possible, then the size or turn angle of the tunnels must be reduced.

Open-wheel race cars actually fall into two main categories: those with and those without underbody tunnels. In spite of the flat bottom in the latter case (F-1), some level of underbody venturis can be generated by curving the under-pan behind the rear axle (most of this was banned at mid 1994 for F-1 cars). Therefore, wing placement will be very important in both cases. Underbody tunnels and skirts can be used very effectively on these cars. Also, the aerodynamic balancing of front/rear downforce is quite simple with the front/rear wing configuration. However, the ground proximity of the front wing can create excessive pitch sensitivity, and if too low, can block the flow under the car, adversely affecting the downforce in the rear venturi area. Finally, the largest disadvantage, at least from the aerodynamic point of view, is the large drag penalty of the exposed wheels. It is possible to reduce their effect by properly curving the side pods and by uing some of the air-deflecting devices listed in Figs. 6.26–6.28.

REFERENCES

6.1. Morel, T., "The Effect of Base Slant on the Flow Pattern and Drag of Three-Dimensional Bodies with Blunt Ends," in Sovran et al. (Ref. 2.19), pp. 191–226.

6.2. George, A. R., and Donis, J. E., "Flow Patterns, Pressures, and Forces on the Underside of Idealized Ground Effect Vehicles," *Aerodynamics of Transportation-II*, Fluids Engineering Division, ASME, FED-Vol. 7, pp. 69–79, 1983.

6.3. Wright, P. G., "The Influence of Aerodynamics on the Design of Formula One Racing Cars," paper in Ref. 2.4, pp. 158–172.

6.4. Fackrell, J. E., and Harvey, J. K., "The Aerodynamics of an Isolated Road Wheel," Paper No. 8 in Ref. 2.18, pp. 119–126.

6.5. Stapleford, W. R., and Carr, W.G., "Aerodynamic Characteristics of Exposed Rotating Wheels," Motor Industries Research Association (MIRA), Rep. No. 2, 1970.

6.6. Poncini, G. F., and Di Giusto, N., "Experimental Methods for Wind-Tunnel Testing of Racing Cars with Ground Effect," paper in Ref. 2.4, pp. 480–492.

6.7 Schekel, F. K., "The Origins of Drag and Lift Reductions on Automobiles with Front and Rear Spoilers," SAE Paper 77-0389, Feb. 1977.

6.8 Duncan, L. T., "Wind Tunnel and Track Testing an ARCA Race Car," SAE Paper 90-1867, Feb. 1990.

6.9 Rogallo, F. M., "Internal-Flow Systems for Aircraft," NACA Rep. No. 713, 1941.

6.10 Frick, C. W., Davis, W. F., Randall, L. M., and Mossman, E. A., "An Experimental Investigation of NACA Submerged-Duct Entrances," NACA ACR No. 5I20, Oct. 1945.

6.11 Mossman, E. A., and Randall, L. M., "An Experimental Investigation of the Design Variables for NACA Submerged Duct Entrances," NACA RM No. A7I30, Jan 1948.

6.12 Sovran, G., and Klomp, E.D., "Experimentally Determined Optimum Geometries for Rectilinear Diffusers with Rectangular, Conical or Annular Cross-Section," *Fluids Mechanics of Internal Flows*, Elsevier Publishing Co., N.Y., 1967, pp. 270–319.

6.13. Boyce, T. R., and Lobb, P. J., "An Investigation of the Aerodynamics of Current Group 6 Sports Car Designs," *Advances in Road Vehicle Aerodynamics*, BHRA Fluid Engineering, pp. 127–145, 1973.

7

REAL-WORLD EXAMPLES

INTRODUCTION

In Chapter 6, three representative race car configurations were identified, along with a variety of aerodynamic trickery. As was noted in the conclusion, the number of such ideas that can be incorporated into a particular design is limited. In this chapter we will more fully explore the particular aerodynamic features (and limitations) for each of these categories using one representative race car from each category. (The selection of the representative vehicles was based primarily on the availability of such data on the particular race car and on the importance of aerodynamics in shaping these vehicles' bodies.) As an introduction before surveying the recent inventions of racing minds, let us look back at a brief historical survey, highlighting the significant developments in race car-oriented aerodynamics in past years.

MILESTONES: HISTORICALLY IMPORTANT DESIGNS

There are four basic factors controlling race car performance: the engine, the tires, the chassis, and the driver. A rapid development in any of the first three can generate a large advantage to any vehicle in the field. In the early days of motor racing (prior to 1950), most of the above technologies were still rapidly changing, while the aerodynamic considerations of the chassis designer were usually aimed only at achieving low drag.

In the early 1960s race car speeds climbed steeply, and racing regulations limited engine power and tire sizes, which effectively reduced the advantage of one team over another in these areas. Designers were forced to look for the "unfair technical advantage" in chassis design (and aerodynamics). Also at this time, airplane aerodynamics was considered to be a mature science, and the transfer of this technology led to numerous innovations in chassis aerodynamics. Regulations soon followed in an effort to limit this technology, and this cat & mouse game of technology versus regulations has influenced race car aerodynamics well into the 1990s.

To demonstrate the aerodynamic evolution of race car design some of the notable vehicles during this process are discussed in the following paragraphs. The selection of the examples is based on the limited material collected over recent years by the author. Some of the innovations presented may have been introduced earlier and by other teams or manufacturers.

The 1924 Tropfenwagen (droplet-shaped car, in German), designed by E. Rumpler and shown in Fig. 7.1, serves as an excellent example for early efforts to reduce aerodynamic drag by streamlining the vehicle's body. Even though this car was not designed for racing, it is presented here, since an original example was taken from the German Museum in Munich and tested in the VW AG wind tunnel in 1979 (Fig. 3.11). While the side view of the car resembles the silhouette of other automobiles of that era, the top view clearly reveals the aerodynamic teardrop shape of the body. The measured drag coefficient for a full-scale vehicle in the VW wind tunnel was $C_D = 0.28$ (Ref. 2.6, p. 14), which is a remarkably low value, even when compared to more recent futuristic low-drag sedans. This car also featured a mid-engine layout which was reinvented in the 1960s by race car engineers, but in the 1920s this design was too much for the traditional automobile buyer and thus resulted in commercial failure.

Fig. 7-1. *The 1924 Tropfenwagen, which had most "desirable features" of a modern race car such as a mid-engine design, a low drag coefficient of $C_D = 0.28$, and yes, four exposed wheels. Yet it turned out to be an unsuccessful road car. Illustration by Brian Hatton.*

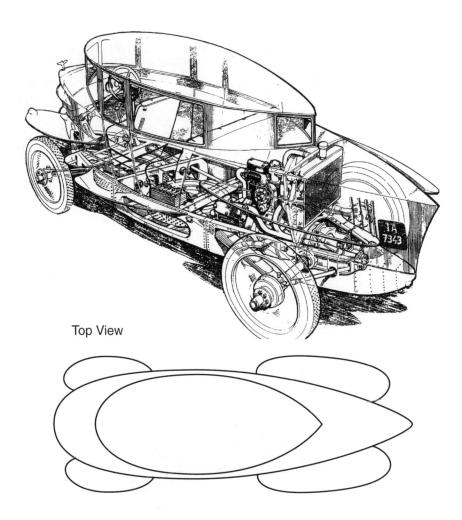

Top View

This trend of streamlining the vehicle's body in order to reduce aerodynamic drag continued in all forms of racing. Most cars had elongated boat-tails with drag coefficients of less than $C_D \sim 0.4$, accompanied by some positive lift coefficient (probably up to $C_L \sim 0.4$). As maximum speed has risen into the 200–300 km/hr range, positive lift, which was felt more on the rear axle, resulted in lateral instabilities, as described in Chapter 5. One logical solution was the addition of large side fins, as seen on this 1966 Peugeot Le Mans endurance racer (Fig. 7.2), which reached 245 km/hr with a 105 HP motor (Ref. 2.6, p. 267). A more recent Le Mans racer and a 1994 Indy car using vertical fins are presen-

Fig. 7-2. *The 1966 Peugeot CD, Le-Mans racer, which used vertical fins to increase lateral stability (courtesy of Peugeot Motors of America).*

ted in Fig. 5.19. For similar reasons most speed-record-breaking vehicles of that era (and even today) had similar stabilizing fins. However, a far simpler solution to the lateral instability is the elimination of the lift, and the use of moderate levels of negative lift to increase the rear tire's cornering stiffness. This approach was adopted after 1965.

The Chaparral 2C race car, one of the most successful designs in 1965, can be considered as the first vehicle to use inverted wings to improve lateral performance. (There are sporadic reports about people using wings on cars as early as the 1920s. The Chaparral 2C probably was the first serious such effort by a major racing team.) This car (shown in Fig. 7.3) used a single-element rear flap mounted between its two tail fins (Ref. 7.1, p. 76). The angle of incidence of this full-span flap could be varied, and Fig. 7.3 clearly indicates that air could flow under the flap's leading edge, making it a legitimate wing.

Fig. 7-3. *First efforts to adjust rear downforce by variable flap on this 1965 Chaparral 2C. Courtesy of Dave Friedman.*

Chaparral cars continued to play the leading role in race car aerodynamics and in the year that followed a high-mounted, inverted rear wing appeared on their 1966 2E Can-Am racer, as shown in Fig. 7.4. Their experience with the 2C car indicated that at high speed the aerodynamic downforce compressed the suspension, making the ride very stiff. On the 2E, the struts holding the rear wings were mounted directly to the rear hubs to transfer the downforce directly to the tires, relieving the large loads from the sprung part of the car.

Fig. 7-4. *The 1966 Chaparral 2E Can-Am racer can be considered as the first race car to use the wing in the configuration used even in the 1990s. Courtesy of Bob Tronolone.*

During 1967 and 1968 the use of such wings was adopted by many F-1 teams, with Ferrari, Brabham, and Lotus leading those early experimentations. Varying of wing incidence during the race was allowed, and a popular choice was to increase wing angle in a turn and reduce it on a straightaway. To avoid an increase in suspension stiffness, most early wings were mounted directly on the unsprung wheel/suspension components. Also, the aerodynamic data of those days on airfoils mounted on vehicles, such as presented in Ref. 2.16, p. 102, indicated that wings needed to be mounted as high as possible in order to avoid the distorted flow near the body (which is really not the case, based on the findings in Chapter 6). A typical example for such an F-1 race car is shown in Fig. 7.5. This design dates from 1967 (Ref. 2.4, p. 159). The combination of high-mounted wings with indirect mounting resulted in several wing failures in

Fig. 7-5. *The 1967–68 Lotus Type 49 with a high wing mounted on the rear hubs. Courtesy of Randy Barnett.*

1968 and 1969. By 1969 new F-1 regulations restricted wing mounting directly onto the sprung part of the body. Furthermore, varying of the wing angle and geometry was prohibited during the race. By the end of 1989, regulations also limited the maximum height and span of wings (the wording of those regulations was somewhat indirect; it can be interpreted to read that the wings must be placed under the 1 m maximum height measured from the ground).

For 1969, Chaparral appeared with a second innovation in the increased downforce battle, in the form of its 2J race car, shown in Fig. 7.6. In this case two large fans (driven by an auxiliary snowmobile engine) were used to suck the air from beneath the car's body, as in a vacuum cleaner (see also Fig. 6.11). The advantage of a separate drive for the fan is that the downforce on the tires is independent of speed (say, compared to wings) and does not vary during gear changing. Therefore, low-speed cornering can be improved as well. The body/ground contact area of the 2J was sealed by flexible Lexan skirts to increase the effect of the low pressure, which was capable, according to the rumors, of creating a downforce of 1g. From the aerodynamic point of view this solution not only provides downforce with low effort (which depends on the effectiveness of the seal between the car and the ground), but also reduces base drag, due to the effect of blowing into the separated flow area behind the car.

Fig. 7-6. *Chaparral 2J was the first fan car that appeared in 1969 and used two auxiliary fans to create suction under the car. Courtesy of Bob Tronolone.*

This idea appeared later in F-1 in the form of the 1978 Brabham BT46B "fan car," shown in Fig. 7.7. The area beneath the engine and gearbox was sealed by flexible skirts and a large fan, driven from the gearbox, sucked air out of the engine bay area. In this case the fan drew cooling air across the horizontally mounted water radiators (above the engine), and blew into the separation bubble behind the car (thus reducing drag). The car was introduced in the 1978 Swedish GP, and immediately won in the hands of Niki Lauda with a margin of about 30 seconds. This instant success raised a strong protest from other teams, and it was immediately banned on the basis that it used a movable aerodynamic device (the fan).

Fig. 7-7. The 1978 Brabham BT46B fan car (top) with which Niki Lauda won the 1978 Swedish GP on its day of introduction, top. A rare rear view of the suction fan of the BT46B (bottom), during the 1978 swedish GP. Top: Phipps Photographic. Bottom: Courtesy of Gordon Murray.

Among the many race car innovations in the 1970s, one must include the six-wheel Tyrrell P34, introduced in mid-1976 (Fig. 7.8). Compared to a much larger front wheel, the four small (10-inch diameter) front wheels were believed to increase contact area with the road and to reduce aerodynamic drag and disturbance. The ingenious front suspension and the adhesion and drag benefits were no match to the additional weight and the unresolved front tire problems, and the concept was abandoned by the team after the 1977 season. Since the car was not competitive from its first day of introduction, regulations limiting the number of wheels of an F-1 car to 4 were introduced only in 1983.

In 1977 the first application of the "inverted wing in ground effect" principle was utilized on the Lotus Type 78 F-1 car, shown in Fig. 7.9. There were several important features in this car (Ref. 7.2) that paved the way for many of the concepts still found in most forms of racing. First, the sides of the car were sealed by movable skirts to create a two-dimensional inverted airfoil effect, which in principle can create large levels of downforce with small drag penalties.

Fig. 7.10 is an excellent photograph, showing this inverted airfoil-shaped side pod. The second, and equally important, outcome of this development was the attention to the flow under the vehicle, which is a major factor in determining downforce and drag. In fact, this aspect of the flow was much improved in the following year (Fig. 7.11) in the Type 79 Lotus, with which Mario Andretti won the 1978 F-1 World Championship. The third important aerodynamic as-

Fig. 7-8. *The principle of smaller wheels equals less drag, and more wheels equals more cornering power was used on this 1977 Tyrell P34 F-1 race car. Courtesy of Randy Barnett.*

Fig. 7-9. *The first ground effect F-1 car with side skirts, the 1977 Lotus Type 78. Reprinted with permission from Ref. 6.3.*

Fig. 7-10. *The inverted airfoil-shaped side pod of the Lotus Type 78 F-1 car (side skirt assembly was removed). After Ref. 7.2, courtesy of Christian Hoefer.*

pect of this car was the very low mounting of the rear wing, which had the additional function of pumping air beneath the car to aid the ground effect. The only drawback of this design was that this type of ground effect was sensitive to the gap between the road and the sliding side skirts (Chapter 6). Thus, by 1980, the side skirts were banned and a minimum ground clearance for the bodywork was established (1981). In 1983, in an effort to end the ground effect wars, a flat-bottom formula was mandated by F-1 regulations.

Fig. 7-11. The improved Lotus Type 79 ground effect car in which Mario Andretti won the 1978 F-1 title. This photo shows Ronnie Peterson in the 1978 Swedish G.P. Note the perfect skirt seal against the track. Phipps Photographics.

The successful ground effect concept introduced on open-wheel F-1 cars gradually migrated to other forms of racing, and by the end of 1978 these ideas were incorporated into the design of enclosed-wheel race cars. The first such car, the Lee Dykstra-designed Busch HR-001, appeared at the opening of the 1979 Can-Am Challenge series (Fig. 7.12). The sides of the car between the front and rear wheels were sealed by a sliding Lexan skirt, and the inverted airfoil idea was implemented by using two large venturis in the space between the gearbox and the inner face of each of the rear tires.

Fig. 7-12. The 1979 Busch HR-001 race car, which was the first to use underbody venturis in the Can-Am Challenge series. Robert Fisher photo.

The indented underbody tunnels (venturis) can be seen clearly in Fig. 7.13, where young Dykstra (at the center) carefully examines the details of his design. The car performance clearly demonstrated the advantage of this high downforce concept by being the fastest in the turns, whereas the drag penalty of the large downforce resulted in somewhat lower top speeds on the straightaway (but the car was still very competitive). A slightly different design contributing to the transfer of ground effect technology to enclosed-wheel racing was the Lola T 530 Can Am car that appeared somewhat later. This particular race car used a rigid, ceramic side skirt with inverted airfoil-like side pods, in the spirit of the Lotus T 78/79. This concept was later refined (after all sliding skirts were banned) and by the early 1980s all Le Mans-type, FISA group C, and IMSA GTP cars had such underbody tunnels (Fig. 6.36).

The effect of the aerodynamic developments listed in the aforementioned brief historical survey had a noticeable impact on race car performance, especially by drastically improving cornering speeds on unbanked road surfaces.

Fig. 7-13. *Clear view of the underbody venturi (viewed from top) of the 1979 Busch HR-001 Can-Am car and its designer, Lee Dykstra (at center). Robert Fisher photo.*

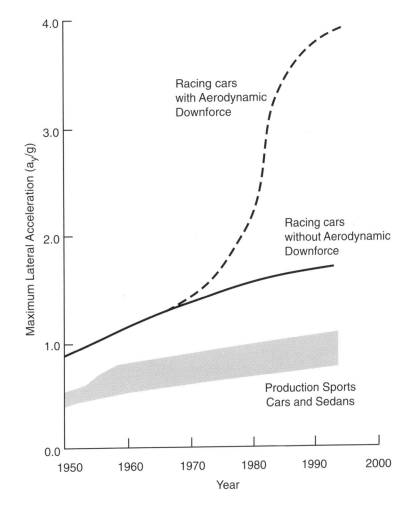

Fig. 7-14. *Generic trends in the increase of the maximum lateral acceleration (in g) of production sports cars and race cars with and without aerodynamic downforce.*

This improvement in performance can be summarized by observing the evolution of the maximum lateral acceleration (during cornering) over the years, as presented by the diagram of Fig. 7.14. The grey area shows the gradual improvement in sports (and production) car handling, which is a direct result of improvements in tire construction. The solid line indicates a somewhat larger envelope of performance due to the softer and stickier tire compounds used for racing purposes.

The gradual increase in race cars' maximum lateral acceleration, prior to 1966, is again a result of improvements in tire and chassis technology. However, the rapid increase that followed is due to the sudden utilization of aerodynamic downforce. The introduction of the ground effect cars in 1978 caused a sharp increase in the maximum lateral accelerations. Of course, those large values represent momentary limits, and it is quite difficult to experience a lateral acceleration of three gs for more than a few seconds. For this reason, in many races where large lateral forces will be generated, the helmet of the driver is strapped to the sides to avoid excess neck stress. If one must speculate about the future of racing, it seems that the $4g$ shown in this diagram is a reasonable limit, and is based on human comfort. But, from the engineering point of view this can be extended to the momentary $8g$ range, which, so far, is reserved for military test pilots.

MORE CURRENT EXAMPLES

As was mentioned before, the shape of most vehicles is usually a result of the regulations governing that particular group of race cars, and is not the optimal shape for the application. We shall follow the generic grouping of race cars adopted before and present examples for passenger-based, enclosed-wheel, and open-wheel race cars. For each of these vehicles I will sketch the main geometrical features affecting the aerodynamic performance, together with some of the dominant features of the flow field. The flow visualizations are based on low Reynolds number testing with about 1/10-scale models, and the results are believed to capture the dominant large-scale effects, such as areas with massive flow separation.

Passenger Car-Based Configuration

The transformation of a mass-produced passenger car shape into a racing car usually requires the lowest level of aerodynamic effort, compared to, say, the effort invested in developing the shape of a prototype or an open-wheel racing car. Furthermore, in this type of racing the level of aerodynamic treatment is usually limited (severely) by the governing regulations. Most passenger car configurations will have a moderate drag coefficient in the range of $C_D = 0.30$ to 0.45, and some level of positive lift in the range of $C_L = 0.10$ to 0.40 (see Table 2.3 and Appendix 1). Therefore, the first aerodynamic task is to reduce their lift, or even create some level of downforce, especially on the rear axle. Typical areas for modifications should include the rear deck and the whole area under the car. The addition of a smooth underbody panel, with possible venturis, can increase downforce and reduce base-flow separation (at the rear). Possible areas of flow separations near the rear window and deck area should be reduced or eliminated for lower drag, while the addition of a rear wing or spoiler can create reasonably large levels of downforce.

As an example, the Mazda RX-7-based 1991 IMSA GTO racer is shown in Fig. 7.15. The vehicle shape is based on the popular RX-7 sports car. Body modifications included an enlarged fairing to house the wider racing tires, a smooth underbody panel, and a rear wing. The important details from the aerodynamic point of view are the small diffuser section starting ahead of the rear wheel with a 6° upward slant (Fig. 7.16), and a highly cambered rear wing, spanning the whole width of the vehicle. The regulations allowed the use of a spoiler or a similar size wing, and of course the latter performed better (see Ref. 2.7). Details on the geometry of the wing's airfoil section and on the pressure distribution can be found in earlier sections of this book (Figs. 6.38, 6.67, 6.68). To fully exploit the benefits of the smooth underbody panel, the cooling flow was ejected at the sides, behind the front wheels, so that the underbody flow was not blocked.

Fig. 7-15. *The Mazda RX-7 IMSA GTO race car, after winning the 1991 championship in Del Mar, CA.*

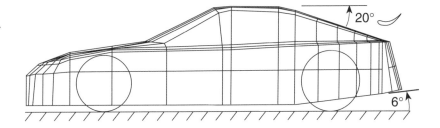

Fig. 7-16. *Side view of the 1991 Mazda RX-7 GTO race car.*

The dominant features of the flow over this vehicle are summarized in Fig. 7.17. The flow over most of the upper part of the vehicle, including the rear window area, is attached. Small regions of flow recirculation can be seen near the windshield pillar, and a major flow separation bubble exists at the rear base of the car. The car had no side windows (the drag penalty due to this opening was quoted in Fig. 6.62). The large cooling flow intake at the front reduces the speed of the incoming air so that the pressure ahead of the heat exchangers approaches the stagnation pressure. The hot cooling air is then ejected behind the front wheels, so that this low density air won't flow to the rear wings. By

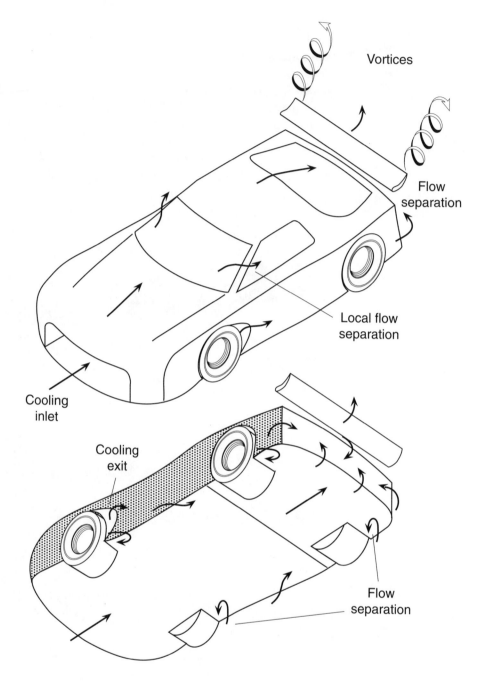

Fig. 7-17. *Schematic description of the flow field over a production car-based racer.*

adjusting the length of the lower horizontal plate at the inlet, the front down-force can be trimmed as suggested by Fig. 6.46 (D). The rear wing has the maximum possible span (full width of the car) and its highly cambered airfoil shape was developed for this particular purpose. The flow over the wing was attached on the actual race car and its lift could have been varied by changing its angle of attack and by adding small Gurney flaps of various lengths.

The second part of Fig. 7.17 depicts the flow features under the car. Typical localized flow separation areas can be found behind all four wheels, and the flow under the car was somewhat restricted by the horizontal, front-inlet spoiler. As a result of the low base pressure at the back, which is enhanced by the rear wing, a lateral inward flow pattern is observed between the front and rear wheels. This flow also feeds the small diffuser created by the upward slant of the rear underbody panel, which increases the downforce (see the corresponding pressure distribution in Fig. 6.38). Typical drag coefficients for such a configuration are in the range of $C_D = 0.4$ to 0.6 and the lower end of this range can be obtained by reducing the regions of flow separation. Such modifications can focus on streamlining the rear end of the vehicle and reducing the separations near the four tires and near the open window, but of course, this is not allowed by most regulations. The range of lift coefficient published for this vehicle (Ref. 2.7) is $C_L = -0.3$ to -0.4, but with some of the above mentioned modifications $C_L = -1.0$ is probably possible.

Prototype Cars

The vehicles included in this group of race cars will have (mostly) enclosed wheels, and the regulations governing the shape of their bodywork is quite relaxed. Such race cars are a designer's dream, and the bodywork can be formed to maximize aerodynamic benefits. The highly streamlined body not only will have reasonably low drag, but also will generate large levels of downforce (not counting the contribution of the wings). This can be achieved with underbody channels and closely coupled rear or even front wings. Typical examples for the most aerodynamic vehicles from this group are the 1992 Peugeot 905 (Fig. 7.18), the 1992 Jaguar XJR-14 (Fig. 6.2), or the Mazda RX-792P (Fig. 7.19) from the same year. Details on the aerodynamics of such vehicles are quite rare in the open literature, but for the first in this group (the Peugeot 905) some details and a photograph of the underbody tunnels are revealed in Ref. 7.3.

Fig. 7-18. 1992 Peugeot 905, group C, Sportscar World Champion. Courtesy of Peugeot Motors of America.

Fig. 7-19. The 1992 Mazda RX-792P prototype race car at the end of the season in Del Mar, CA.

The Mazda race car was selected as an example for this group because of the simple, straightforward aerodynamics of the body and because, to the best knowledge of the author, this was the first vehicle to use extensive numerical fluid dynamics in the early stages of the shape development (Ref. 2.11). The numerical grid shown in Fig. 7.20 was created in January 1991, long before the vehicle was built. The bottom wing was initially placed low to increase the flow in the underbody tunnel and was referred to as a body flap, while the "actual" rear wing was mounted at the highest position allowed by regulations. (Because of delays in the manufacturing of this vehicle, the fabrication of the composite biplane wing was delayed to the second half of 1992 and the car was run initially with a single (lower only) aluminum wing.) The beaver tail behind the two rear wheel fenders and the sharp trailing edge at the exit of the tunnel were optimized by numerical computations so the flow was completely attached in these regions (and the immediate benefits were increased downforce and reduced drag). The concept of two rear wings was already in use in 1991 in F-1 cars and it was natural for it to appear later that year also on the Jaguar XJR-14 (the team had strong F-1 connections).

A schematic description of this car's geometry and some of the flow field features are presented in Fig. 7.21. The upper body had a highly streamlined shape with practically no visible areas of flow separations. The primary (oversized) cooling inlet was located in front of the vehicle and the cooling exits were in front of the windshield and at the two sides, behind the front wheels. This allowed a smooth underbody with two large tunnels that formed a sharp trail-

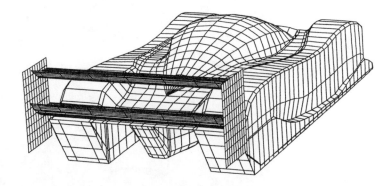

Fig. 7-20. *Computational grid for the aerodynamic development of the RX-792P and a view of the actual vehicle, which was built one year later. Note the sharp trailing edge of the bodywork.*

Fig. 7-21. *Schematic description of the flow field over a prototype race car.*

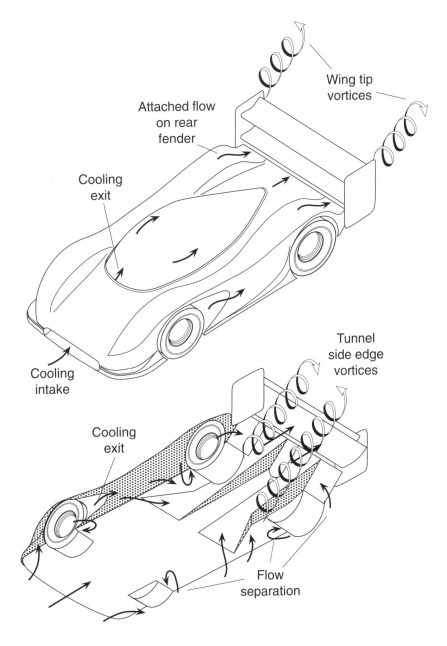

Wing tip vortices

Attached flow on rear fender

Cooling exit

Cooling intake

Tunnel side edge vortices

Cooling exit

Flow separation

ing edge at the exit, to minimize base drag due to rear flow separations. The lower wing was placed behind this trailing edge in a manner similar to the flap of a multi-element wing, and the flow was attached both on this wing and inside the tunnel.

The lower part of Fig. 7.21 shows the direction of the flow under the car. The most interesting feature is the inflow, toward the low pressure tunnels, behind the front axle (see typical pressure distributions for similar cars in Figs. 6.40 and 6.65). This inflow, as it turns around the sharp edges of the tunnel, forms a strong vortex which helps the flow on the tunnel's upper wall to stay attached. The two vortices from both tunnel sides extend behind the vehicle, as shown in the figure. Due to the tunnel suction, a strong lateral flow exists behind the rear wheels, which creates a smaller vortex there that increases both downforce and drag. The trimming of the front/rear downforce ratio was obtained by varying the lower rear wing flap angle and by adding small nose strakes (Fig. 7.19).

The level of downforce that can be obtained with such vehicles is close to $C_L = -4.0$ with drag coefficients in the range of $C_D = 0.6$ to 0.8 (see Table 2.3). Published data (Ref. 2.11) on the car in Fig. 7.19 quote the values of $C_L = -3.8$ and $C_D = 0.7$. However, with some modifications the downforce can reach levels of $C_L = -5.0$ while the lift/drag ratio may hover near 6. Typical areas of improvement for such a vehicle should focus on increasing the flow under the large intake and between the front wheels, to allow more flow into the tunnels, and on reducing the flow separation behind the two rear wheels and the gearbox. Also, the computations showed large spanwise lift variations on the lower wing, and for a better design a laterally varying airfoil section must be used. The addition of internal guide vanes in the underbody tunnels (as in Fig. 6.42), when properly placed, can increase the aerodynamic efficiency so that the above quoted large aerodynamic coefficients can be obtained.

Open-Wheel Race Cars

Open-wheel race cars are by far the most complicated vehicles, from the aerodynamic point of view, primarily due to their four large exposed wheels. As a matter of fact, the shape of these race cars, thanks to regulations, is closer to an aerodynamic nightmare than to an ideal high-speed streamliner. For example, if the side pods could be as wide as the wheels, which of course should have been covered, or if the underbody could be shaped along the whole vehicle length, then a far more aerodynamic formula could have been devised. To demonstrate the difficult initial condition for the design of the rest of the bodywork, let us observe the schematic description of the flow field over four wheels as shown in Fig. 7.22.

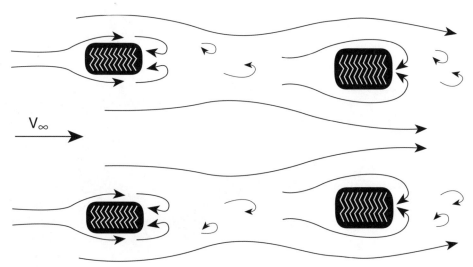

Fig. 7-22. *Schematic description of the separated flow field created by four wheels.*

In this case as well as in the case of an isolated wheel, which was discussed in Chapter 6, the flow behind each wheel is completely separated, and large values of drag and lift can be expected (see Table 6.1). The added frontal area of the four wheels may be as high as 65% of the vehicle frontal area, and with the values presented in Table 6.1 the drag contribution of the four exposed wheels can reach values of $C_D \sim 0.2$ to 0.5, with lift (positive!) of $C_L \sim 0.3$ to 0.4 (based on the complete vehicle's frontal area). Thus the bodywork of the vehicle must be fitted within the highly disturbed flow field and no matter how sleek the geometry is, the drag of such a vehicle will be considerably higher than that of a prototype race car with a similar level of downforce. Moreover, an efficient shape of the body and of the side pods (when they are not specified by regulations) is dictated directly by the flow between these four wheels, which incidentally resembles a Coca Cola bottle from the top view. By following this natural shape and by using the body's curvature to direct some of the flow behind the wheels in an effort to close the large separation bubbles there, the drag contribution of the wheels can be somewhat reduced. As an example to this school of design (Coca Cola), the top view of an F-1 race car is shown in Fig. 7.23. This design of the side pods is a quite large departure from the earlier styling practice of open-wheel race cars as depicted in Fig. 7.9 and 7.11, where the side pods were used to shield the flow behind the front and ahead of the rear wheels.

Because of the highly complex flow over an open-wheel race car, which is dominated by major separated flow regions, many tricks were and still are being tried in the name (or for the sake) of aerodynamic improvements. Many of these brave aerodynamic styling exercises were never substantiated by proper evaluation methods nor were carefully optimized. Therefore, the vehicle that was selected to represent the open-wheel race car group has one of the simplest and most straightforward configurations. This car, the 1992 McLaren MP4/7A, with the powerful (possibly up to 830 HP) V12 Honda 3.5 liter, naturally aspirated engine, was one of the most dominant racers that year (Fig. 7.24). It won

Fig. 7-23. *The 1994 Ferrari F-1 race car in the Montreal GP. Note the Coca Cola bottle-shaped body from the top view.*

Fig. 7-24. *The 1992/3 McLaren MP4/7A F-1 car, representing the clean lines of the early 1990s design. Courtesy of Tag/McLaren.*

5 races that season but finished second to the powerful duo of Williams-Renault (Fig. 6.3).

The schematic description of the vehicle shape and some of the dominant flow features are presented in Fig. 7.25. Because of the complicated shape of the streamlines, a particular feature, such as flow separation, is shown in one view only. (It should have been visible in both views, but was not duplicated for sake of clearness and simplicity). The flow separation behind the four wheels, for example, is shown at the upper view, and most details are similar to those presented in previous figures (Fig. 6.23 or Fig. 7.22).

The flow over the front and the upper rear wings is fairly standard and well behaved (and attached). The front wing is raised somewhat to allow flow under the body, to eventually feed the rear diffuser, and to enter the cooling intakes. The presence of the large nose cone reduces somewhat the wing efficiency (as demonstrated by Fig. 6.75). The large cutout at the center of the wing allows sufficient flow to reach the cooling inlet, while the longer chord near the tips supplements the needed lift. The elongated front-wing end plates act as deflectors to blow air behind the wheels to reduce their drag. At the same time they help direct the wing-tip vortices away from the cooling inlets (see also Fig. 6.73). Because of the flat-bottom requirement for F-1 cars, a horizontal plate is added behind the front wheels (under the driver), as was shown in Fig. 6.49. The flow under the slightly elevated nose cone impinges above this plate and creates a stagnation point with high pressure, creating a downward force on this plate.

The aft section of the bodywork is built around the large rear wheels, which deflect the flow behind the narrowing tail of the body so that the flow stays attached there. The horizontal plates ahead of the rear wheels generate additional downforce, based on the principle described in Fig. 6.49. The venturi at the rear section operates as described in Figs. 6.59 and 6.70.

One interesting aspect is created by the flow escaping through the longitudinal gap between the rear wheel and the curved-up bottom plate, creating a vortex under the car. This vortex helps to attach the flow in the small venturi, and

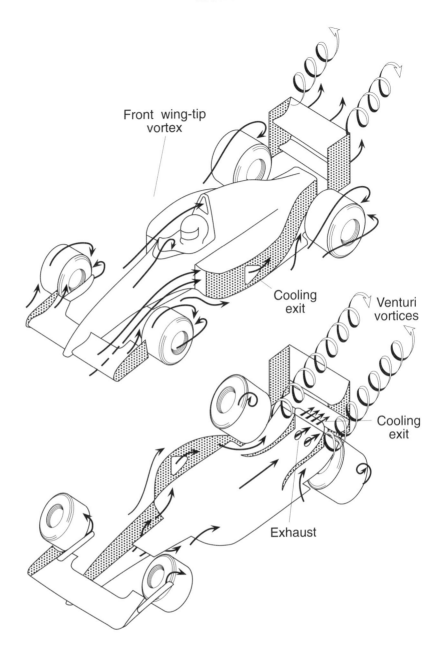

Fig. 7-25. *Schematic description of the flow field over an open-wheel F-1 race car.*

Front wing-tip vortex

Cooling exit

Venturi vortices

Cooling exit

Exhaust

its high-speed core reduces the pressure on the lower surface of this curved-up plate. The lower rear wing clearly helps to induce additional low pressure for both the cooling flow exit at the tail and for the diffuser exit, increasing the flow rates there, which in turn increases the downforce of the venturi. The geometry of this venturi is highly simplified in this Figure and the exhaust exit is actually partitioned by an extra set of splitter plates, as shown in Fig. 6.59.

The engine air intake above the driver's head is fed by the almost undisturbed air flowing above the top section of the vehicle. The large structure behind the driver houses a diffuser that slows down the air entering the airbox. The windshield is small enough not to disturb the above flow but sufficient to divert most of the flow from the driver's helmet (creating a small flow separation behind the windshield). Most of the cooling flow entering the two side intakes passes inside the body and is exhausted at the tail. This allows reduction of the base drag, as discussed in reference to Fig. 6.59. In this particular case, though, an additional cooling exit was located at the sides.

The flow field behind such a race car is highly disturbed by the many vortices leaving the vehicle. The most visible are the trailing vortices of the two wings and the wakes of the rear wheels, but the venturi vortices, and the pulsating engine-exhaust flow are not negligible.

The aerodynamic efficiency of open-wheel race cars is worsened by the lift and drag of the wheels. The maximum downforce is usually limited by the allowed wing sizes and can be in the range of $C_L \sim -2.5$ to -3.5 for F-1 cars (some unofficial claims in excess of -4 were voiced) while Indy cars with underbody tunnels can develop up to $C_L \sim -3.7$, according to Table 2.3. Drag is usually high, and better quantified by the downforce to drag ratio, which is probably within the range of 2 to 3 (with 2.92 quoted in Ref. 2.14 for an Indy car).

CLOSING REMARKS

When observing the metamorphosis in the shape of competition vehicles over the last few decades, one can only be fascinated by the tremendous importance of aerodynamics in influencing these changes. This becomes even more important in view of the fact that vehicle performance is directly dictated by engine and tire performance, and aerodynamics, in that sense, is only a secondary factor. The most dramatic developments in race car aerodynamics took place in the late 1960s and 1970s. After that era, "refinements" is a more proper word to describe the aerodynamic evolution of the various vehicle shapes.

It seems that the basic knowledge in the field has matured. Therefore, new challenges due to regulation changes can be met faster, but regulation changes will remain the dominant factor that *indirectly* controls the shape of a particular race car.

The developing trends indicate the need for leading-edge technology both in wind tunnel methods and in computational fluid dynamics, so that the design cycle can be shortened and the cost reduced. As an aerodynamicist, it is also a great pleasure to close the chapter on the days when vehicle shape was designed by an "artiste" with a "vision" (but no education), and to march into the reality that almost everything is designed by sound theory to fit the aerodynamic needs.

Beyond the 1980s, it is not surprising to see aerodynamics dictating engine design (say, a V with less than 60°) to fit in a narrow nacelle, or to dictate that the inner U-joints be moved inside the transaxle to allow better flow in the underbody tunnels. It finally seems as if aerodynamics has grown to be equally important in winning races as the other two traditional disciplines of tire and engine technology (the driver factor is another case altogether!).

REFERENCES

7.1 Falconer, R., and Nye, D., *Chaparral*, Motorbooks International, 1992.

7.2 Christian Hoefer, "Lotus 78—Modern Formula-1 Technique," ATZ 80 (1978), 7/8, p.306, Fig. 4.

7.3 Bamsey, I, "Peugeot 905: Sportscar World Champion," *RaceCar Engineering*, Vol. 2 No. 4, pp. 51–61, 1992.

APPENDIX 1: DRAG COEFFICIENTS

The major drive behind aerodynamic research for passenger cars is fuel economy. Consequently, most of the data published so far on this matter is related only to a vehicle's drag force. Also, the fuel consumption of a vehicle is usually related to the total aerodynamic resistance. Thus, when comparing various vehicles, their total resistance $C_D A$ is a product of the drag coefficient C_D multiplied by the frontal area (see also Eq. 4.12). The following list provides drag coefficient data for a variety of cars. The Table is based on a more complete list that can be found in Ref. 2.6, pp. 196–198. Model year is not listed in the source, but assume that most of these models are early 1980s (prior to 1985). Based on this data, it takes the VW Beetle about 30% more power to overcome its aerodynamic resistance than the much more powerful Chevrolet Corvette (at the same speed).

Vehicle Type	Drag Coefficient C_D	Frontal area A $[m^2]$	$C_D A$ $[m^2]$
Mini cars			
Fiat Uno ES	0.33–0.34	1.83	0.60–0.62
Peugeot 205 GL	0.35–0.37	1.74	0.61–0.64
Renault 5 GTL	0.35–0.36	1.79	0.63–0.64
Honda Civic 1.2	0.37–0.39	1.72	0.64–0.67
Opel Corsa TR	0.38–0.39	1.72	0.65–0.67
Citroen LNA	0.38–0.40	1.71	0.65–0.68
Citroen Visa 17 RD	0.38–0.40	1.76	0.67–0.70
VW Polo Coupe	0.39–0.40	1.72	0.67–0.69
Mitsubishi Colt 1200 GL	0.39–0.42	1.80	0.70–0.76
Ford Fiesta 1.1	0.40–0.41	1.74	0.70–0.71
Fiat Panda	0.40–0.42	1.70	0.68–0.71
Suzuki Alto	0.46–0.47	1.59	0.73–0.75
Daihatsu Charade TS	0.47–0.49	1.71	0.80–0.84
VW Beetle	0.48–0.49	1.80	0.86–0.88
Citroen 2 CV	0.51–0.52	1.65	0.84–0.86
Economy and medium size			
Opel Kadett GSi	0.30–0.31	1.90	0.57–0.59
Citroen GSA Special	0.34–0.35	1.83	0.62–0.64
Ford Sierra 1.8	0.34–0.35	1.94	0.66–0.68
Citroen BX 16 RS	0.34–0.36	1.91	0.65–0.69
VW Golf GTI	0.35–0.36	1.91	0.67–0.69
Renault 18 Turbo	0.35–0.37	1.88	0.66–0.70
VW Jetta C	0.36–0.37	1.89	0.68–0.70
VW Passat CL	0.36–0.37	1.89	0.68–0.70
Mazda 626 GLX 2.0	0.36–0.38	1.92	0.69–0.73
Mitsubishi Galant 1600 GLX	0.36–0.38	1.88	0.68–0.71
Ford Escort XR 3i	0.37–0.38	1.85	0.68–0.70
Alfa Romeo 33 1.3	0.37–0.39	1.82	0.67–0.71
Opel Ascona GT 1.8i	0.37–0.38	1.87	0.69–0.71
Toyota Camry GLi	0.37–0.39	1.94	0.72–0.76
Renault 9 GTL	0.37–0.39	1.85	0.68–0.72
Audi 80 CC	0.38–0.39	1.86	0.71–0.73
Mitsubishi Lancer 1500 GLX	0.38–0.41	1.81	0.69–0.74
Peugeot 305 GTX	0.38–0.40	1.84	0.70–0.74
BMW 318i (320i)	0.39–0.40	1.86	0.73–0.74
Fiat Ritmo 75 CL	0.39–0.40	1.87	0.73–0.75

Vehicle Type	Drag Coefficient c_D	Frontal area A [m²]	c_DA [m²]
Ford Escort 1.3 GL	0.39–0.41	1.83	0.71–0.75
Nissan Cherry GL	0.39–0.41	1.83	0.71–0.75
Volvo 360 GLT	0.40–0.41	1.95	0.78–0.80
Honda Accord 1.8 EX	0.40–0.42	1.88	0.75–0.79
Nissan Stanza SGL 1.8	0.40–0.42	1.88	0.75–0.79
Mazda 323 1.5	0.41–0.43	1.78	0.73–0.77
Nissan Sunny	0.41–0.43	1.82	0.75–0.78
Talbot Horizon GL	0.41–0.44	1.85	0.76–0.81
Alfa Romeo Giulietta 1.6	0.42–0.44	1.87	0.79–0.82
Toyota Corolla 1300 DX	0.45–0.46	1.76	0.79–0.81
VW Golf Cabrio GL	0.48–0.49	1.86	0.89–0.91
Full-size sedans			
Renault 25 TS	0.30–0.31	2.04	0.61–0.63
Audi 100 1.8	0.30–0.31	2.05	0.62–0.64
Mercedes 190 E (190 D)	0.33–0.35	1.90	0.63–0.67
Mercedes 380 SEC	0.34–0.35	2.10	0.71–0.74
Mercedes 280 SE	0.36–0.37	2.15	0.77–0.80
Mercedes 500 SEL	0.36–0.37	2.16	0.78–0.80
BMW 518i (520i, 525e)	0.36–0.38	2.02	0.73–0.77
Citroen CX 25 GTi	0.36–0.39	1.99	0.72–0.78
BMW 323i	0.38–0.39	1.86	0.71–0.73
Alfa Romeo 90 2.0	0.38–0.40	1.95	0.74–0.78
Mazda 929 2.0 GLX	0.39–0.44	1.93	0.75–0.85
Saab 900 GLi	0.40–0.42	1.95	0.78–0.82
Volvo 740 GLE	0.40–0.42	2.16	0.86–0.91
Volvo 760 Turbo w/intercooler	0.40–0.42	2.16	0.86–0.91
Peugeot 505 STI	0.41–0.43	1.97	0.81–0.85
Peugeot 604 STI	0.41–0.43	2.05	0.84–0.88
BMW 728i (732i/735i)	0.42–0.44	2.13	0.89–0.94
BMW 745i	0.43–0.45	2.14	0.92–0.96
Ford Granada 2.3 GL	0.44–0.46	2.13	0.94–0.98
Sports cars			
Porsche 924	0.31–0.33	1.80	0.56–0.59
Porsche 944 Turbo	0.33–0.34	1.90	0.63–0.65
Nissan 300 ZX	0.33–0.36	1.82	0.60–0.66
Mazda 626 Coupe	0.34–0.36	1.88	0.64–0.68
Opel Monza GSE	0.35–0.36	1.95	0.68–0.70
Renault Fuego GTX	0.34–0.37	1.82	0.62–0.67
Honda CRX Coupe	0.35–0.37	1.72	0.60–0.64
Audi Coupe GT 5E	0.36–0.37	1.83	0.66–0.68
Chevrolet Corvette	0.36–0.38	1.80	0.65–0.68
Chevrolet Camaro Z 28 E	0.37–0.38	1.94	0.72–0.74
Mazda RX–7	0.36–0.39	1.69	0.61–0.66
Toyota Celica Supra 2.8i	0.37–0.39	1.83	0.68–0.71
VW Scirocco GTX	0.38–0.39	1.74	0.66–0.68
Porsche 911 Carrera	0.38–0.39	1.78	0.68–0.69
Honda Prelude	0.38–0.40	1.84	0.70–0.74
Mitsubishi Starion Turbo	0.38–0.40	1.84	0.70–0.74
Porsche 928 S	0.38–0.40	1.96	0.74–0.78
Porsche 911 Carrera Cabrio	0.40–0.41	1.77	0.71–0.73
Jaguar XJ-S	0.40–0.41	1.92	0.77–0.79

APPENDIX 2: WIND TUNNELS

The following tables are a partial list of wind tunnels used for general automotive and race car testing. The first list of facilities is based on information provided in Ref. 2.6, p. 426. Most of those wind tunnels serve for general automotive studies and do not necessarily have a rolling ground simulation. All of the facilities concerned with race car testing are listed in the second group and have rolling ground simulation in the test section.

Automotive Wind Tunnels

Name of Facility	C (m^2)	L (m)	V$_{max}$ (km/h)	Test Section	K	P (kW)
Behr	5.24	14.00	120	O	6.0	147
BMW	20.0	12.5	160	SW	3.66	1676
Caltech	7.3	3.35	210	C	NA	625
Chrysler	4.74	8.6	190	O	5.56	560
Daimler-Benz	32.6	10.0	270	O	3.53	4000
DNW	90.25	15.0	220	C	4.8	12700
"	48.0	16.0	400	C	9.0	12700
Fiat, 1	12.0	11.60	160	O	4.0	560
Fiat, 2	30.0	10.50	200	O	4.0	1865
FKFS, 1	6.0	15.8	200	O	4.16	1000
FKFS, 2	22.5	9.5	220	O	4.41	2550
Ford (Cologne)	24.0/8.6	10.0	182/298	O	4.0	1650/1960
Ford (Dearborn)	23.2	9.15	201	C	3.80	1865
General Motors	65.9	23.0	240	C	5	2950
Inst. Aero. St. Cyr	15.0	10.0	144	SW	5.0	516
JARI	12.0	10.00	205	C	4.06	1200
Lockheed-Georgia	35.1	13.10	406	C, MG	7.02	6700
Mazda	24	12.0	230	C/O	6	1600
MIRA	35.0	15.24	133	C	1.45	970
Mitsubishi	24	12.0	216	C/O	NA	2350
Nippon Soken	17.5/12	12.5/8.5	120/200	C	3.66	1450
Nissan	21.0	10.00	119	C	2.86	NA
Opel	4.30	NA	120	C	NA	460
Pininfarina	11.75	9.5	150	O	6.2	625
Porsche	22.3	12.0	230	SW	6.06	2200
Toyota	17.5	8.00	200	C	3.66	1500
Sofica	11.0/4.3	16.5/14.0	80/170	C	NA	380
Volkswagen, 1	6.0	7.2/6.0	170/180	O	6.0	460
Volkswagen, 2	37.5	10.0	180	O	4.0	2600
Volvo, 1	4.32	8.6	190	O	6.60	500
Volvo, 2	27.06	15.8	200	SW	6.0	2300

C–Nozzle cross section; L–Length of test section; V$_{max}$–Maximum wind speed; Type of Test Section: O–Open, C–Closed; SW–Slotted walls; MG–Moving ground; K–Contraction ratio; P–Drive power

Race Car Wind Tunnels

Name of Facility	W (m)	H (m)	L (m)	V$_{max}$ (km/h)	Test Section	K	P (kW)
Activa (Brabham)	1.83	1.37	3.96	110	C, MG	5	215
British Aero. (Warton)	5.5	5.0	6.6	76	C, MG	2.32	220
British Maritime Inst.	2.75	2.13	7.31	180	C, MG	8	220
Comtec (March)	2.3	2.3	6.3	140	C, MG	N/A	300
Cranfield	2.4	1.8	5.2	180	C, MG	7	373
Dallara	1.7	0.9	2.75	100	C, MG	2.08	37.5
Flowscience (GB)	2.7	2.1	5.5	216	C, MG	5	380
Footwork	2.0	2.0	4.0	180	C, MG	4.6	224
Imperial College	3.05	1.52	8.5	126	C, MG	3.3	100
Lotus	1.54	1.23	3	108	C, MG	3	17
MIRA	2.0	1.0	6.0	144	C, MG	N/A	N/A
Ohio State University	3.0	2.1	5.2	145	C, MG	14	1490
SIMTEK	1	1.3	2.5	133	O, MG	3.5	N/A
Southampton, 1	1.7	2.1	4.42	180	C, MG	5	150
Southampton, 2	3.5	2.6	9.01	180	C, MG	5.3	380
Swift	2.75	2.44	6.7	225	C, MG	5.3	373
Swiss Federal (Emmen)	2.45	1.75	3.8	200	O, MG	4.8	410
Toyota (AAR)	1.52	0.89	3.5	160	C, SW, MG	6	130

W–Width; H–Height; L–Length of test section; V$_{max}$–Maximum wind speed; Type of test section: O–Open, C–Closed; SW–Slotted walls; MG–Moving ground; K–Contraction ratio; P–Drive power

Index

A

Ackermann angle, 154
Aerodynamic downforce, 2, 48
  braking, 159–160
  cornering, 3, 4, 5
  cornering speed, 160–161
  enclosed wheel race cars, 237
  performance, 4–5
  pitch sensitivity, 170–173
  side skirt gap, 201
  speed, 161
  suspension, 170–173
  tire load, 4
Aerodynamic forces
  components, 2–3
  creating, 6–8
  measuring, 6–8
Aerodynamics
  multivehicle interactions, 174–177
  performance effects, 157–177
  performance measurement, 9–10
  terminology, 23–30
Airfoil
  angle of attack, 102
  boundary layer, 107
  drag, 107
  highly cambered, 140, 141
  laminar bubble, 110
  leading edge, 113–114, 115
  lift coefficient, 103, 112
  pressure distribution, 110–115
  Reynolds number, 108–110
  shapes, 138–144
  surface irregularities, 144
Airfoil lift
  airfoil thickness, 106
  angle of attack, 102–103
  camber, 100, 102
    attached flow, 105
    flow separation, 105
    trailing edge, 105
  chord length, 6
  defined, 99–115
  leading edge, 100, 106
  lift force, 2
  pressure distribution, 102
  stagnation point, 100–101
  stagnation streamline, 100–101
  streamline, 100–101
  symmetric, 100
  trailing edge, 100
Airfoil moment, 108, 109
Angle of attack
  airfoil, 102–103
  drag, 189, 191
  lift, 102–103, 189, 191
Axle, longitudinal weight transfer, 152–154

B

Benetton-Ford F-1 car, 13
Bernoulli's equation for pressure, 34–39
  application, 35
  terminology, 36
BMW M3, 16, 17
Body. *See* Vehicle body
Boundary layer, 26, 30–34
  airfoil, 107
  defined, 30
  laminar flow, 31
  skin-friction coefficient, 31–32
  thickness, 30
  turbulent flow, 31
  velocity distribution, 30–31
  wind tunnel, 73–76
Brabham BT46B fancar (1978), 247–248
Braking, 5
  aerodynamic downforce, 159–160
  straight-line, 159–160
Busch HR-001 race car, 250, 251

C

Camber, airfoil lift, 100, 102
  attached flow, 105
  flow separation, 105
  trailing edge, 105
Center of gravity, 163–164
Center of pressure, 163–167
Central wing, 225
Channeling, 238
Chaparral 2C race car, 245, 246
Chaparral 2J race car, 247
Circulation control airfoil, high lift wing, 127
Closed circuit lap time, speed, 161–162
Closed-return wind tunnel, 65
  disadvantages, 66
Coast-down test, drag, 59–60
Cockpit, open, 223
Compact commuter car, 16
Computational test method, 55, 89–96
  advantages, 96
  current capabilities, 94–96
  disadvantages, 96
  types of codes, 94–96
Conservation of momentum, 90
Continuity equation, 90, 91, 92
Cooling drag, 214–215
Cooling exit, 219–221, 222
Cooling intake, 218–219, 220
Cooling system, 214–224
  speed, 216–218
  static pressure coefficient variation, 214–215
Cornering, 154
  aerodynamic downforce, 3, 4, 5
  maximum lateral acceleration, 250–252
  skirt, 201–202
Cornering speed, 160–161
  aerodynamic downforce, 160–161

D

Deflector plate, 197–198
Deformation force, flexible material, 147
Delta wing, 225–226
Density, 27, 28
  air, 29
  water, 29
Diffuser, 204–205, 238
Dive plate, 212
Dodge Ram truck, 15
Drafting, 11, 175–177
  drag, 176, 177
  lift, 176
Drag, 45–52
  angle of attack, 189, 191
  ground proximity, 189, 191, 194
  isolated open wheel, 196
  reduction by streamlining, 2, 3
  side-slip angle, 188–189
  spoiler, 209
  underbody tunnel, 183
Drag coefficient, 47, 58
  airfoil, 112

ABOUT THE AUTHOR

Dr. Joseph Katz is Professor of Aerospace Engineering and Engineering Mechanics at San Diego State University. He received the degrees of BSc, MSc and DSc, the latter in 1977 in Aerospace Engineering after which he spent two years at the NASA Ames research center full-scale wind tunnel facility. During his academic career he taught and developed numerous graduate and undergraduate courses in both the Aerospace and the Mechanical engineering departments, including two courses dealing with vehicle dynamics. His wide research interest spans between typical aerospace disciplines where he was active in developing computational and experimental aerodynamic methods, and vehicle related research with emphasis on engine cooling and vehicle dynamics. He is the author of more than 60 journal articles in computational and experimental aerodynamics. His previous book (coauthored with A. Plotkin) is "Low Speed Aerodynamics: From Wing Theory to Panel Methods," (McGraw-Hill 1992). As a result of his active research in aerodynamics and his teaching experience in vehicle handling and dynamics, he consulted for various race-car teams and has became involved with race-car aerodynamics and design. Over the past thirteen years he has worked on many types of road vehicles including open wheel (F-1, CART) and enclosed wheel (IMSA GTP, GTO) race cars, and has contributed to their shape, cooling and wing development. In recent years he worked closely with designer Lee Dykstra on the MAZDA GTO (winner of driver and constructors title in 1991) and GTP projects. In both cases extensive numerical aerodynamic models were used to shape the vehicles prior to the construction of any mock-up, wind tunnel model or the actual car itself.

The author's love for automobiles does not end at the office. At home he is polishing his mechanical skills in rebuilding classic cars, and his sizable collection of high-performance vehicles endangers the free parking area left in his whole neighborhood.